SEVEN
OF THE
CROSS

Thrillogy Press Edition 2019
ISBN:978-1-950376-02-5
Epub edition:978-1-950376-03-2
First Published by ECHO PARK PRESS LLC
Copyright © 2009 by Terry Fritts, All rights reserved.
ISBN-13: 978-0-9791514-8-4
Library of Congress Control Number: 2009933705

All rights reserved under International Copyright Conventions, including the right to reproduce this book or portions thereof in any form.

The image on the first title page is the emblem of the Spanish Inquisition. The Inquisition officially began in Spain in 1478 and definitively ended in 1834 but had mostly been forgotten by the end of the sixteenth century.

Other Books by Terry Fritts

BIO-TERROR SERIES

TAKA
KONA SNOW
KAPU ʻĀINA
(Forbidden land)

The Kevin Bridges Spiritual Warfare Series

CONSUMING FIRE
BROTHERHOOD OF THE DIVINE

SEVEN OF THE CROSS

A KEVIN BRIDGES SPIRITUAL WARFARE NOVEL

BY

TERRY FRITTS

THRILLOGY PRESS

Kevin Bridges Spiritual Warfare Series came as a surprise. I had just returned from Russia with an idea of writing a spiritual warfare novel about archangels and End Times. As I began writing, I had several bizarre vivid dreams. I remembered them all in detail which guided the direction of the first book **Brotherhood of the Divine**. The book took on a life of its own with characters and historical events arriving at the right time. Kevin Bridges became a wonderful character that needed to be explored so I wrote a prequel, **Seven of the Cross**. It deals with fallen angels and it too spurred some characters I hope to explore in later books. It also inspired me to write another prequel featuring Keven Bridges, **Consuming Fire**. **Consuming Fire** is a very intense look at evil and the power of prayer. In this new Thrillogy Press edition of the series, all three books have been edited and slightly modified from the originals to allow continuity of character and story.

Seven of the Cross is a work of fiction. Any similarity between characters in the book and real people is coincidental, except, of course, the historical figures that did exist and did play a part in a particular era or event and the modern-day rulers in Spain who are mentioned in the story. However, some of the actions attributed to those historical figures are part of the fiction story that is woven into the actual historical events.

ACKNOWLEDGEMENTS

I want to thank my wife for all her support and for reassuring me that yes, it was time to retire from teaching and spend more time doing the things we enjoy together, like traveling, visiting with grandkids, and researching for my novels.

Pauline and I had a fabulous time in Barcelona and an unforgettable Valentine's Day in Sevilla. (Sorry about the rental car.) Madrid and Ronda were incredible and play a major role in this novel. Glad our daughter Katy recommended Spain.

I want to thank my editors and proof readers, especially Jennifer, for all their hard work.

SEVEN OF
THE CROSS

SEVEN of the CROSS

CHAPTER ONE

"Obedience"

"**I am your servant,** I am a living sacrifice to the world around me. Lord, let your will be done through me. Lead me…"

The dark man was jarred from his prayers as several children scrambling to see the processional knocked him from his knees and into the wall. He winced as his thigh once again began to throb.

"Urchins," he yelled through his pain, but the children had weaved their way through the legs of the adults and were gone. They now sat on the curb where they would have a clear view of the processional and of the accused.

He climbed slowly to his feet and wiped the perspiration from his face. Perspiration from both the pain he suffered and the unrelenting summer heat of Madrid. He too wanted to watch as the guilty were marched to their sentencing and ultimate fate. He could see the dim light of the candle bearers reflecting high off the sides of the houses as they approached. With their approach came the surge of the crowd, pinning him against the wall as he struggled to overcome the nauseating pain in his leg.

The crowd scared him. Not the size of the crowd, he was used to such large gatherings, it was that this crowd, or the faces of the people in this crowd that scared him. These people were not normal. They were freaks. Freaks with horrendously twisted faces, faces of evil. Lost souls with no direction, no purpose, and no destiny, many of whom more deserved to be paraded to their death than those that now approached. Of this he was certain. But, he was different. God had ordained his destiny. He averted the contentious looks of these lost souls as they gazed upon him. He cared not what they thought of him, for what did they know? He commanded a certain respect from these people, for he wore the robes of a man of the church. Most of these souls would never share in the splendors of heaven. Not like him. He was special. He had heard the voice. The voice that had commanded him. The voice that guided him. The voice of God. Or so he thought.

The cross felt warm against his chest. Comforting. Its warmth flowed through his body easing the pain that ravaged his leg. He could feel the moisture of his blood as it soaked through the scapular that he had wrapped around the seething wound and now dripped onto his foot as he walked. It had been several days but still the mass of raw flesh had not fully scabbed over. He knew this was a small sacrifice to pay compared to the sacrifice that Jesus made to guarantee the faithful's place in heaven. Now it would be his turn to save many of these freakish souls standing before him, pushing and shoving, trying to gain a better view of the approaching processional.

The hooded man needed to move. The crowd had grown too large in the narrow alleyway and he'd be unable to push his way to get the view he needed. He had to see. She'd be there. God had told him so. He'd know when he saw her.

"Out of my way," he screamed shoving several men aside as he headed towards the plaza where he knew the ceremony would end. There were several entrances into the Plaza Mayor. He circled the building to his left and easily made it into the porticoes that surrounded the plaza. It was a warm evening and hundreds of people had crowded the plaza awaiting the arrival of the processional. Several acrobats performed their stunts hoping for a small bit of money for their effort, but only the children seemed to show any interest tonight. Numerous charlatans had staked out areas within the vast plaza trying to cheat or deceive those foolish enough to show an interest. He had often challenged these evil men in the past, but tonight he had work to do.

Several workmen were impatiently waiting to remove the stands that had been built for the inquisition that had found these lost souls guilty. It had been many years since Madrid had seen a trial of inquisition. The hatred for the Protestants had subsided and the conversos, or Jews, who had converted to Catholicism were long since dead and their children and grandchildren were now prominent members in Spanish society and the Catholic Church.

There would be no scaffolds built and no stakes at which to burn the guilty. Of the seven brought before the tribunal, four were women accused of crimes of superstition, two men for heretical propositions, and a young priest for solicitation.

The four women accused of superstition were by their own admission witches. They were at most risk of being condemned to die by the tribunal, but the witch-hunt fervor that seemed to flourish in France, England, and Germany did not reach to Spain. It was decided that these women would be imprisoned for two years. A harsher penalty was expected but their admission to being witches did not come till after several hours of excruciating torture. The tribunal took this into consideration when assigning punishment.

The heretical propositions, or verbal offences by the two men accused, were merely questionable statements about the Holy See that a business competitor swears to have heard. Was it not for the fact that this accuser had close ties with King Philip's court; the tribunal would have dismissed the charges outright. The tribunal sentenced the men to pay a nominal fine and march in the processional with the guilty at the auto de fe.

The young priest, Father Adega, was accused of solicitation of a prostitute during confession. She had come to church to confess her sins of sexual transgression when she claimed the priest solicited the same favors for which she had come seeking absolution. He of course denied such an exchange ever took place, but it was her word against the young priest's and there was a strict vigilance over the actions of those in the church. He would be sentenced to several lashes, but would remain a priest.

The crowd began to part as two rows of godly men entered the plaza. Each man carried a deep violet paschal candle over four feet in length. Many of the faithful were so short they struggled to keep the candle from hitting the cobbled street below. Behind these rows of men came the archbishop, a priest and several altar boys. The archbishop carried a larger more ornate scarlet paschal candle adorned with several jewels and ornaments. The first two altar boys, or thurifers, were rather plump lads and carried two covered golden liturgical vessels called boats which held the incense and the spoon for spreading the aromatic mixture across the burning coals. The priest stood slightly in front and in-between these two altar servers and swung a matching golden thurible from golden chains censing the people as the processional snaked slowly along. Next came three more altar boys. The two on the outside carried oil torches trimmed in gold. The third and huskier of the three boys stood in the middle carrying a pole holding an emblem featuring a golden cross with a sword and branch with an inlay of a dark green jade. Two more columns of candle bearers holding dark green candles followed close behind constraining the convicted within their ranks. They also kept the mobs at bay from delivering premature justice upon these poor souls. Next came the bearers of the crucifix. It took more than a dozen strong men to support and transport the larger-than-life cross with the carved replica of the crucified Jesus. They struggled to keep the giant icon upright as they shuffled along but only managed to keep the head of Jesus slightly above their own.

    The processional had started at the Templo Eucarístico de San Martín. The reconstruction of the templo had just recently been completed with the installation of the final stations and icons. Of course, the ceremony had begun with a Mass and prayer service followed by the procession of the green cross. It was the procession and reading of the sentence that drew the large crowd. For most, this was the first and would be the last auto de fe they would ever witness. A few in the crowd may have witnessed such an event in their youth, but this day's spectacle would bear little resemblance to those held at the height of the Inquisition. In fact, this inquisition and auto de fe were designed to advertise the opening of the new church more than to prosecute and punish heretics.

    The dark man's eyes darted from face to face. "She must be here," he said. "God open my eyes so I may see the one you have called me to. Is it the priest's accuser?" he asked in his prayer. He knew the accuser must always be present at the reading of the charges and sentencing. It had to be that harlot who had accused the young priest. Surely, God had sent him to avenge her false accusations. She must be made to pay for her lies and sins, like the other before her had been made to pay.

The tribunal ascended the stand where they would pronounce sentencing on the guilty, although, the guilty all knew their penance or sentence. The city officials were already in place as was Diego Astorga Céspedes, Archbishop of Toledo, along with his secretary. Several priests from the archdiocese and several local Madrid church officials found their seats. It would be the archbishop who would pronounce the sentences.

"I call you all before God to pray for forgiveness for these seven souls and to pray for…"

Seconds after the archbishop started his prayer, the bells of the new Templo Eucarístico begin to chime incessantly. He tried to continue but the bells and the murmur of the concerned crowd made it impossible for him to be heard. He first turned to Pastor Santorio who was responsible for the new parish. "What is the meaning of this?"

"Forgive me your grace, but I know not why the bells toll."

"Brother Bruno, go find out what is so urgent and tell them it must stop immediately, they are ruining the auto de fe."

"Yes, your grace," Bruno replied. Bruno Mancini was the archbishop's secretary, and had been for several years. He was a wise and shrewd man who the archbishop trusted completely. Without hesitation he leaped from the platform and started running towards the northwest exit from the plaza.

"Brother Mancini," the monsignor called. Bruno immediately stopped. "Make sure these bell ringers are not the parishioners in charge of guarding the Eucharist for it must never be left unguarded. If so, they risk excommunication as far as I am concerned," the pastor added.

Bruno looked at the archbishop who nodded for Bruno to continue to the church.

Let's not be so hasty, monsignor," the archbishop responded. "Do not forget that this inquisition and auto de fe is little more than a charade to show-off your new parish church and to scare many of those Catholics who have become lax in their faith back into the fold. Perhaps this interruption was part of your plan you neglected to tell me about."

"Absolutely not, your grace," the pastor replied.

As Bruno exited the plaza, he saw several men waving their arms and running towards the plaza from the direction of the templo.

"It's a miracle, it's a miracle," one of them was yelling.

Bruno grabbed the man by the collar of his coat yanking him off his feet. "What miracle?" Bruno demanded.

The man dangled in the air thrashing his arms. "Mary, the blessed Virgin Mary," the man yelled and began to cry. The cries soon turned to sobs. "The Madonna is sad. She cries tears of blood, the blood of Jesus."

Bruno dropped the man who scrambled to his feet and continued running towards the Plaza Mayor falling several times along the way.

At the sounding of the first bells, the hooded figure's head snapped to face the direction of the church.

"They must know," he wheezed. He allowed himself to smile through his pain, "Just as I had planned. But why do they continue to toll the bells? They mustn't toll the bells."

He watched as several men ran into the plaza and straight to the tribunal stand. He had to get closer to hear what was being said. Surely, this would not interfere with the auto de fe.

        ❧   ❧   ❧

"Your grace, your grace, a miracle has occurred. A miracle at the templo," the man gasped.

"What is this miracle you speak of?" the pastor asked.

"The Virgin, she cries tears of blood," the man exclaimed.

Bells from other churches between the plaza and the templo began to join in.

Several of the clergy gathered on the stand dropped to their knees to pray. Many of the parishioners who had carried the candles in the processional and overheard the man speaking to the archbishop broke their ranks and headed back towards the templo. The processional was collapsing.

"What's the meaning of this?" one of the comisarios of the tribunal asked. "We must complete the auto de fe."

"It seems God has intervened and chosen a different outcome for the accused," the pastor replied.

The crowd was quickly leaving the plaza and the ceremony couldn't continue. The alguacil in charge of detaining the guilty turned to the two inquisitors standing beside the archbishop. "Should I lock them back in the jail?"

"No, it is as the pastor has said, God has decided their fate. Free them."

"Blasphemy!" the hooded man screamed. "These heretics must suffer for their crimes." No one heard the man as the crowd turned into a swarming uproar as word of the miracle spread.

"Jesus has paid for your sins and transgressions with his bloody tears," the alguacil announced to the seven prisoners. "God has decided the processional was punishment enough for your crimes."

"No," the hooded man screamed, "it mustn't be."

Father Adega, the priest accused of solicitation, rushed to the archbishop, knelt and kissed his ring. "Thank you, your grace, for your compassion in releasing me…"

Before the priest could finish the archbishop and pastor had started to move off the stand and join the crowd heading towards the templo.

"What about the witches?" the hooded man screamed. "They have admitted their heresy and deserve the most serious punishment of relaxation. They should be burned at the stake." No one could hear his shouts.

No burning would take place that night in the square. The alguacil cut the ropes that bound the hands of the witches. "God has shown his mercy tonight. I advise you to seek out our merciful God and repent of your evil ways. You must leave the city and denounce Satan or I will see to it that someday a pyre will await your body and Satan will claim your blackened soul."

The four women knew recalcitrance would only bring them more trouble and cast their eyes downward without replying as the bindings were cut. Once free they wasted little time in going their separate ways blending into the crowd and leaving the square. Only one paid heed to their release, the man in the brown hooded robe.

"Enough with the bells," Bruno screamed holding his ears as he approached the church. Almost immediately the bells stopped. Not because of Bruno's request, but because the bell ringer could see that the crowd gathered in the plaza for the auto de fe was now headed out of the plaza and moving past the shops and homes towards the templo.

Bruno entered the sanctuary and saw the monstrance holding the Eucharist with two parishioners standing guard. On the left side he saw a crowd gathered around the large marble statue of the Madonna. Even from the rear of the church he could see what appeared to be blood running down the Virgin's cheeks, then dripping onto her lower torso. Several monks were already on their knees praying before the statue as parishioners began to stream in joining them in prayer.

"Brother monks," Bruno bellowed, "we must preserve this for the archbishop to see. We need all these people out of here until the archbishop arrives."

The monks knew of Bruno's stature in the church as the archbishop's vicar and quickly ended their prayers. The church doors were shut and the parishioners already inside were guided out a door near the stairs leading to the crypts.

"There appears to be drops of blood leading down into the crypt room," one of the parishioners pointed out to the monk escorting him from the church.

The monk stopped and touched one of the droplets. "It is blood," he exclaimed and dropped to his knees to pray. The controlled exit was in danger of turning into another mass of prostrated believers when Bruno intervened.

"All of you out this way," he thundered in a voice no one dared question. He pulled the monk to his feet. "What is your name?"

"I am Raul, Brother Raul Toribio," the monk answered. "Brother Toribio, allow no one to enter the crypts without my permission and detain any who may try to leave by this staircase."

"Yes, your Grace," the monk replied.

"I'm not your Grace, I simply work for the archbishop, understand?"

"Yes, Brother Mancini," said the monk.

One of the monks who had been tolling the bells called down from above. "His grace and the monsignor are nearing the church. What should we do?"

"Open the door of course," Bruno replied.

"But there are so many people with them," the monk explained.

"Then I will open the door," Bruno replied.

Bruno threw back the latch and stepped out and stood before the doors forcibly shoving several people off the steps to clear a path for the archbishop and pastor.

A cry went up from the crowd demanding to see the miracle.

"There is no miracle until the archbishop decrees that a miracle has indeed taken place. You are welcome to wait here, but for now the church will remain closed."

Several people shouted their displeasure with Bruno's edict and some even challenged his right to close the church.

The archbishop turned to address the crowd. "Brother Bruno is correct in his order. Until I view this alleged miracle and report my findings to the Holy See and his Holiness rules on this matter, no one will be allowed to view the Madonna. I shall have it removed from the sanctuary where we can study it properly."

A groan arose from the crowd. The monsignor whispered something to the archbishop. "Perhaps we should allow the faithful to view the Blessed Virgin, but under stringent controls. It would do a lot to forward the faith of many in Madrid who have become remiss in their devotion."

"We shall see," the archbishop replied as he turned and entered the church.

℘ ℘ ℘

Three of the women convicted of superstition left the square through the north portal. It was the most direct route to the templo and the crowds were thick. A few newer buildings were scattered among the older shops and homes between the plaza and the new templo. The plaza was centered in the old section of Madrid. Many of the houses and shops had been around for centuries. To the west was the palace surrounded by the old Moslem and Christian walls built in the 9th and 12th centuries. The palace had been built in the 16th century on the sight of the old mayrit, which was the 10th century outpost fortress of Mohammed I, the Emir of Cordoba. Many of these walls had been removed to make room for the palace and grounds, but several still remained.

The fourth woman scurried towards the southwestern corner of the plaza where few people remained. She lived alone in a small barren room of one of the old Moslem houses that made up part of the ancient fortress walls overlooking the orchards and fields in the valley below. The man in the hooded robe hurried to try to catch her but was slowed by the searing pain in his leg.

"I mustn't lose her," the hooded man cried. "Please Lord, help me in my task."

No sooner had the hooded man finished his prayer did two men grab the woman and pull her into a dark narrow alley.

"Let me go," she tried to scream, but one of the men smashed a cloak into her mouth to quiet her, splitting her lip and loosening her rotted teeth.

"Silence witch," the other man said as he threw her to the ground pinning her arms while his friend pulled up her dress ripping the front.

"No one cares about a sinner such as you," the first man slurred drunkenly.

The hooded man heard the struggling as he reached the darkened alley. "Thank you, Lord," he said knowingly. He entered the alley just as the second man was trying to pull down his own pants. He shoved the man causing him to tumble, tripping over his lowered pants and knocking his partner away from the hold he had on the woman's arms. She scrambled to her feet pulling her dress around her. The presence of the hooded stranger gave her confidence and she spat bloody spittle on both the men cursing and kicking at their heads while they lay on the ground.

The two men were too drunk to fight back. The hooded man grabbed the woman's arm. "We should leave before the wine restores their courage."

She spat once more at the men and hurried away with the man who had rescued her.

"The streets are not safe tonight. Allow me to walk you home," the hooded man said. The two moved quickly away.

The young woman began to laugh.

"What do you find so amusing?" the hooded man asked.

"I mean no offense," she replied. "It is that only moments ago your church was about to punish me for not believing in your god and now your god has rescued me."

"My God is a forgiving God," the man replied.

"Your God may forgive, but I can see in your eyes that you do not forgive. You are a lost soul. You serve a different god," she replied.

The hooded man was stunned by her accusation. "How dare you say such blasphemy? I have given my life to the church."

"And what has the church given back to you?" She paused giving him time to reply, but no response came, only garbled mutterings from beneath the hood.

"Your church has forsaken you and you have forsaken your church," she explained. "It is time you realized what god you serve."

They continued to walk a short way further. "This is the house where I live, at least until tomorrow. Why don't you come in and I'll give you what those two drunken fools tried to steal from me."

The hooded man looked up at the woman and smiled.

The witch began to laugh and closed the door behind them. She knew she'd found another of Satan's disciples and the hooded man now knew what god he truly served.

༄ ༄ ༄

"Is it some sort of trick?" the archbishop asked.

"No, my Grace, it appears to be real blood," Bruno replied. "Of course, we'll have our experts at the Vatican confirm this."

"Well how did it get there? Did somebody paint it on? Did the men who delivered the icon have anything to do with this?"

"Bring me a ladder," Bruno thundered. Within moments the ladder was in place and Bruno was leaning against the cold marble Virgin poking and scraping with the knife he always carried under his tunic.

"There is no way anyone could have put the blood here," Bruno called down. "Someone, throw me a rag." Bruno wiped away the fresh blood that had collected in the two small nodules near the outer corners of the half-closed eyes. No sooner had he cleaned away the bloody tears, did he see more blood begin to seep from the lower portion of the eye and spread upwards towards the outside corners. There it gathered then flowed down the Madonna's cheeks leaving an almost circular stain where the blood coagulated then dropped onto the lower portion of the marble icon. The process was slow but continuous.

"You," Bruno said to one of the monks praying before the Virgin. "You get two bowls to collect the blood as it falls."

"It looks to still be crying," the archbishop said. "What do you make of this Bruno?"

"I think God is trying to tell us something," Bruno replied.

"You think this is a true miracle?" the archbishop asked.

"That's for you to officially determine, not me," Bruno replied smiling.

"No, my friend, that's for the Holy See to determine based on my report, but unless you tell me different, I have no doubt we're witness to a miracle."

"Yes, but just what is the significance of such a miracle as this?" Bruno asked.

"That will be your task to find out," the archbishop replied. "May God aide you in your task. Now it's time to pray."

"I would suggest your Grace pray elsewhere while we get an enclosure constructed around the Madonna. It's too heavy to move," Bruno said.

"A wise suggestion," the archbishop replied.

"Your Grace, would you reconsider allowing the faithful to come pray before the crying Virgin?" Father Santorio asked.

The archbishop looked to Bruno. "Would it interfere with your investigation?"

"I don't believe so, but not until we build the wall separating it from the rest of the church."

"I will leave it up to you," the archbishop replied turning to leave with the monsignor.

"The rest of you get some wood and some curtains," Bruno said to the several monks still gathered around the Virgin. "I want this separated but accessible. Leave room for people to come in to see it and pray, but make sure they can get in and out without causing trouble."

"Brother Bruno," the monk returning with the two-bowls called, "Brother Raul wants to know how much longer he must stand guard over the stairway to the crypts?"

"Goodness, I forgot all about Brother Raul," Bruno said as he climbed down the ladder.

An ominous shiver ran down Bruno's back. Bruno felt an overwhelming urge to look back at the Madonna. The tears of blood seemed to have doubled in intensity. Bruno knew it was a sign. "You three," Bruno called to the monks. "Let the others build the enclosure. I need you three to pray. This miracle is Virgin Mary warning us to prepare for battle. Satan grows strong in Madrid. Evil is close at hand and we need to pray and ask for strength to stay faithful. Pray. Pray hard and long. God will hear those who believe."

ও   ও   ও

The cross burned against his chest. It called to him. It consumed his thoughts. He no longer felt the pain that had engulfed his body. Only the cross. He felt nothing but the burning as it lay against his chest.

"She is the one," the voice said in his head. "She offers herself as a martyr. She's the one I've sent to you."

"Yes Lord, I will do as you command," the hooded man replied.

"What did you say?" the woman asked, but no answer came. "Why do you wear the cloth of the church you do not serve? Our lord Satan would not be pleased at such an insult." The witch laughed as she removed her torn dress then turned to face the hooded man.

"Well, aren't you going to take off your clothes?" she asked. "You can't very well do anything wearing that monk's tunic."

Still the man didn't reply. She reached over, grabbed the brown cloth and pulled it over his head. His hands immediately went to the cross. He held tightly to the metal shaft below the strangely shaped bulbous cross and continued his incoherent mutterings.

"What happened to your leg?" the woman asked. "It's bleeding horribly."

The cloth he had wrapped around the wound could hold no more of the blood that oozed from the massive wound on the man's thigh and had slipped down his leg. As she stared at the bloody mess, she failed to notice the man had removed the chain that held the cross from around his neck.

"It's in the shape of a cross," she said. "It looks like someone cut a cross out of your leg. Who would do such a thing?"

"I would," the man replied as he smashed the sharpened end of the cross through her forehead and into her brain.

"Thank you, Satan, for calling me," the witch whispered with her dieing breath. Her body shuddered then slowly slipped down the metal spike till the inside of the skull snagged on the barb-like point of the cross as blood gushed from the massive wound.

"Oh no, we mustn't get blood on that lovely skin," the man said catching her before she hit the ground. He lifted her body onto the small table placing her facedown with the head hanging over the end to allow the body to bleed out.

"If I only had a bucket to catch the precious life draining from your brain," the hooded man said.

He picked up the dress and ripped away a portion of the material and laid it on the floor away from the pooling blood. He pulled a knife from a pocket of his tunic, pulled her hair away from the string that bound it and sliced away most of her hair. He wrapped the hair in the material he had cut from the dress. Then he carefully carved a large oversized cross into her back about a half inch deep. No blood flowed from the sliced flesh. He lifted one corner of the carving and slowly cut the cross shaped meat and skin away from her back. He rolled it up and tied it with the string she had used to bind her hair. He placed both the bundle containing the hair and the skin in the pocket of his tunic.

"I mustn't delay," the hooded man said to himself. "Much to do, much to do before morning." He pulled her body from the table sitting her in the room's one chair. He carefully leaned her head back against the wall so the cross would stick prominently upright from her pierced skull.

"Thy will be done," the man said as he pulled the hood over his head and quietly left the house.

CHAPTER TWO

"Deception"

"I must've really pissed somebody off," Kevin said to the female clerk in the medical office.

"Why's that?"

"Why else would they have me reading old medical files? Anybody with a third-grade education could do this."

"Excuse me?" the clerk responded obviously offended.

"Just kidding," Kevin said with his wry disarming smile. "I only meant it as a joke. I had to get you to notice me somehow."

"Duly noticed," she replied in a matter-of-fact tone that made Kevin cringe.

"So, what'd you do to get banished to this menial brainless task?" the clerk asked sarcastically.

"Ouch," Kevin said. "I really was joking."

"I know, I just wanted to see you squirm a little more," she replied. Now it was her turn to smile.

"What I did was admit to my boss that I really wasn't a Catholic but an evangelical Christian," Kevin replied.

"And that pissed your boss off, why?" the clerk asked.

"Well I am, or at least I thought I was, the chief miracle investigator for the Vatican," Kevin replied. "I'm starting to think they would like to keep the work in the family if you know what I mean."

"I'd think they'd like the idea of a non-Catholic trying to prove that a miracle occurred. It gives the impression of a non-biased investigation."

"Thanks for the positive spin, but I don't think that's the case," Kevin replied.

"I thought I read somewhere that Father Oder was leading the investigation into the miracles of John Paul II?"

"Oh, he is, but he is the point man that deals with the media. It's guys like me who do the down and dirty stuff," Kevin explained, trying to recall when he had mentioned the reason for his visit.

"And you consider this the down and dirty stuff?" the clerk asked.

"I do when I find something like this," Kevin said turning the computer screen so she could read it.

"I don't believe it. That SOB has been lying to us this entire time. He never even had a brain tumor," she said.

"So it'd seem," Kevin replied.

"This proves that the radiologist and the doctor were both aware of this. Why would they risk their careers over something as stupid as this?"

"I wouldn't call the beatification of a Pope stupid. If in fact they got away with this and this was considered the miracle that allowed John Paul II to be canonized, I would imagine the three of them would figure out a way to profit rather nicely from it all," Kevin suggested. "I can only hope the other two identical claims will be as easy to disprove as this one."

"Two other claims?" the clerk asked.

"That's right. On Friday I head to Krakow to investigate an identical claim and then next week I'm off to New York."

"Are you telling me two other men have claimed to have had their brain tumors disappear after placing a picture of Pope John Paul II on their heads?"

"Rather coincidental wouldn't you say?" Kevin replied.

"Sounds to me like you don't believe any of these miracle claims."

"No, I do believe in miracles. I've seen God's power and healing a brain tumor is nothing compared to what he is capable of. It's just my job to be skeptical until the facts prove me wrong."

"I'm afraid you'll find few Parisians who share your belief," the clerk said.

Kevin just nodded his head. "An unfortunate fact I'm afraid. I'm going to need a copy of this."

"Just push print. It will send it to the printer in the reception area. By the way, my name is Lucienne," she said sweetly.

"A beautiful name for a beautiful woman," Kevin replied.

"I bet you say that to all women you accuse of having a third-grade education."

"A grand faux pas to be sure," Kevin replied. "Allow me to make it up to you by taking you to dinner." Kevin reached down to gently touch her hand and let out a yelp.

"I know that static shock can really get you," Lucienne said.

"It was a shock, but not from static. Your hand felt like a piece of dry ice. I think I burned myself," Kevin replied.

"Don't be absurd," Lucienne replied grabbing Kevin's hand. "See perfectly normal," she said as she moved in close and kissed him.

Kevin almost pulled away, but the warmth of her lips on his seemed to weaken his knees and caress his entire body.

"I'll meet you at Le Grand Colbert at nine. That will give me time to run home and freshen-up" Lucienne whispered pulling away. "Don't forget to pick up the papers you printed."

"Yes, of course," Kevin replied feeling a bit dazed and confused. Kevin looked back at the information on the computer, but when he looked up Lucienne was gone.

"Something's not right," Kevin said and rushed out to the lobby. Lucienne was nowhere to be seen.

"Excuse me, but did some papers come through that I sent to this printer?" Kevin asked the receptionist.

"Let me look," she scooted her chair about five feet to the right where a large printer sat below the table. "This must be what you want." She handed the papers to Kevin and went back to her desk without even looking up.

Kevin didn't remember seeing her when he first came in earlier that afternoon and became suspicious. "Working a little late tonight, aren't you? The office was supposed to close two hours ago."

"That's right, but my boss told me I had to stay until you were finished, which I hope you are because I have a friend waiting for me at a bistro just down the street who has called about half dozen times wondering where I am," the receptionist replied obviously displeased.

"I'm so sorry," Kevin replied sheepishly as the lady put on her coat and turned off the computer and printer. "Lucienne should have told me, both of you didn't need to stay."

The receptionist looked curiously at Kevin but did not reply. She just wanted out of there and the less conversation the quicker she would get away.

"Thanks for your help." Kevin said as they walked down the steps and past the doorman.

Several taxis were waiting on the street. Kevin jumped into the one at the front of the line.

"Hotel L'Horset, 18 Rue D'Antin," Kevin said.

"Oui monsieur," the driver replied.

Kevin pulled out his cell phone and called the bishop who headed the Doctrinal Office at Vatican City. Kevin was specifically instructed to report all his findings directly to the bishop who in turn would pass along the information to Father Oder. At least the information the bishop thought it necessary and relevant to pass on. Kevin didn't care for this arrangement. Too many times in the past information he thought relevant never seemed to make it out the Doctrinal Office, but when he brought it up, he always received the same lecture about not seeing the entire picture or that it was a papal decision.

"Kevin, it's good to hear from you," the bishop said when he answered the phone. "Was it a real miracle?"

Kevin knew the driver would be listening to everything he said and was reluctant to respond.

"Sir, I believe we should talk when I return to Rome tomorrow."

"That must mean you were able to disprove the miracle," the bishop replied. "Is there someone listening?"

"Yes, sir and yes sir, I am on my way back to the hotel now. I have the papers that will verify my findings."

"Good job, Kevin. I look forward to seeing what you found. What time do you arrive tomorrow?"

"My plane leaves at 11:15 a.m. and arrives at Fiumicino at 1:20 p.m."

"Why not Ciampino, it's much more convenient?" the bishop asked.

"Sure, just send one of the papal jets to pick me up and I'll be happy to fly into Ciampino," Kevin replied. "Unfortunately, Air France only flies into Leonardo di Vinci Airport."

"I'll be sure to have a car waiting to pick you up," the bishop replied. "God bless you, my son."

"Thank you, sir," Kevin replied as the call disconnected.

At least the Vatican didn't skimp on Kevin's Hotel. The Hotel L'Horset was an elegant and charming four-star hotel located within a quarter mile of the center of Paris. It was a small hotel and although it lacked a restaurant, several excellent ones were within easy walking distance including Le Grand Colbert, where Kevin would be meeting Lucienne in less than an hour.

Kevin changed into a clean shirt and put on his dinner jacket that he always carried while traveling in Europe. Europeans tended to dress up to go out to dinner much more so than Americans and even though there was nobody prouder to be an American than Kevin Bridges, in the world climate today, it was best to be an inconspicuous proud American.

"Just in case," Kevin said to himself as he packed away his dirty clothes and tidied his room. "Who knows what might happen tonight. I am in France and when in France..." Kevin had a habit of talking to himself. Usually it was his way of working out problems he would encounter on his investigations. Tonight, it was a different kind of encounter he was hoping for, that is, until he remembered when he first touched Lucienne's hand. He looked at his finger tips and saw that the skin on two of them looked slightly white and burned.

"That's not possible," he said. A sense of dread came over Kevin. "I got a bad feeling about this." When Kevin got the feeling something was not right, it usually wasn't. He looked at the clock and realized if he was going to be on time for dinner he had to leave immediately.

The sense of dread did not get better when he reached the lobby. There were several people sitting in the bar and Kevin got the feeling every one of them was staring at him and in fact, most were. Even the doorman emoted displeasure at having to end his conversation with the clerk and open the door for Kevin to leave.

"Do you need a taxi, sir?" the doorman asked.

"No thank you, I think I will walk," Kevin replied.

"As you wish, sir," the doorman replied methodically.

When Kevin turned the corner onto Avenue De L'Opéra he recognized two men he had seen in the lobby bar. He knew immediately they were following him. They both had the look of hired thugs, no doubt engaged to dissuade Kevin from his investigation.

"I don't have time for this," Kevin said to himself. "Luceinne is waiting for me." He ducked into a doorway and hid in the shadows. "Let's just find out who hired you two." He readied himself to jump the two men when they passed.

Kevin wasn't the most patient person and a man can stay poised to pounce for only so long. After about five minutes and still no sign of the men, Kevin found himself in a predicament.

"Damn," he said softly. "If I come out now it could be me walking into a trap, but if I don't come out, I'll surely be late for my dinner date. Maybe those two weren't even after me. Maybe I'm just being paranoid." Kevin continued to debate with himself for another minute.

"The hell with it!" he said and finally stepped back onto the street. He looked around but the two men were nowhere to be seen. He thought it best that he not walk the rest of the way to Le Grand Colbert just in case the two thugs were waiting in some shadowy doorway for him. He would take a cab.

It took Kevin three tries before he finally got a taxi to pull over. Most Paris taxi drivers do not like to pick up passengers who are not at designated taxi stands, especially when they only intend to go four blocks away. Kevin could tell the driver was not pleased and paid him almost three times the fare. "Money well spent." Kevin said to himself.

It was exactly 9:00 o'clock when he entered the restaurant.

"Good evening monsieur, do you have a reservation?" the hostess asked.

"Not unless my lady friend made one," Kevin replied looking around the restaurant for Lucienne.

"What name would it be under?"

"I'm afraid I only know her first name, Lucienne. If it's not under that name I wouldn't know. She said to meet her here at nine," Kevin replied.

"I'm sorry monsieur but I have no reservation for Lucienne," the hostess replied.

"Perhaps she made it under a different name," Kevin said.

"No monsieur, I have no such reservations."

"She's about five feet ten inches tall with long ebony hair. Maybe I should look around to see if she is here already," Kevin said.

"I'm sorry sir, but that will not be possible. I can assure you that I have not seated a single lady all evening. I regret that we do not have a bar where you can wait. Perhaps you should wait outside until she arrives." The hostess was becoming a bit snippy in her attitude.

"Could you please seat me so I can order some wine while I wait?" Kevin replied.

The hostess took her time looking over the seating chart and reservation list before responding. "I believe I may have a table available."

Kevin could see at least a dozen empty tables.

"This way please," the hostess said.

Kevin followed her towards the back of the restaurant passing several tables along the way until she reached a table next to the restroom doors.

"Is it possible to seat me at one of those tables along the wall so I can see when my date arrives?" Kevin quipped.

"Of course, monsieur," the hostess replied with a complete lack of sincerity.

Kevin was really starting to dislike the attitude of the Parisians.

"I'll show them," he thought to himself, "I'll order a bottle of California wine."

The wine steward was more than happy to serve him a bottle of Georis Cabernet Sauvignon from Carmel Valley, California for $130 a bottle.

By 9:40, Kevin was over half-way through the bottle of wine and annoyed that Lucienne had stood him up. The hostess made it a point to walk past his table several times with a smirk that left little doubt as to her amusement over Kevin's situation.

By 10:00 the wine was gone and Kevin decided he would wait no longer and ordered the spicy fish soup and a Grand Colbert salad, which was simply a Caesar salad, but excellently prepared. To make the best of the evening he ordered a thirty-five-year-old port to complete his meal.

When Kevin left the restaurant, the two thugs who he thought had followed him from the hotel earlier were waiting for him. Unfortunately, he didn't see them until the first one's fist was in his face.

"A friend of ours thinks you need to mind your own business," the man said as he smashed Kevin's jaw knocking him into the gutter.

The men stood there waiting for him to get back up.

Kevin pulled his handkerchief from his dinner jacket pocket and held it against his face.

"And what business might that be?" Kevin replied.

"Don't be stupid," the second man said and swung his foot at Kevin's head.

One bottle of wine did have an affect, but not enough to slow Kevin's reflexes. With his free hand he blocked the man's foot and used the man's own momentum to knock him off balance. He crashed hard to the ground hitting his head and momentarily dazing him. Before the other man could react, Kevin used his handkerchief to scoop up a healthy pile of recent dog crap, leaped to his feet and smashed the contents of the handkerchief into the mouth and face of the first attacker.

"Ah crap," the man managed to say before puking all over his friend lying on the ground.

"Exactly," Kevin replied. "You just better be glad none of that got on my favorite dinner jacket or you might have really pissed me off. Now go tell this friend of yours that Kevin Bridges doesn't like to be threatened."

A group of people had gathered outside Le Grand Colbert seemingly disgusted by Kevin's actions and began cursing him.

"Excuse me," he said as he headed back inside the restaurant. The bystanders were quick to get out of his way.

"I just need to use your toilette," Kevin said holding his hand up for the hostess to see. She didn't quite understand until the smell reached her nostrils, but before she could refuse Kevin was headed back to the rear of the restaurant.

Kevin had just finished washing his hands when two of the waiters and one of the chefs, who was holding a meat cleaver, pounded on the door of the restroom.

"Monsieur, we must insist you leave at once, or we will call the police" the waiter said.

"I was just on my way out," Kevin replied.

"Monsieur, we find what you did disgusting," the hostess said from behind the group of men.

"What I find disgusting is the total lack of respect for this fabulous city by you Parisians. Look at your streets; they are covered in dog feces. I understand that three people a day are hospitalized due to falls caused by slipping on the messes left on the sidewalks."

Just as Kevin walked out the door a taxi pulled up to let out a party on their way to dinner. Kevin looked around for the two thugs but they were nowhere to be seen.

"Hotel L'Horset," Kevin told the driver soft enough so none of restaurant employees who followed him out could hear.

"Oui monsieur," the driver replied. As the taxi turned onto the Rue du Quatre Septembre the first police car turned onto Rue Vivienne.

Before Kevin exited the taxi, he looked around to make sure the two thugs were nowhere in sight. He was in no mood to do battle again, especially since this time they would be angry and no doubt better prepared. To his surprise, there were two police cars parked in front of the hotel and several policemen milling about the lobby.

"Great," Kevin said. "How did they find me so quickly?"

As soon as Kevin entered the lobby the police came straight to him.

"Mr. Bridges we have a few questions we would like to ask you."

"I know I shouldn't have gone back into the restaurant smelling like that, but what else was I to do. And as to why those two thugs tried to jump me, I've no idea," Kevin explained.

"Pardon, monsieur, but what are you referring to?" the officer asked.

"Yikes," Kevin thought to himself, "now I've stuck more than just my hand in it." He proceeded to explain what had happened at Le Grand Colbert and about the same two men following him when he first left the hotel.

"If you took a taxi, how did they know where you were going to dinner?" the officer asked.

"They must have known where I was going," Kevin replied.

"Who else knew you were going out to dinner?"

"Only Lucienne, the woman I was to meet there," Kevin replied. Suddenly, the policeman became much more serious.

"Where is this Lucienne?"

"I have no idea; she never kept our dinner date. Just what's going on here and why so many questions?" Kevin asked.

"What is this Lucienne's last name and where does she live?" the officer asked.

"I don't know. I met her at a medical records office today where I was working," Kevin replied.

"By working do you mean trying to prove a miracle?" the officer asked somewhat skeptically.

"I guess you have been in touch with my boss. Just what exactly is going on here? I'm answering no more questions until I get a few answers myself," Kevin replied.

Before the policeman could answer, the elevator door opened and his supervisor stepped out. "Mr. Bridges I presume, a pleasure to meet you. My name is François Bontecou, lieutenant with the Paris Prefecture of Police." The officer passed the lieutenant the notes he had written.

"Nice to meet you lieutenant, but could you please tell me what is going on," Kevin asked.

"But of course. It appears that someone entered your room while you were at dinner," he started to explain.

"Was anything stolen?" Kevin asked.

"We were hoping you could answer that for us. Was there anything in your room of great value?"

"Nothing at all," Kevin said, although he already knew it was the papers he had found disproving the miracle that the thief was after.

"Are you sure you had nothing related to your investigation here in our city that the thief may have wanted?" the lieutenant pressed.

Kevin knew there was more going on than they were telling him. They had already contacted the Vatican and knew why he was in Paris. They were probably already checking his story about going to dinner and running into the two thugs. Kevin knew it would be best to tell the truth. "I did have the papers that related to the alleged miracle that I was working on."

"Just exactly what did those papers show?" the lieutenant asked.

"I found proof that the man claiming to have had his brain tumor disappear never had a brain tumor to begin with," Kevin explained. "Do you think the two thugs that tried to jump me broke into my room and stole my papers?"

"No," the lieutenant replied, "we know who broke into your room, we have them on video."

"Who was it?" Kevin asked.

"We were hoping you could tell us," the lieutenant replied. "Please come this way, I'd like you to see the tape."

Kevin followed him into a room behind the reception desk. A bank of monitors showed every floor, the lobby, the elevator interior and outdoor views of the front and back entrance to the hotel. On the fourth floor in front of Kevin's room were several policemen going in and out of his room and an ambulance gurney in the hallway. "I don't like the look of that," Kevin said. The lieutenant didn't reply, but pushed a button. On a larger screen a previously recorded picture of an empty fourth floor came on the screen.

"Oh, my goodness, that's Lucienne," Kevin said. He watched as she walked up to his door and seemed to walk right in. "Did she have a pass key? I didn't see her use a key." Kevin said. "I thought the doors were always locked."

"They are," the manager said. "She broke the lock. That's why we sent hotel security to your room when the alarm went off in here." The lieutenant looked sternly at the manager who had said too much. He got the message and left the room.

Kevin continued to watch as the hotel security guard moved slowly towards the door, seemed to call out, and then entered the room. The door closed behind him. The lieutenant stopped the video.

"I take it she got away," Kevin said. "And from the looks of the gurney in the hallway, things must not have gone well for the security guard."

"An excellent observation and deduction," the lieutenant replied. "What can you tell me about the woman, this Lucienne?"

"Not much more than I already told the officer. She assisted me at the medical clinic today as I was looking through computer files. I said something that offended her, so I offered to make it up by taking her to dinner. Now I know why she never showed."

"You never got a last name?"

"No, but I'm sure the medical office can get you that information," Kevin replied.

"We called the owner of the office. According to him no one named Lucienne works or has ever worked for him."

"That's not possible. She helped me for at least two hours. Ask the receptionist, she'll know, she locked up when we left," Kevin explained.

"She saw Lucienne leave with you?" the lieutenant asked.

"No, Lucienne walked out before me. She was gone by the time the receptionist and I walked out. But she must've seen Lucienne leave before me," Kevin said.

"We did speak to her. We found her partying at a local bistro her boss said she frequents. She wasn't too happy to have her date interrupted. She claims there was no other woman working with you this evening."

"That's ridiculous," Kevin said. "That was Lucienne in the video. But why would she steal something that I can easily replace in the morning?"

"Can you?" the lieutenant asked. "The medical offices were burned to the ground less than two hours ago."

"This all makes no sense what-so-ever. Tell me what happened to the hotel security guard?" Kevin asked.

"I understand you worked for the FBI before you took your present job with the Vatican," the lieutenant said.

"You're well informed," Kevin said.

"Why is it you gave up such an interesting career and took the job as miracle investigator for the Catholic Church? I know you're not Catholic. Was it for the money?" the lieutenant asked.

"No, not at all, although I do admit I'm paid very well for what I do. I was working on a serial murder case in the South when I realized the only rational explanation was that Satan himself was behind the murders." Kevin explained.

"Attributing a series of murders to Satan is a rational explanation?" the lieutenant asked.

"It was to me. The more I explored the possibility the more real it became, but try to tell that to your boss. He reacted pretty much the same way you are," Kevin laughed. "I did finally catch the man who was responsible for the murders, but he was just doing Satan's work. I know this probably sounds ridiculous to you, but there was just too much that couldn't be explained."

The lieutenant remained quiet for a moment. "I think you better come upstairs and have a look at your room."

൞   ൞   ൞

The television, dresser, and desk had all been pushed against the room's window. In their place was the crucified body of the security guard. His body hung from two large spikes that had been hammered through his palms and into studs in the wall.

"How did he die?" Kevin asked

"The coroner says his heart stopped."

"So, he was dead before he was placed on the wall?" Kevin asked.

"We're not sure," one of the crime scene investigators replied.

"If he was alive, he would've been screaming bloody murder," Kevin replied. "Surely, someone would have heard him and come to investigate."

"He wasn't able to scream, his mouth was seared closed," the investigator said.

"Was it fear that stopped his heart?" Kevin asked.

"Possibly, but I think it was something else. I think it was frozen. Look at the tissue around his chest. It looks like it was burned by liquid nitrogen. His entire torso is still ice cold," the investigator said.

"Liquid nitrogen in the shape of a hand," the lieutenant said.

Kevin's fingers suddenly started to burn. The dead skin on the security guard matched the dead skin cells on Kevin's fingers.

"Lucienne did this!" Kevin exclaimed.

Everyone in the room looked at Kevin. "You think a woman could do something like this alone?" the lieutenant said.

Kevin didn't want to say what he really thought. "Those two thugs probably helped her."

"No one else entered this room," the lieutenant said and paused. "Nor was anyone seen leaving the room."

"Then how did she get out?" Kevin asked. "There are no doors to adjoining rooms and the furniture is blocking the window."

"And the window is locked from the inside," one of the investigators added.

"This investigation seems to be right up your alley Mr. Bridges," the lieutenant said.

"Thanks, but I have my own case to work on," Kevin replied, "but if you would like a suggestion, why don't you try to find those two thugs who tried to jump me. They have to be involved in this."

"We'll find them, you can be sure of that," the lieutenant replied.

"Is there anything else missing from the room?" the lieutenant asked.

"From what I can see, only the papers from the medical office are missing. They were in that empty briefcase that's now lying on the bed," Kevin said.

"Where was the briefcase when you left?" asked the lieutenant.

"Under the desk, which was right about directly under that left spike in the wall," Kevin explained.

"Anything else you think we should know about?" the lieutenant asked.

"If I think of something, I'll be sure to let you know," Kevin replied. "Now can I get my suitcase? I'm sure the hotel has an empty room. I drank an awful lot of wine and have to get up very early in the morning so I really need to get some rest."

The lieutenant nodded his head and one of the investigators brought Kevin his suitcase.

"I'm not sure what your plans are for breakfast tomorrow Mr. Bridges but there is more we need to talk about. I'll call for you at 8:00 in the morning. I know this terrific restaurant that makes superb crepes. Oh, by the way I saw you were planning on returning to Rome later in the morning."

"That's right," Kevin replied.

"You may want to consider delaying your return until we know a little more about what's happened here."

Kevin had had just about enough advice from the lieutenant but held his tongue. "I'll give that some thought," Kevin replied.

"I'll have two of my men guard your door tonight to make sure you have no more surprises," the lieutenant said.

"And to make sure I don't try to leave town," Kevin wanted to say but didn't. At least the lieutenant hadn't asked Kevin to turn over his passport. European Union citizens didn't need a passport to travel around Europe, and even though Kevin worked for the Vatican, he still used his United States passport when traveling. However, if it was ever necessary, Kevin also had what he considered his 'get-out-of-jail-free' card. The Pope had issued him a Vatican diplomatic passport making him immune to prosecution or lawsuit in a host country. Tomorrow he just might get the chance to use it.

CHAPTER THREE

"Wrath"

Madrid had flourished since the end of the Siglo de Oro, the golden century, despite the decline of the Spanish Empire throughout Europe. Now that Philip V had returned to the throne after the death of his eldest son, Spaniards hoped to recapture some of that past glory that seemed to had faded when Spain was forced to cede many of their colonies and territories.

Many of Madrid's older buildings were being torn down, old fortress walls razed and new structures, plazas, and gardens were replacing them. Philip's desire was to turn Madrid into a viable economic center and many of these new structures were built to house the ever-growing population. And with the influx of people the need for new churches to meet their spiritual needs increased. The Templo Eucarístico de San Martín was one of the first major projects to fill that religious need.

The pastor had orchestrated a fine plan in arranging for an Inquisition Tribunal and the auto de fe that was to follow. Those whose faith had lagged would be frightened into renewing their spiritual life so as not to suffer the same fate as those accused and convicted. It also gave the pastor the opportunity to impress the local bishopric and enhance his chances of promotion to such a position. An excellent plan until the bells began to toll.

༄ ༄ ༄

"Brother Raul, has anyone tried to exit the crypt?" Bruno asked.

"No one my grace, I mean, Brother Mancini. Nor has anyone asked to enter." Raul replied.

"Well let's just see where this blood trail leads us. I have a feeling we may find the source of blood coming from the Madonna," Bruno said.

Bruno grabbed a candle and started down the steps. "Stay with me Brother Toribio, no telling what we may find," Bruno said.

Raul wasn't the bravest monk and immediately started to pray. "Protect us Father from…"

"Latin, pray in Latin. Satan hates it when you pray in Latin," Bruno explained. Immediately, Raul's prayers changed to Latin.

"A lot more blood drops down here," Bruno said as he reached the bottom of the steps and entered the crypt.

There were several candles burning inside the crypt displaying a most grizzly scene. Lying in the middle of the floor, as though he had been crucified, was a young boy whose face was covered in blood. "This is not good," Bruno said crossing himself.

Raul remained behind Bruno but peered around him to see what was not good. "Oh, dear God, that's Jose, he's one of the acolytes. It was his job to replace all of these candles after the crypt closed for viewing."

"I thought the crypt remained open until 10:00," Bruno said.

"Not tonight. It was closed at six when the Mass for the auto de fe began."

"Yes, but isn't there a monk assigned to monitor the door from the sanctuary after it has been locked? That's the only way the monks can return to the cells from the sanctuary isn't it?" Bruno said.

"Actually, that door is always kept locked. It's only monitored during the times the crypt is open for visitation. I'm sure no one has been there since six o'clock when the Mass started. Most of the monks use the door leading from the monastery directly to the street. That door always has someone watching it. Except this evening when everyone went to watch the auto de fe."

"There appears to be a deep puncture in his forehead. Help me lift the body," Bruno said. "Let's get him upstairs."

"His back is stuck to the floor, and it looks like someone cut his hair off." Raul said pulling hard. Suddenly the body broke free of the floor with a ghastly sucking sound.

"Turn him over," Bruno ordered.

They turned over the body and laid the boy on his stomach.

"It's a sign from God," Raul said. "Look, a cross has been carved into his back."

"More likely a sign from Satan," Bruno replied. "It looks like someone cut out a cross from the skin of his back."

"Lord preserve us," Raul said dropping to his knees to pray.

"In Latin I told you," Bruno ordered. "Satan hates it when you pray in Latin." Bruno carefully probed the boys back then turned the head to look at that wound. "There should be more blood," he said, looking around the room.

Raul ended his prayer and looked up. "The candles were not replaced at the far end of the crypt. Look, there by the bench. That is the tunic Jose would've been wearing."

"It's soaked in blood," Bruno said. "The boy's body appears to have been bled dry before he was moved."

"Who could've done such a thing?" Raul asked.

"Many a mind can be twisted by Satan's temptations," Bruno replied.

"Could Jose's blood be the source of the Virgin's tears?" Raul asked.

"I don't see how," Bruno replied, "but still, a lot more blood than what we see here should have seeped from the body."

"I understand," Raul replied. "The Virgin cries for what has occurred in the Lord's Holy Temple. It is truly a miracle."

"Tell no one of what we have found," Bruno explained, "at least not yet. I need to speak with the archbishop about how to proceed. Did the boy have family in Madrid?"

"No, he came to us when his parents were killed by *moriscos*," Raul explained. "He lived here at the church."

"We must move him to one of the monk's cells. Do any of the monks know how to draw?" Bruno asked.

"I don't understand," Raul replied.

"You know draw," Bruno pretended to draw a picture on a tablet." "Do any of your brothers have artistic talents?"

"Brother Benito is very talented," Raul replied.

"Good. Once we get Jose's body to the cell, I want you to have Brother Benito copy the carving on Jose's back. It is very important he get it exactly right. Do you understand?" Bruno said.

"Yes."

"I also want you to write down exactly how we found the body, when Jose was last seen, and everything that happened since the Madonna began to cry. As a matter-of-fact, I need you to keep a daily record of all that transpires with regards to the Madonna. How long she cries and how much she cries. I also want samples of the bloody tears collected everyday and sealed in a bottle."

Bruno grabbed one of the candles and walked around the edge of the room. A trail of blood drops similar to the ones found on the stairs ended in front of one of the crypts where they were smudged, as if someone's had walked in them.

"Did you walk over here Raul?" Bruno asked.

"No brother, I did not," Raul replied.

Bruno lifted the candle and began to read the inscription on the crypt:

> "Ask and it will be given to you; seek and you will find; knock and the door will be opened to you.
> For everyone who asks receives; he who seeks..."

Before Bruno could finish, a voice called from the stairs outside the crypt.

"Brother Bruno. His grace would like to speak with you."

"I guess we better let the archbishop know what we've found," Bruno said. "Let's get this poor soul out of here."

When the two men reached the top of the steps one of the other brothers was already cleaning the blood drops. When he saw the body of the dead acolyte he dropped to his knees in prayer.

"Pray later," Bruno insisted. "Help Brother Raul take this boy to an empty cell. I need to speak to the archbishop."

"You'll find him in the church office with Father Santorio," the monk replied. "There's also an alguacil waiting there."

"Bad news must travel fast around here," Bruno said. "Too fast!"

Bruno was sweating when he entered the pastor's office. "You needed to see me, your Grace?"

"I will be leaving for Rome in two days to report what I've seen to the Pope. I hope you'll have some information I can tell him as to why this is happening and if it's indeed a miracle," the archbishop explained.

"I have made some interesting discoveries yet there is much to learn about this. Be assured, I'll have the information to you before you leave on your journey," Bruno insisted.

The archbishop knew Bruno didn't want to share his 'discoveries' in front of the alguacil. "This man has brought very troubling news about a grisly murder. Circumstances suggest that someone in the church may have been involved."

"Why do you believe the church to be involved with this alleged murder?" Bruno asked.

"The victim was one of the witches whose punishment was rescinded. She was freed from the auto de fe after the Madonna began to weep and the bells tolled," the alguacil replied.

"As I understand it, the auto de fe was symbolic. There was no severe punishment to be accorded," the archbishop said.

"The witches were to be sentenced to two years in jail but, when freed, they were told they must leave the city and denounce Satan. I went to her house to remind her to be gone by the morning and discovered her body," the alguacil replied sheepishly.

"More likely you went to steal one last night beneath her covers," the pastor said.

"Forgive me Father," the alguacil kneeled before the pastor.

"You believe someone in the church passed judgment on this woman and murdered her?" Bruno interjected.

"I'm not sure what to think, but I know this is an evil beyond what the local authorities are capable of handling," the alguacil replied. "I believe this is a matter for the church."

"Go with this man and see if what he says is true, Bruno," the archbishop said to his trusted friend.

"Have one of the monks go with you. Take a cart to bring the body back here," the pastor explained.

"You cannot bring a worshipper of Satan to this holy place," the archbishop said. "Even in death this witch is still one of Satan's disciples."

"Take the body to the blacksmith shop behind the stables. The church owns the building and there's a room inside with a table where you can lay the body. There you'll be left alone to conduct your investigation," the pastor explained.

"I hope that will not be necessary," Bruno replied. "I should be able to perform a summary examination of the corpse at the scene. If further examination is required, I'll bring the body to the stables as you suggest monsignor. If not, I'll have the body removed to the cemetery outside the city for burial once I've completed my task."

"I'll have Brother Tomás fetch the cart and meet you in front of the church," the pastor said to both Bruno and the alguacil.

"If you could please wait for me outside," Bruno said to the alguacil, "I need to speak to the archbishop and pastor in private for a moment"

"Of course, and Father please forgive me for my sins," the aguacil said to the pastor.

"Save your confession for church tomorrow, my son," the pastor replied ushering the alguacil out of the room.

"There has been another murder," Bruno began to explain. "One of the acolytes, a boy named Jose; I found his body down in the crypts. His head had a deep puncture wound and there was a large patch of skin missing from his back. I was on my way to report this when I was summoned to your office."

"Where's the body now?" the pastor asked.

"I told Brother Raul to take it to one of the empty cells, but I think it would be better if it were moved to the stable where I could examine it more closely," Bruno explained.

"I'll arrange for it while you're away with the alguacil," the pastor replied.

"Do you believe this murder has anything to do with the Madonna's bloody tears?" the archbishop asked.

"It'd be foolish for me to rule that out," Bruno replied, "but there's much to learn before I can say anything for certain."

"Do whatever is necessary," the archbishop implored. "We must not allow the church to be victim to some hoax nor do we want news of this murder to create panic and foreshadow what may be a most miraculous sign from God."

"Trust in me as I trust in God," Bruno replied.

"We always do," the archbishop replied.

When Bruno exited the church, he had to push through the large crowd still hoping for a chance to witness the alleged miracle of the Virgin. Brother Tomás and the alguacil were waiting about fifty yards west of the church where Calle de San Martín merged into Calle de los Tadescos. It was at least a twenty-minute walk to the house where the witch's body was discovered. Twenty minutes Bruno felt he didn't have time to waste. Still, the archbishop thought the alguacil's plea for assistance necessitated Bruno's involvement. Bruno was considered one of the most learned men serving the Holy See. Bruno was in fact a prelate, a dignity granted by the Pope giving Bruno all the privileges and rights equal to that of an archbishop, but without the jurisdiction over a specific territory. Bruno's jurisdiction was a personal duty to perform a constant service in the retinue of the Pope. Even with the papal brief giving him equal standing with the archbishop, Bruno chose to remain, at least in name, the archbishop's secretary. It allowed him the freedom to perform his duties without being the focus of attention. It also allowed him to continue his personal research in medicine and science with freedoms greater than those the church granted to Leonardo Da Vinci two hundred years earlier. However, it was much of Da Vinci's research that guided Bruno's studies and that he referred to often in his current investigations.

"So just what makes you think someone in the church may have something to do with this witch's murder?" Bruno asked the alguacil.

"The cross; such an odd cross; haunting. Who but a man of the church would carry such a cross?" the alguacil replied.

"Did anyone actually see someone from the church at her house?" Bruno asked.

"No, but two drunks complained that a monk knocked one of them down when he was only trying to talk to the woman," the alguacil said.

"How did you find these two drunkards?" Bruno asked.

"They were arrested trying to molest one of the local prostitutes not far from the murder. They complained as to why they were being arrested when a monk had just assaulted them and got away with it. As we questioned them a few more details came out," he said.

"What details?"

"That the monk was wearing brown robes that even covered his head and that they were trying to do more than just talk to the woman when the monk stepped in to help her," replied the alguacil.

"This monk who saved her, you also suspect him of killing her?" Bruno asked.

"Only because of the cross. It's such a horrible sight," the alguacil explained.

Again, the alguacil couldn't stop talking about the cross, a fact that didn't go unnoticed. As they approached the house, several people had gathered trying to get a look inside the small room, but a second alguacil forcibly kept them back.

"Step aside," Bruno demanded. The power of his voice parted the peasants like a wedge splitting a log.

"Go home, all of you go home. There is nothing for you to see here," the alguacil ordered. "Unless of course you wish to spend the remainder of the night locked up."

That was all it took for the crowd to quickly disperse. They knew the local jail was no place to spend a night.

"Lord protect us," Bruno said as he, Tomás and the alguacil entered the room where the witch's body sat.

Tomás dropped to his knees and began to pray.

"She would've been pretty if she wasn't such a retch," the alguacil said standing in the doorway refusing to cross the threshold.

Bruno slowly walked around the body looking both at it and at the floor searching for clues as to who might have done such a gruesome act. He saw strands of long black hair on the floor and it appeared that the woman's hair had been cut. His eyes were constantly pulled back to the woman's face and the strange cross protruding from her forehead. It was odd, but she appeared to be smiling. The similarity between the blood pooled below the end of the table was almost identical to the scene back at the church. However, there was much more blood here.

"A very haunting cross indeed," Bruno said, still not touching the cross or the body but moving in to get a closer look.

Suddenly, Bruno reached out, grabbed the cross and tried to pull it from the woman's head.

"It seems to be caught up. Tomás, hold her head while I pull," Bruno ordered.

"Yes monsignor," he replied but was none to pleased to touch the pagan corpse.

"Go ahead, she won't bite you," Bruno said.

Tomás did as he was told and grabbed the top of the head.

"It appears someone has cut away her hair," Tomás said.

"Just hold her tight," Bruno replied.

The bottom of the cross was pointed and fit in the pierced skull like a key in a lock. Bruno had to turn the cross slightly to pull it free of the woman's head. Unfortunately, as the cross exited the wound much of her brain came out with it.

"I'm going to need a bucket for this," Bruno said turning to the alguacil who now looked very pale and ill.

"I'll go find one," he replied trying to keep from vomiting.

"Tear me a piece of cloth from the blanket in the cart," Bruno told Tomas. "I don't want anyone to see this cross."

A bucket was produced and the brains dangling from the point on the cross were placed inside. Bruno carefully wrapped the cross in the cloth and placed it in his satchel.

With a small rag Bruno wiped away the blood and tissues near the wound entrance. It was almost identical to the wound he saw on the acolyte's head.

Bruno lifted the witch's body slightly away from the wall to confirm what he already knew to be true. Just as with the acolyte, a large patch of skin had been cut away from her back. Bruno decided this was information the alguacil didn't need to know. At least not yet. Bruno took the rest of blanket Tomás had given him and wrapped the body as carefully as possible to insure neither Tomás nor the alguacil would see her mutilated back. Fortunately, the raw exposed back tissues did not rest against the wall making his task easier.

"What do you intend to do with the body?" the alguacil asked.

"We will take it to the stables behind the church so I can examine it and then bury it in the cemetery outside the city," Bruno explained.

"What do you expect to learn from this examination?"

"I would expect to learn who killed her and why," Bruno replied. "But what I expect often is not what I find, at least not at first. I assure you that whatever I learn I will share with you and the tribunal."

"And what if you find it is one of your own who is responsible?"

"Then God and the tribunal will both pass judgment on his soul," Bruno replied.

"May whoever did this rot in hell and suffer the tortures of Satan," replied the alguacil.

"My guess is they already are," Bruno responded. "Now let's get her out of here."

CHAPTER FOUR

"Intentions"

"Good morning Mr. Bridges. I hope you had a restful night's sleep," the lieutenant said when Kevin opened the door. "I see you're already dressed; shall we head to breakfast?"

"I do have to eat and I'm mighty curious as to what you have turned up in your investigation, so I guess the answer is yes, lieutenant," Kevin replied.

"Excellent, but please call me Francois," the lieutenant replied.

"Uh-oh," Kevin thought to himself. He knew if the lieutenant wanted to be on a first name basis, something was up. "Thank you, Francois and please call me Kevin, Mr. Bridges is my father."

Francois laughed a little too hard at Kevin's joke raising even more suspicion of Francois' motives.

"Tell me Francois, did you have any luck finding those two thugs who jumped me?" Kevin asked.

"I'm surprised you didn't first ask about this woman Lucienne," Francois replied. "It would seem to me that finding the murderer who deceived you would be of more interest."

Kevin shrugged, "That was no woman that was Satan."

Francois stopped and stared at Kevin, "I'm sorry I cannot share your religious fervor, for I did see this woman, the one you call Lucienne, enter the room. Of course, blaming Satan for the murder would make it simpler to solve," Francois said almost mockingly.

"I wouldn't expect you to believe it was Satan. What reasonable man would believe such a thing?" Kevin replied. "Then again, explain to me how this woman murdered, then lifted and crucified a man almost twice her size on the room wall, moved all the furniture against the room's one window, which was locked from the inside, and then managed to escape without ever exiting the room. At least she didn't leave according to the hotel's video surveillance. And I know we didn't discuss this, but I'm guessing this all happened in what, maybe one or two minutes before back-up security arrived. Not to mention he was killed by his heart being frozen. I'm sure your forensics people have told you it would take almost five minutes to freeze a heart solid, and that is if it was dropped into a bucket of liquid nitrogen."

"It is rather mystifying," Francois replied sheepishly.

"Well you let me know when you figure it out, but I won't hold my breath," Kevin replied.

"I don't understand," Francois responded, "What do you mean you won't hold your breath?"

"I apologize. It's an American colloquialism and a rather sarcastic one at that. I meant no offense," Kevin replied.

"None taken, for I was rather rude as well," Francois said. "We did find the two men on the video from earlier in the evening. The two who you claim attacked you. It seems they were the doctor and radiologist who instigated this miracle hoax."

"Good, my faith in the Paris Prefecture is renewed," Kevin laughed.

"Unfortunately, they were found murdered in an alley very near the Grand Colbert," Francois explained.

"Am I a suspect in their deaths?" Kevin asked.

"No, there were sufficient witnesses that accounted for your whereabouts after your initial confrontation with the two men until you arrived here at the hotel," Francois explained.

"Well at least there is some good news," Kevin replied. "Let me guess, they both died of heart failure."

Francois smiled, "No, they both died of brain aneurisms. Their heads had been frozen."

Before Kevin could respond Francois continued. "Ahh, here we are. This place serves the best crepes in Paris."

"I hope so, all this walking has made me hungry," Kevin replied.

As they entered it was obvious by the crowd that this was indeed a popular place to eat.

"Looks like we will have to wait for a table," Kevin said.

"Ah, there she is," Francois said as he nodded towards a woman sitting alone at a table by the window.

"There's who?" Kevin asked following behind Francois.

"Kevin Bridges, I'd like you to meet Elizabeth Purdue. Elizabeth works with Interpol. It seems the murder of the hotel security guard is remarkably similar to another recent murder in Poland that Elizabeth is working on."

"Nice to meet you Elizabeth," Kevin replied, "but why is it I get the feeling I am being set-up?"

"A bit paranoid are we, Mr. Bridges? And please call me Liz," she held out her hand. Kevin hesitated before taking it. "I promise it won't burn you."

"You must know the story about Lucienne?" Kevin said gently shaking her hand.

"That's why I'm here, but I must say I certainly don't put much credence in your theory Mr. Bridges," Liz replied.

"Please call me Kevin and I wouldn't believe my theory either if I hadn't seen things for myself," Kevin said.

"You both might be interested to know that a local medical supply company was robbed last night and reported that a canister of liquid nitrogen was missing. I think that might explain our frostbite heart attacks and frozen heads."

"Not in the least," Kevin replied. "I'm sure your crime scene specialists will eliminate that theory shortly. Liz, tell me about this murder in Poland and how it ties in with this case." Francois didn't like having his theory dismissed so quickly by Kevin. Even less did he like the interest Kevin seemed to show for Liz.

"I think it's you who needs to be answering and not asking the questions Kevin," Francois said.

"No, that's quite all right. I believe Kevin and I are both working on the same cases. At least that's what I'm here to find out," Liz explained to Francois. She turned to Kevin. "I was called to assist in Poland earlier this week when several bodies were discovered. Three men had died from cardiac arrest due to their hearts freezing. I had investigated a similar case last year in Yorkshire. One of the local Krakow police had been in Yorkshire observing during that investigation and thought to call me when the bodies were discovered in Poland. It turned out all three of these men were connected to a miracle claim submitted to the Vatican to support the beatification of John Paul II. I called the Vatican and they told me about you, Kevin. When I arrived last night at your hotel I intended to check in and speak with you this morning but you can imagine my surprise when I found out why the local prefecture was swarming the lobby. Francois filled me in on what had occurred in your room and suggested we all meet this morning."

"Francois knows a lot more about what's going on here than I do," Kevin said. "I told him everything that happened yesterday."

"Francois filled me in on his investigation but I think we have or very soon will hit a dead end with the investigation here. I was hoping you could tell me where you think this Lucienne will strike next," Liz said. "If I'm going to catch her, I need to be a step ahead of her, not two steps behind."

"It seems I'm further behind than you are," Kevin replied. "I was headed to Krakow in a couple of days to start my investigation of the miracle claim there. This is the first I've heard about the deaths."

"I guess I just saved you a trip," Liz said.

Kevin wasn't sure just how much he should tell Liz, if anything at all. He could tell both Francois and Liz still had suspicions about his involvement, but that only made sense since they had nothing else to go on. He also had to agree with Liz that there was little else to be learned about Lucienne and the murders from this investigation. What he needed to do was head to New York as soon as possible before more bodies were found with frozen hearts.

"New York," Kevin said. "We need to head to New York right now. There was a third miracle claim identical to the ones here and in Poland."

Liz immediately pulled out her cell phone to book a flight that day.

"I'm afraid Liz will have to make that flight on her own. I'm going to need you to stay around for a few days until we conclude our investigation," Francois said.

"You'll never conclude this investigation," Kevin replied. "This is one of those that will go down as unsolved."

"That may very well prove to be true, but it still doesn't change the fact that I'm insisting you stay in Paris while we continue our investigation," Francois said.

"I thought you might say that," Kevin said. "That's why I brought my passport."

"There is no need to surrender your passport, I trust that you will not leave the country," Francois said.

"Well I'm glad you have so much faith in me, but that's not why I brought my passport," Kevin said holding it open before the lieutenant. "I have diplomatic immunity. You cannot keep me here."

"Should I make the reservations for two?" Liz asked smiling, knowing how angered Francois was.

"Most certainly," Kevin replied closing his passport and smiling at Francois. "Of course, I'll be happy to answer any further questions you may have when I am finished with my investigation in New York."

"Make reservations for three," Francois said, "if this murderess Lucienne is headed for New York, then so am I." Now it was Francois' turn to smile.

"The plane leaves in three hours," Liz said, "we can continue our conversation on board."

"And we most certainly will," Francois added. "Can you find your way back to the hotel, Kevin?"

"I believe so. I'll see you all at the airport, *au revoir*," Kevin said.

"No, your Grace," Kevin explained. "There's no chance of finding the proof, the medical office was destroyed, but I'm sure the other two claims are somehow connected. From what I learned from the Interpol agent, the people I planned to interview in Krakow are dead so there's no point following up there. I should head to New York, today if possible."

"From what you've told me, this Lucienne already knows of your plans. What makes you think she'll not have already destroyed any evidence there as well?" The bishop asked, but before Kevin could answer, the bishop continued.

"No, I've spoken with Father Oder and we have decided it is no longer necessary for you to investigate these other two claims."

"But your Grace," Kevin replied. "This Lucienne is no doubt one of Satan's agents and she must…"

"Kevin," the bishop interrupted. "It's your job to investigate miracles for the Vatican, not to battle Satan or track down murderers. Leave that task for the clergy and Interpol."

Kevin knew there was no point to argue the matter further. The bishop obviously already knew about Liz tracking Lucienne. "Then I shall return to Rome immediately and give my report to Father Bamonte." Father Francesco Bamonte was known as one of the leading exorcists in Rome. "He should know about the remarkable powers that Lucienne seemed to possess."

"No, you're needed elsewhere," the bishop replied. "A Madonna in a Madrid church has begun to cry tears of blood. I need you to fly to Spain immediately and investigate this alleged miracle. I've already dispatched a papal jet. It should arrive within the hour."

Kevin was beginning to question just why he had left the FBI. "What about my report?"

"Send it to me. I'll be sure the information gets to the right people."

"Yes, your Grace," Kevin replied, knowing someone or something was conspiring to keep him off this investigation.

"Trust in God, my son. Fulfill the great commission and the church will prevail. Remember, God works in mysterious ways," the bishop explained and hung up the phone.

"Well, I know you certainly do," Kevin said, shaking his head in disgust.

※ ※ ※

"You're late," Francois said as Kevin entered the airport. "We thought we would have to leave without you."

"You do," Kevin replied. "I've been ordered to fly to Spain immediately. I was told to leave the hunt for murderers to the proper authorities. That would be you and Liz."

"That's absurd," Liz replied sounding disappointed. "Is there something you're not telling us?"

"No, honestly, I can't believe they pulled me off the investigation either," Kevin said. "I was looking forward to showing you New York. Both of you," Kevin added taking his eyes off of Liz and finally acknowledging Francois.

"Why are they sending you to Spain? Does it have to do with these miracles you two talked about," Francois asked.

"I'm being sent to look into an alleged miracle, but one that has nothing to do with the one I've been investigating here. A church in Madrid claims that its Madonna, which has been there for over two-hundred seventy years, is now crying tears of blood," Kevin just smiled and shook his head.

"I've heard of this happening all over the world. I even heard your Madonna showed up on a toasted *fromag*e sandwich. Someone actually paid thousands of dollars for it. That's simply ridiculous."

"Maybe ridiculous to an agnostic, but not to the pious devotees of Catholicism," Kevin explained.

"I have many more questions I need to ask you about your investigation," Liz said. "We don't even know where we're going or who we're looking for."

"That's why I brought you this. Here's a copy of the files and my notes regarding these three miracle claims. Here is my cell phone number if you have any questions. I still have friends with the FBI in New York if you get into trouble or need anything. I've already called one of the agents to let him know you are coming. His name is Carlo, Carlo Caressa. Anything you need, Carlo can get for you. Believe me, you can trust Carlo with anything, including your lives. I explained the situation to him and told him to keep things quiet until he hears from you. He'll be waiting at the airport to speed your arrival along. It can take up to a couple of hours getting through customs at JFK."

"How will we recognize Carlo?" Francois asked.

"I'm sure he will see you long before you see him," Kevin explained. "I described you both to him. I told him to look for a raven-haired goddess accompanied by an Inspector Clouseau look-alike, no disrespect intended, Francois."

Kevin's statement caused Liz to giggle.

"Carlo is a rather burly man. That's a polite way of saying he could stand to lose about fifty pounds. Last time I saw him he had a short beard that was more white than brown," Kevin said.

"I'm sure he'll be easy to spot," Liz replied.

"When do you leave?" Liz asked.

"A Vatican jet is waiting for me now on the other side of the airport," Kevin replied.

"If the Vatican sent a private jet then it must be very important," Liz replied.

"It must be. Not often do I rate such luxury," Kevin replied.

"I wouldn't get too used to it if I were you," Francois piped in.

"I also included a copy of the report I am sending back to the Vatican concerning what I believe happened here yesterday. Don't let all the talk about Satan spook you, it's a little hard for non-believers to understand."

"Who said anything about being a non-believer? Liz replied.

"This is the final boarding call for Air France Flight 006 to New York City," the public-address system blared. "All passengers please report to Terminal 2 gate E41 immediately. Your plane is ready to depart."

"I'll take good care of Liz," Francois assured Kevin with a sly smile.

Liz was about to respond but knew male chauvinism was one of those dreadful French traits ingrained in the culture. She knew there would be plenty more opportunities to let Francois know what she thought about him. "I will be in touch," Liz said gently squeezing Kevin's hand.

Her touch was warm and it made Kevin smile. "Be careful, both of you. And make sure you read my report."

CHAPTER FIVE

"Preparation"

The acolyte's body was already lying on the table in the stables when Tomás and Bruno arrived with the witch's corpse. Raul sat at a table furiously writing a record of what had transpired that day, just as Bruno had ordered. The smell of death hung heavy in the small room, for the boy's body had begun to putrefy in the unrelenting Madrid heat.

"Brother Raul, would you please help Brother Tomás unload the body from the cart and place it next to this one, but first cover the boy's body. I want as few people as possible to know about the mutilated skin and keep the witch's body covered." Bruno noticed a most definite reaction in Raul's movement at the mention of the word witch.

"As you wish, Brother Bruno," Raul replied

"Fear not that she was a pagan," Bruno said trying to ease Raul's concern. "Her soul has surely been claimed by Satan and her body is but an empty shell."

"It's not that she was a witch," Raul replied. "It was your order to keep the boy's and the witch's bodies covered. It leads me to believe these deaths are somehow connected in an ominous way."

"A very astute observation," Bruno commented. "God in all his wisdom has sent a worthy assistant to aid me in my investigations."

"Thank you, monsignor," Raul replied, "but I now must assist Brother Tomás and get a bit of fresh air."

"You never get used to the smell," Bruno replied. "At least I never have."

The oppressive heat made the unpleasant task of moving the body from the cart to the room in the stables even more difficult for the two monks. Both Tomás and Raul were sweating heavily when they plopped the body onto the table. The roughness of the drop forced some of the pent-up gases out of the witch's body bringing along with it some rather rancid smelling wastes.

"That smells horrible," Tomás whined.

"Next time perhaps you'll be a little more careful when you are dealing with the dead," Bruno advised. "Now I have even more of a mess to clean up."

"My apologies, monsignor," Tomás said.

"Tomás, I want you to tell Raul where and in what position we found the body. And try to remember every detail of the room," Bruno ordered.

"Raul, write down Tomás' version and later I will dictate my version to you as well. I need to get some of my things from my room in the monastery then speak with the archbishop if he is still awake. I also need to check on the progress of the construction of the partition sealing off the Madonna. I should return in less than an hour."

"Yes, your grace," Raul replied.

Bruno was too tired to correct Raul again.

> "And with the measure you use,
> it will be measured to you.
> And with the measure you use,
> it will be measured to you."

Recited the monk in a sing-song lilt. He stretched the skin he had cut from the witch's back, tacking it down with small nails. "One must be careful, one mustn't tear such beauty," the monk said out loud. He grabbed a ceramic bowl full of salt and his own urine and poured it on the outstretched skin. "*And with the measure you use, it will be measured to you.* Maybe a little more for you as well, niño," the monk said pouring the mixture onto a second skin tacked onto the table next to the witch's.

Candles flickered, creating a myriad of shifting shadows in the small cave-like room where the monk worked. In the corner was a pile of bones heaped recklessly when he had cleared away the remains of long-ago interred predecessors. Several identical cells connected to the main catacomb that had served as the burial chamber for generations of monks. Generations who were long since forgotten by the templo and monastery's present enclave of pious believers. When the monastery was first rebuilt almost a hundred years earlier, the catacombs had been sealed when new crypts were built in front of the former entrance. When the monastery and templo were recently expanded and made anew, it was the monk who had discovered the hidden catacomb and chambers. A discovery he thought best kept to himself. Now these chambers served as his personal shrine, his adytum, the most sacred part of the templo, forbidden to the public, the innermost shrine of shrines, and his own private inner sanctum. It was here that he first heard the voice of his god.

৯   ৯   ৯

The hour had turned late and like any sensible man, the archbishop had gone to bed soon after Bruno left with the alguacil to view the witch's body. Bruno saw no reason to disturb his rest. Besides, he had not even examined the bodies so there was little information to pass along. His most pressing concern was where he would find the tools necessary to do a thorough examination. He had come to Madrid with the archbishop who was there to observe the auto de fe and preside over the dedication of the new templo. Bruno gave no thought to bringing with him the tools that would now be necessary. Of course, he always carried a satchel of small tools, potions, and herbs he had found to come in handy during his frequent travels. More than once had the contents of his satchel saved someone's life, including his own. Bruno carried the satchel with him almost everywhere he went. Now in the privacy of his monastic cell he took out the cross he had removed from the witch's head. Before he could unwrap it, someone knocked at his door.

"Yes, who is it?" Bruno grumbled.

"Sorry to disturb you, monsignor, but I completed transcribing Brother Tomas' story and thought you might need some help carrying your belongings to the stable," Raul replied outside the door.

"That was quick," Bruno replied.

"Brother Tomás is not a man of many words," Raul replied smiling.

"Come on in. I'm about to look at something and you can write down my comments about it," Bruno said.

As Raul spread his papers on the table to prepare to write, Bruno unwrapped the cross.

"Write this down," Bruno ordered. "Description of the cross removed from the witch's head. August 21, the year of our Lord 1725. The cross is two fingers short of a foot tall and eight fingers from point tip to point tip wide. The supporting structure of the cross is made of iron approximately half a finger in diameter with a double-barbed tip at the bottom, arrow-point tips on the cross-bar ends and a rounded knob on top a little more than two fingers wide. Did you get all that Raul?" Bruno asked.

"You're speaking a little quickly, but I believe I did get it all," Raul said.

"Excellent," Bruno replied. "When I'm finished, I'll need you to draw this for me as well."

"Yes monsignor."

"Let's continue. The most striking feature of the cross is the outer structure that appears to be made of human skin," Bruno dictated.

"Human skin! What kind of a madman would make a cross of human skin?" Raul interjected.

"We'll discuss that later, let's continue," Bruno replied unflustered. "The skin appears to have been de-putrefied and tanned, although, there are some signs of hair remaining on the skin. The skin appears to have been stuffed with human hair to give the cross a bulbous appearance. The outside edges of the skin-structure have been stitched with a thick thread which also winds in a sinuous pattern around both the upright and crossbar. This bulbous structure stretches the width of the cross-bar and fits snugly into the base of the arrow-tips which have been fitted to accommodate this bulbous pouch. The length of this skin pouch is roughly eight fingers and there are additions to the underlying iron structure that fit over the ends of the pouch. Do you have all that? "Bruno asked.

"Give me a moment," Raul requested.

Bruno did not always have a lot of patience, but did realize he spoke rather quickly.

"I'm ready, go on," Raul said.

"Let's take a break for a moment," Bruno said. "A very gruesome cross wouldn't you agree?"

"Terrifying, Raul replied. "Could the cross have been made from the skin taken from the acolytes back?"

"Not this cross," Bruno replied. "It would take several days of tanning to get the skin prepared to make such a cross. However, I have little doubt that the skin taken from his back is destined for a similar satanic use."

"Tomás told me that the witch's back was disfigured," Raul said. "Was the skin removed from her back as well?"

"It was, but I did not share any information about the extent of her disfiguring with him. The fewer people who know the facts, the easier it will be to find the murderer."

"But isn't Satan the one doing this?" Raul asked.

"Satan of course is behind it, but it's not Satan himself performing these demented murders. It's one of his disciples. More than likely someone close to the church who believes he's doing what God has instructed him to do. I have little doubt that this murderer believes it's the voice of God, not the voice of Satan, that guides his actions," Bruno explained.

"That's madness! Who in their right mind would think God was telling them to do such perversities?" Raul asked.

"You answered your own question," Bruno replied. "This murderer is not of a right mind. I'm sorry to say I've seen many a godly man fall from the path of righteousness. Admittedly, not many fall this far, but it does occur."

"You said you believe this murderer is someone close to the church. Do you mean a parishioner or possibly even one of the brothers in the church?" Raul asked.

"I cannot say at this point. There are several parishioners always at the church keeping watch over the perpetual adoration of the Eucharist. The sanctuary doors are never locked." Bruno said

"Yes, but the door from the sanctuary to the monastery and crypts is always locked," Raul replied.

"This is true, but with all that went on here yesterday and last night it would've been possible for anyone to access the crypts and murder the acolyte. In fact, the outer door leading from the monastery to the street was left unlocked and unguarded during much of the auto de fe. However, I believe it's someone who knows the workings of the church extraordinarily well who is responsible for the acolyte's murder."

"And for the witch's murder?" Raul asked.

"Yes, I believe it was the same person who killed them both, but that's just my opinion until the facts prove it to be true. It is those facts that you and I are about to go gather now," Bruno replied.

"But first pass me that box next to the table, and be careful it's very breakable."

"I've one more question," Raul said as he carefully lifted the wooden box and placed it on the table. He could hear liquid splashing in bottles.

"And that is…?" Bruno said.

"Do you believe the Madonna cries because of these murders?"

"We've yet to prove that the Madonna is truly crying those tears of blood," Bruno replied. "But yes, I do believe the tears are related to the murders. Whether it's the Madonna crying for those who do not believe in Christ's teachings and the sacrifice he already paid or the murderer himself through some sick but ingenious hoax who causes these tears I cannot say. Yet I do believe they are connected."

Bruno opened the box and removed two glasses and a large bottle of a ghastly looking greenish liquid.

"What's that smell?" Raul asked.

"It's green anise. Actually, it's both green anise and a sweeter alicante anise mixed with Artemesia Absinthium, better known as grand wormwood. A monk in a small monastery near Barcelona distills it for me. He calls it 'absenta'. They use it at the monastery for medicinal purposes. I on the other hand rather enjoy the taste. You'll also find that it will help conceal the smell of death as we work on the two corpses in the stable."

"But isn't wormwood extremely bitter?" Raul asked.

"The bitterness is well hidden by the anise and believe me, once we begin our work, not only will you appreciate the overwhelming aroma of this green nectar but you'll find it will put your mind at ease without dulling your senses, and I need you alert to write down everything I say."

"As you wish, monsignor," Raul replied hesitantly.

"Good, then drink up."

CHAPTER SIX

"Fellowship"

"Surprise, surprise, surprise!" Kevin said in his best Gomer Pyle voice.

"How is this peossibuell?" Francois countered in his best Clouseau accent, causing everyone to laugh.

"I bet you thought you'd seen the last of me for awhile," Kevin said.

"Oh no, I knew we'd be seeing each other again," Liz said, "and honestly, I'm not even surprised to see you here."

"Not even a little?" Kevin said.

"She even told me on the plane that she believed you'd figure out a way of getting here and that she wouldn't be surprised if you beat us to New York," Francois said.

"That's right, I could tell that you're too stubborn to just let go of an investigation that meant so much to you. I knew you'd find a way to join us," Liz said.

Kevin didn't have the courage to say that it wasn't his stubbornness that brought him to New York, but a mandate from his boss.

"God moves in mysterious ways," Liz added, smiling at Kevin as though she could read his thoughts.

"Though I must say I'm quite surprised by both your presence and Liz's intuition," Francois added.

"Let me introduce you to my good friend Carlo Caressa. Carlo has arranged for you to by-pass the customs lines," Kevin explained.

"How ya' doin'," Carlo said shaking both Liz's and Francois' hand. "If you two will follow me I think I can have us out of here in just a few minutes."

"Maybe us, but not our luggage," Francois replied.

"Have a little faith in the powers of the FBI," Kevin said.

When they entered the room, their luggage was already waiting for them.

"Now I truly am surprised," Liz said laughing.

"I've arranged with the Department of Justice for both of you to be allowed to carry a weapon while in the United States," Carlo explained. "It was a simple process for you, Liz, since you are an Interpol agent. It was a bit more difficult to arrange it for you, Francois; it seems the DOJ has a few bones to pick with the French Police."

"I don't understand 'bones to pick'," Francois replied.

"It just means that there is some smug bureaucrat in Washington who calls French fries, 'freedom fries', and thinks Frenchmen are arrogant and that France still owes America for the Normandy invasion," Kevin replied.

"I appreciate your effort," Francois said to Carlo, "and I'm sorry to say that it's true that many of our young people don't realize that if it wasn't for the United States, we would be speaking German."

"My friend Carlo has had a team of agents watching the office of the surgeon who diagnosed the brain tumor and then signed the affidavit confirming that it had miraculously disappeared. It just so happens that the brain in question belongs to a second surgeon whose office is located in the building with the doctor who validated the claim," Kevin explained as they headed out of the airport.

"I wasn't sure what kind of budgets you had for accommodations," Carlo began to explain. "I know money is no object for the Catholic Church but for the sake of convenience and budget, I booked all three of your rooms at the Bayview Park Hotel. Not the fanciest place in New York, but near the medical offices and the Lourdes Grotto."

"Did you say Lourdes Grotto?" Francois asked. "I didn't know such a place existed outside of Southern France."

"It's actually a replica of Our Lady of Lourdes," Kevin said knowing he now had to come clean about why he was in New York. "When I got on the papal jet in Paris, I had new orders from the Vatican. The Madonna in Spain was still crying, but the spring that fed the stream beneath the statue of the Virgin Mary at St. Lucy's Catholic Church in the Bronx had started gushing blood. At least that's according to the message the Vatican received from the local diocese."

"I thought that spring dried up years ago," Liz said.

"It did. For the past thirty years or so it's been New York City tap water feeding the stream in the grotto replica. Even so, it attracts hundreds of people a week who come and collect the water, drink it, and even bathe in it, believing it has divine power to heal."

"That's ridiculous," Francois retorted.

"Tell that to the five million people who make the pilgrimage each year to the original springs in Lourdes. I doubt that they find it ridiculous," Kevin replied.

"I read something about that place in this morning's paper," Carlo interrupted, "but there was no mention of blood that I can recall. The article said something about closing it down for renovation or something like that and a lot of people raising a big stink about it."

"Believe me, there's a lot more to the story," Kevin said. "That's actually why I'm here and not in Spain. The Vatican decided this was a much more pressing event that needs to be investigated immediately."

"I noticed you didn't refer to it as a miracle," Francois noted.

"The Vatican doesn't like to overuse that word. The bishop of the local diocese has reported the incident and the possibility of it being a miracle. Until a thorough investigation is done, it will remain an event," Kevin explained.

"So, it's not a miracle until you say it is," Francois replied. "That must make you a very important man having the power to interpret nature or God's actions."

"It's not a miracle until the Pope proclaims it as such," Kevin replied tersely. "Feel free to jump into this conversation anytime, Liz."

"What and ruin my entertainment," Liz replied smiling "Boys will be boys."

"Here's the car," Carlo said hoping to change the subject. He popped open the trunk and began putting Liz and Francois luggage next to Kevin's.

"I would appreciate it if you could have my luggage taken to my room at the hotel," Liz replied as a gentleman wearing a three-piece suit joined their group. "Interpol requires me to report immediately to the office upon arrival and brief them on the investigation. If you will excuse me, I'll meet you all at the hotel in an hour or so."

The three men stood silent for a moment apprising the dapperly dressed man who seemed to appear from nowhere.

"Do you still have my cell number?" Kevin finally asked.

"I do, and mine is written on this card," she replied handing one to Carlo, Kevin, and Francois. "If anything happens in the next hour be sure and call me."

"Of course," Kevin replied.

The three men all watched as Liz got into a new black Mercedes CLS 550.

"Looks like Interpol has a better budget than the FBI," Francois said as all three men turned and looked at the scratched and dented Mercury Grand Marquis waiting at the curb.

꙳ ꙳ ꙳

"Were you able to get what I asked for? I heard the church closed off the grotto," Liz asked.

"It was closed off to the public, not to us," the man replied opening a briefcase and removing two jars of blood.

Liz took both jars and placed them inside her purse.

"Are you sure the blood is necessary?" the man asked.

"The power of the blood of Christ gives us power over Satan," Liz replied.

"You more than anyone should know that is just a metaphor symbolizing the blood Christ shed on the cross as our salvation and giving us power over Satan," the man replied.

"Of course, but blood flows from the Virgin at Our Lady of the Lourdes for a reason."

The gentleman pressed the issue no further.

"Are you sure both doctors are on vacation?" Liz asked.

"Yes, a medical convention in Madrid, Spain. One day of meetings in Madrid, then two weeks of golf and sightseeing," the man replied. "The perfect solution for allowing them to write a vacation off as a tax deduction."

"Do we know if Lucienne has arrived?" Liz asked.

"We can't be certain, but some of our people have reported a strong unfamiliar evil presence in the city," the man said.

"I'm sure Satan's demons create a constant veil of evil over this city," Liz surmised.

"Yes, but we have many forces faithfully engaged in spiritual warfare. The city is by no means lost. The battles will continue as they have for centuries," he explained.

"I would venture to say that when Lucienne set foot in New York, the blood began to flow."

"That would be a logical explanation," the man replied.

"She surely must know by now that the doctors are out of the country," Liz said.

"Maybe, maybe not. Since you called, we have watched the medical building. Several evil spirits have recently arrived and began watching the building as well. Their numbers continue to build which leads me to believe Lucienne will soon arrive," the man said.

"With the doctor's away, what does she hope to gain? The Vatican already has the proof that this was indeed a miracle attributed to Pope John Paul II. The other two claims were simply to raise doubt about the real miracle," Liz said.

"Yes, but if similar deaths occur here as they did in Poland and France, there will be those who will doubt that a miracle did occur here."

"There will be those who will doubt regardless of what happens here," Liz replied.

"And there always will be," the gentleman replied, "but the true believers will know."

"How many people are in the medical offices?" Liz asked.

"It is a large building with dozens of people working inside and dozens more coming and going continuously. The doctor who had the brain tumor has closed down his office while he is away on vacation, so there is no one working there. The doctor who diagnosed the tumor shares an office with two other surgeons who did not go to the convention.

Only one of them is in the office right now. The other is at a local hospital trying to remove a cancerous tumor from a young boy's lung."

"I will pray for him," Liz interrupted.

"There are several nurses and support personnel working in the shared office. The radiologist and MRI technicians who took the pictures of the doctor's brain with the tumor and later without the tumor also have an office in the building. They too would be at risk from Lucienne," the gentleman explained.

"I think we better get there right away," Liz suggested.

"That is where we are heading, but won't your friends be upset when they discover you challenged Lucienne without them?"

"This is a battle they cannot fight. I must face her alone. I just hope we're not too late. I don't want anyone else hurt or killed," Liz said.

ൟ   ൟ   ൟ

"If you don't mind, Francois, I need to make a quick stop at St. Lucy's Church. You're welcome to come along or we can drop you at the hotel if you'd prefer," Kevin offered.

"No, I'd enjoy seeing this miracle you're here to investigate. Besides, with Liz meeting with her Interpol colleagues I don't want to be sitting alone in some hotel bar when the action begins," Francois replied.

"That's fine, but don't go using the word 'miracle' around the church. I don't want to stir up emotions more than they already are with the crowd that I'm sure has gathered," Kevin explained.

"And if anything does start to stir at the medical building my agents know to contact me immediately. In fact, it's only a few blocks from the church," Carlo reassured.

"No, I'm anxious to see this replica of Our Lady of Lourdes. I in fact have visited the original twice before," Francois said.

"I thought you said you thought it ridiculous that people visit the grotto?" Kevin retorted.

"Ridiculous that they visit a replica, not the real Our Lady of Lourdes in France," Francois replied grinning.

"What say we stop for a few 'freedom fries' on the way there," Carlo replied curtly.

Now it was Kevin's turn to smile.

"Hey, hey, hey! Take a look at that babe," one of the agents staked out in the building across from the medical building said to his partner. "Didn't Carlo say that this murderess was a looker?"

"Yeah, but every other woman you see you think is a looker," his partner replied. "That's about the tenth one you thought was our suspect. And enough already with the Fat Albert imitation."

"Sounds like a grumpy old married man talking," the agent said.

"And proud of it," his partner replied.

"What color hair did Carlo tell us she had?" the agent asked.

"Black. The eyewitnesses in France said she had long black hair," his partner replied.

"Who was this eyewitness?" the agent asked.

"Ex-FBI, you might even remember him, guy's name is Kevin Bridges. Carlo said they also got her entering the hotel lobby and the room on video."

"I remember that name. Wasn't he the agent who busted that serial killer down in Louisiana?" the agent asked.

"Yeah, that's right. Had something to do with some religious mumbo-jumbo or something," his partner replied.

"Voodoo!" the agent replied eerily.

"Whatever the hell it was, I just remember hearing it scared the shit out of everybody on the case. Several of the agents retired and Kevin quit the agency. Anyone still around who was part of the investigation won't talk about it. Carlo told me Kevin now works for the Vatican as an investigator."

"Investigator of what, perverted priests?" the agent joked.

"If what Carlo told us is true, I would say it's a little more challenging than busting pedophiles."

"Let me get this straight. This raven-haired good-looking lady kills a hotel security guard twice her size by freezing his heart, nails him to the freak'n wall, steals a briefcase, rearranges all the furniture, and disappears from a locked room with no other way out in less than a minute," the agent said.

"Sounds like bullshit to me too." his partner replied.

∽   ∽   ∽

"It's God's will, how can you deny us this gift from God?" the man yelled in the face of one of the deacons.

"We need salvation; we need relief from the hardships. God is trying to give this to us and the church won't allow it," another woman yelled. The crowd was quickly working itself into a frenzied unruly mob.

The church deacons stood guard at the main entrance to keep the curious away while still allowing those in need to enter the sanctuary for prayer. All doors inside the sanctuary leading out to the grotto and the gates leading into the grotto from Mace Avenue had been either locked or chained. Outside the church, several policemen now patrolled the crowd on horseback to keep the overly zealous from trying to scale the fence.

Carlo pulled his Grand Marquis partially on the sidewalk in front of the school across the street from the grotto, which immediately caught the attention of one of the mounted policemen.

"FBI," Carlo shouted out the window holding up his credentials.

"Jesus Christ, I didn't know this was getting to be such a big deal. Don't leave it parked here for long, this crowd is getting bigger by the minute and I don't want any other wise guys think'n they can pull up on the sidewalk," the officer explained sounding quite irritated by all that was happening.

"Why don't you wait by the car, it might help ease the tension. I should only be a few minutes. I need to let the parish priest know I'm in town and see if there is anything new I need to know about," Kevin said to Carlo. "You're welcome to join me if you'd like, Francois."

"Indeed, I would. I've never seen a real miracle in person," Francois replied. "Besides, I'd like to see if this grotto looks anything like the real Our Lady of Lourdes."

As they crossed the street to the church, cries arose from the crowd as several men exited the sanctuary and started to hang curtains on the fence to obstruct the view of the grotto from the street.

"Rip them down!"
"Blasphemy!"
"You cannot hide God's miracle from us!"
"Tear them down!"

A struggle ensued between the men on the inside of the fence trying to hang the curtains and those on the outside trying to tear them down.

"We're gonna need some back-up here," the mounted officer said into his radio as he spurred his horse between the unruly crowd and the fence.

"Move back, everybody move on back or I'll have you hauled in," the officer warned.

"I hope your God knows what he is doing," Francois commented watching the chaos escalate.

"God always knows what he's doing," Kevin replied. "It's man who always seems to mess things up."

Kevin showed his Vatican identification to one of the elders standing by the door.

"Reverend Father O'Malley told us to expect you. He said to bring you immediately to his office," the deacon said pushing several people aside to allow Kevin and Francois to enter the church.

"I'm sure the Reverend Father wouldn't object if you first showed me the Virgin in the grotto," Kevin replied.

The elder did not wish to disobey the priest's instructions, but he was more afraid to disobey a request from an official Vatican representative. "I'm sure the Father will understand," he replied.

They entered a small room at the front of the sanctuary where a door led outside into the grotto area. Several men were taking out more curtains to place over the fence to block the view as the local diocese had ordered.

"Looks like the police finally got some reinforcements," Francois noted. "The curtains seem to be staying in place."

Kevin wasn't interested in the curtains; his attention was directed at the thirty-foot-tall amalgamation of stones.

"The blood started flowing two days ago. At first, we thought it was a problem with the municipal water company so we turned off the tap," the elder explained.

"Does look at bit like the original Our Lady of Lourdes," Francois commented, "Except of course for the blood running out from under the Virgin Mary."

"I need to get a sample of that blood," Kevin said. "Please get me a jar with a lid."

"No need," the deacon replied. "The proprietor of the gift shop has been collecting jars of the blood since it started flowing. He plans to sell them if the Vatican gives permission. He even writes the time and date when it was collected on the lids. How many jars do you need? We've already sent several to the diocese and another representative from the Vatican picked up a couple of jars earlier this morning."

The deacon's last statement caught Kevin's attention. "Did you say another representative from the Vatican?"

"Yes sir, a tall man in a suit. I didn't get his name, but he was driving one of those new fancy Mercedes sedans," the deacon replied.

"You sure he was from the Vatican?" Kevin questioned.

"He said he was, but I didn't see any identification or nothing," the deacon replied. "It was early this morning before Reverend Father told us to check everybody coming into the sanctuary. I do know he met with the Father."

Francois and Kevin's eyes met. Each man knew something wasn't right about what they just heard.

"Maybe it's that one," the agent said.

"You mean the one with the sunglasses and scarf?" his partner replied.

"Yeah, that's the one."

"Well her hair doesn't look black to me," his partner replied. "Besides, there's a guy with her. Carlo said nothing about her having a partner."

"Well keep an eye on the office jut in case, she looks like she could be from France," the agent replied.

"Right, Sherlock. What exactly does a lady from France look like?" his partner replied facetiously.

The agents were distracted by the sound of screeching tires and honking horns.

"Don't you hate it when rich guys think the traffic laws don't apply to them? That SOB in the Mercedes just ran the light almost causing an accident," the agent said.

"No kidding, where's a cop when you need one," his partner joked as he watched the car skid to a stop in front of the medical building.

"Probably some doctor running late from his golf game," the agent said.

"Wait a minute, check out that woman who just jumped out of the car," the partner said. "That could be her."

"See if she enters the office," the agent said.

"Hey, what the hell is going on? The window in the office looks like it's fogging up."

"Let me see. Call 911, no, call Carlo first, that's smoke, I think the place is on fire," the agent said.

His partner pushed a button on his cell. "Carlo, something's going down. Get your ass here pronto."

"Did you see the woman?" Carlo asked.

"Yeah, well maybe, we're not sure. Someone we thought could be the woman just ran in the building and now the office looks like it's filled with smoke," the agent replied.

"Wait a minute, that ain't smoke or steam, that's frost. The freak'n window is frost'n over," his partner said.

"One of you get in there now, the other watch the exit," Carlo yelled, "I'm on my way."

༄ ༄ ༄

"Look, water is beginning to flow from beneath the Virgin," one of the deacon's praying near the grotto yelled.

Several people in the crowd gathered outside the fence overheard him yell and began to wail their displeasure.

"This was God's gift to his faithful and you stole it from us."

"You've angered the Most Highest and now we'll pay."

"Father please forgive them, they know not what they do."

"Looks like the faithful are losing their faith," Francois commented as the wails and jeers continued.

"Someone must've turned on the water valve," one of the deacons shouted and ran to where the spigot was located. "No, it's still shut just as it has been since the miracle began two days ago."

"We need to get to the medical building," Kevin suddenly said.

At that instant, the horn of the Grand Marquis started honking incessantly.

"Sounds like your friend Carlo needs us," Francois replied.

"Let's go," Kevin shouted and began to run.

"Wait, what shall I tell the Reverend Father?" the deacon shouted.

"Tell him, I'll…"

The deacon couldn't hear Kevin over the shouting and the horn.

༄ ༄ ༄

By the time the first FBI agent exited the building across the street, the Mercedes had disappeared. "What's the office number?" he called into the radio.

"Four-Two-Four. Carlo and FDNY are on the way," his partner radioed back.

Inside the building Liz had reached the fourth floor. She walked directly to the office knowing what was waiting for her inside. The handle to the office door was covered in ice and a freezing mist emanated from the wooden door.

"*It is God who arms me with strength and makes my way perfect*," Liz prayed, then lifted her hands towards the door which shattered into a million tiny pieces.

Inside the room was Lucienne. She stood over the radiologist with her hand upon his chest.

"You are too late again, Elizabeth," Lucienne proclaimed.

"Be gone demon," Liz shouted.

"Fool, you know not the strength lord Satan has granted me," Lucienne said seeming to grow larger as she stood.

"And you know not the power of the blood of Jesus Christ," Liz said pulling out one of the jars of blood taken from the grotto.

Before Liz could open the jar, the FBI agent stepped through the doorway and knocked the jar from her hand.

Liz lifted her hand and the man flew back against the wall.

"Now is not the time nor is this the place where we are destined to battle," Lucienne said picking up the jar of blood. "There will be blood when we next meet, but it will be mixed with hail and fire." Before Liz could respond Lucienne threw the jar of blood at the window which exploded into thousands of razor-sharp shards.

"The Lord rebuke you," Liz screamed.

Carlo arrived at the medical building and the three of them were exiting the Grand Marquis just as the window blew directly above them.

"Inside quickly," Kevin shouted pushing several bystanders inside the doorway.

The shattered glass fragments riddled down upon Carlo's car piercing the metal and leaving thousands of needle-size holes in the roof and trunk. The second FBI agent had just reached the front of the building and was unable to get inside before the shards fell. His body was shredded by the razor cloud of glass.

"What the hell is going on, Kevin?" Carlo shouted.

"It must be Lucienne," Kevin said running out to try to pull the dead agent to safety. Carlo and Kevin both grabbed an arm but the agent's limbs fell apart in their hands. As they looked up a second cloud seemed to fly out from the side of the building, but this was a cloud of locusts that flew off into the sky.

"My agent said that a woman jumped out of a Mercedes and ran inside just as the windows began to frost over," Carlo said.

"Liz," Kevin shouted and took off running for the stairs.

"Francois, you stay here and wait for back-up," Kevin shouted, then realized Francois was nowhere to be seen.

Liz rushed to the body of the radiologist and placed her hands on his frozen torso and began to pray. She did not see Lucienne's companion enter the room from the radiology lab. The man had a knife and was about to plunge it into Liz's back when a shot rang out jarring Liz from her prayer.

"What have you done," Liz said to Francois who stood in the doorway holding a gun.

"You should be thanking me for saving your life," Francois said. "That man was about to stab you."

"I was protected by God. He could have done me no harm. Angels protect you when you pray," Liz explained, still stooping over the body of the radiologist.

"Liz are you okay?" Kevin said running into the room.

Carlo was right behind him and took the gun from Francois' hand.

"He didn't need to kill him," Liz said.

"What hit me?" the agent said still crumpled on the floor at the base of the wall.

"This man needs immediate medical attention," Liz said keeping her hand on his chest. "Lucienne tried to kill him but he has a chance to pull through if we get him to a hospital."

"What happened to Lucienne?" Kevin asked.

"She's gone," Liz replied. "She wasn't ready to fight. She was just trying to get our attention."

"What do you mean wasn't ready to fight?" Carlo asked. "She killed one of my agents; I'd say she now has my attention."

"Killed who?" the agent said as he slowly tried to stand.

Carlo helped the agent to his feet steadying him. "Your partner is dead. The broken glass from the window fell on him."

"That's not possible," the agent moaned as Carlo tried to comfort him.

"Where did Lucienne go?" Kevin asked Liz again.

"She didn't say, but I'd bet she still plans on killing the two doctors. She is trying to cast doubt on the miracle by

Pope John Paul II. Satan wants to delay the sainthood as long as possible," Liz explained.

"That makes no sense, the Vatican already has the proof validating that this was truly a miracle brought on by John Paul II," Kevin replied.

"Doubt spreads like a cancer in the minds of weak men," Liz said. "Satan is skilled at what he does."

"Now what?" Francois asked. "Somehow this murderess has again escaped and you two talk like she is the devil."

"Not the devil," Kevin said, "but undoubtedly doing Satan's bidding."

"You're starting to creep me out with all this Satan talk," Carlo said. "I got a dead agent, a dazed agent, a dead man, a man near death on the floor, blood splattered all over the room, about a million holes in the roof of my car, and only one suspect as far as I can tell."

"You think Liz is responsible for all of this?" Kevin said incredulously.

"I don't know what to think," Carlo replied as paramedics rushed into the office.

"There was another woman," the dazed agent said, "just like you described, long black hair and very beautiful."

"Then where the hell is she?" Carlo demanded.

"I don't know. I came into the room and saw this woman facing off with the other black-haired woman," the agent began to explain.

"Her name is Liz," Kevin interrupted.

"The black-haired one was standing over the radiologist and this one, sorry, Liz, was facing her holding something. I thought it was a gun and knocked it out of her hand. When it fell, I saw that it was a jar of what looked like blood. The black-haired one picked it up. The next thing I know I'm slammed into the wall. It must have knocked me out, because I don't remember anything after that."

By now several dozen police and fire personnel were on the scene and more were arriving by the minute.

"We need to search the building, Lucienne could still be inside," Francois insisted.

"Lucienne is gone," Liz repeated. "I am sure by now she is on her way to Spain."

"Spain? Why Spain?" Francois asked.

"That is where she will find the two doctors that she came to kill," Kevin answered. "I think the best thing we can do now is all go to the hotel. There are going to be a lot of questions to answer and the sooner we all answer them the sooner we can head to Spain."

"We won't be taking my car to the hotel and I'm afraid your luggage and whatever was in it, is history," Carlo said.

"I'll call Interpol, they will send a car," Liz said.

"I still don't understand how you knew to get here to the medical building when you did," Kevin said to Liz.

"There will be plenty of time for answering questions when we get to the hotel," Liz replied tersely.

"I'll have all the airports watched and run a passport search for everyone headed to Spain," Carlo said. "With an agent dead, you can be sure the FBI will be all over this until this Lucienne is found."

Kevin wanted to tell Carlo that he would be wasting his time but knew that when an agent was killed in the line of duty emotions ran high and Carlo was grasping at anything and everything to find the murderer. As much as he loved Carlo, he knew Carlo couldn't understand what was really going on, for even Kevin had a hard time believing it.

CHAPTER SEVEN

"Diligence"

"There's more damage to the boy's skull than I first thought," Bruno dictated. "There's a chunk of skull missing at the point of penetration. A flap of his scalp hid it from view when we first found the body. I'm positive the same type of cross, if not the same cross, was used to pierce the boy's skull in the same manner as the witch's."

"A bit slower, monsignor, if you please," Raul requested.

"No time, write faster, already the stench penetrates the absenta, pour us both another cup," Bruno ordered.

As Raul poured the green liquid, Bruno went down into the storage room where the blacksmith tools were located. Bruno opened several cabinets until he found one that held woodworking tools. He shuffled through them removing many from the pegs that held them in place until he found just what he was looking for.

"A little big, but it will serve its purpose," he commented as he climbed the steps and re-entered the room. Raul handed him the cup and Bruno took a large swig. "Just a sip for you, brother," Bruno cautioned, "just enough to cover the smell. You're not used to the affects of this elixir. The stimulants hide the power of the alcohol and I need you to write faster not slower."

"Yes monsignor," Raul replied sipping the liquid and sitting back down to continue his writing.

"I noticed some pieces of the boy's brain caught on the jagged edge of the broken skull. I need to see inside," Bruno explained.

He placed the saw on the boy's forehead and pulled. "I'm afraid you'll have to hold the head while I saw," Bruno said.

Raul hesitated.

"Hold it with that rag, this shouldn't be too messy."

Raul did as ordered, but turned away so as not to watch the top of the head shear off.

"That was easy," Bruno said. "Now back to your journal." Bruno pulled away the top of the skull. "The skull is brittle showing mineral deficiency in the boy's diet. As expected, most of the brain has been removed."

"What do you mean, been removed?" Raul asked.

"That's right; you weren't with me at the witch's house. When I tried to remove the cross from her head it was stuck. I had to turn it like a key in a keyhole, lining it up just right so I could pull the cross out. With it came a goodly portion of her brain. That's it in the bucket under the table," Bruno explained.

Raul didn't want to look, but his curiosity got the best of him. "Fascinating," Raul said.

"Very good," Bruno replied, "the absenta must be working, you seem to be dealing with this much better. Now continue to write." Bruno moved over to the witch's body. He inserted a rod into the wound in her head. "Just as I surmised, her skull is much thicker than his. The cross must have become lodged in her head and the murderer didn't have time to remove it. Something must have interrupted his dastardly crime. The question is why would the murderer need the brains of his victim?"

Bruno proceeded to cut off the top of the witch's skull as he had the young acolyte.

"I would think it more curious that he needed the skin from their backs," Raul suggested.

"Not at all," Bruno replied, "we know what he plans to do with the skin, especially now that he had to leave his cross behind."

"You think he plans to make more of these satanic crosses?" Raul asked.

"Why else would he take the skin? In fact, this is one of the best clues we have so far, that is, besides the cross itself," Bruno explained as he laid the cross on the table next to Raul. "Look at the skin. Look how well it has been tanned and preserved. Whoever tanned this skin knew very well what he was doing. I've seen fine leather Cordovan gloves that were not of such quality."

"That explains why he took the brains," Raul said. "Tanners use the brains of animals mixed with urine and dung to work the skin. They mix it all together and knead the skin in with the odiferous mixture."

"I'm sure it could not smell as bad as this," Bruno said gesturing to the two bodies.

"In fact, it smells very similar to this, with the rotting flesh, dung, and urine. That is why you'll find no tanneries within the walls of the city," Raul said.

"It sounds like you have an expertise in this craft," Bruno exclaimed.

"No, when we were young, my brother and I often visited tanneries with my father. He'd buy straps for the riding bits that he'd make and sell."

"Your father is a blacksmith?" Bruno asked.

"My father is dead, but his trade was that of a blacksmith," Raul replied. "And your brother, did he follow in your father's trade?"

"He did," Raul replied curtly.

"It'd take a talented blacksmith to create the iron frame of this cross," Bruno said twirling it in the air. "Perhaps your brother would recognize the workmanship."

"Perhaps," Raul said hesitantly.

Bruno could tell Raul was uncomfortable speaking about his brother. That was a conversation that could wait till later.

"If the skin on this cross didn't come from the boy or the witch, then that means there had to have been another victim of this satanic madman," Raul said.

"That is very likely," Bruno replied. "How long would it take to tan the skin so well?" Bruno asked.

"At least two weeks and more likely a month or more," Raul replied.

"That doesn't limit our time frame for the additional murder by much," Bruno replied. "Tomorrow we'll share what we discovered with the alguacil and see what he knows about other recent murders."

"Will we be telling him about the murdered acolyte?" Raul asked.

"We should, but in the best interest of the church we won't," Bruno replied, "but that ultimately is up to the archbishop."

"Does that mean you're through with the examination of the bodies?" Raul asked.

"Not quite," Bruno replied pulling a sharp knife from his satchel. Raul watched as Bruno sliced away pieces of skin from both the witch's back and from the boy's back. "I'll take a larger piece from the witch's back so we can tell them apart."

"Why will we need to tell them apart?" Raul asked.

"I want to find out if this cross we have is made from a woman's or a man's skin," Bruno replied. "Since you seem to know so much about tanning, I thought we should try it for ourselves. We have a bucket full of brains sitting under the table, there's plenty of dung in the stables and outhouse, and I certainly can supply the urine."

"But Brother Bruno, I've never tanned leather myself, I've only watched the men working in the tanneries, and that was years ago," Raul replied.

"Then I guess we better take a journey outside the city to see the process," Bruno replied.

"Well, until then, I do know we need to keep the skins cool and in a salt solution, so until I can get some salt in the morning, I guess our urine will have to do," Raul suggested.

"The things one must do for science," Bruno said as he added his urine to the bucket containing the witch's brain.

Raul followed Bruno's lead relieving himself in the bucket dreading even the thought of the task that lay ahead.

The hooded man left the skins to soak on the table and entered the main catacomb. He lit a small torch and turned to the left following the tunnel until he came to a verse carved on the side wall.

Ask and it will be given to you; seek and you will find; knock and the door will be opened to you.

Surrounding the verse were several sets of numbers. The monk reached beneath his robe and pulled out the iron framework of a cross to replace the one left behind in the witch's skull. He was yet unsure if it would be the witch's or the young acolyte's skin that would finish the cross.

"Not yet complete, but still a perfect fit," he said as he pressed the design melded onto the point of the spear, the number seven into an exact matching indentation etched into the wall. He heard a slight click and immediately pressed the spear point into the second seven. The tip of the spear had been forged to fit the numbers perfectly. A clanking noise was heard as two iron bars dropped from their locking position allowing the hooded man to pivot the large hidden door sideways. He slipped behind the wall as the massive rock wall swiveled back into position and the two iron bars clicked back into their secured receiver. He stood at the top of a stone staircase which disappeared into the darkness below. A darkness now known only to him and the unfortunate few whom he had selected.

Two hundred years ago the cavernous room he now entered was the most feared and secretive place in Madrid. Hundreds lost their lives to the Inquisitor whose edict to cleanse Spain of the heretics, the impure, and the unrighteous, turned into a macabre sadistic frenzy of pain and death.

As he slowly descended into this man-made hell, he lit the torches spaced every three steps. With each torch lighting, the Inquisitor's tools of punishment and death slowly came into view. The smell of rotting corpses was overwhelming.

"Forgive me," a faint voice whispered from someplace in the darkness. "Please forgive me, I am not a sinner."

"We are all sinners," the monk replied. "Some of you are just destined to pay for those sins."

"Water, can I please have some water?" the voice continued.

"It's water you want is it? Well I can surely give you that," the hooded man replied.

He had reached the bottom of the steps and the glow of the burning torches sent dancing shadows around the room. Near the bottom of the steps was the rack, probably the most popular instrument of torture used by the Inquisition. It was an efficient means of extricating a confession from the victim who was lashed to the board by their wrists and ankles. Rollers at each end of the rack could then be turned in opposite directions until every joint in your body was dislocated. Once bound to the rack the possibilities of even more sadistic means of torture seemed almost limitless.

Attached to the ceiling suspended above the rack and tied to the wall was a pendulum. The ball of the pendulum had a sharpened edge extending almost ten inches from the bottom of the sphere.

Further along the wall, past the rack, was an alcove which held a large butcher block table and a single chair. Attached to the table and all along the wall behind the table were a variety of shackles and chains. On the table was a device called a head crusher and in the crusher was what was left of the man's head who sat in the lone chair with his hands shackled to the table.

"Just another turn for good measure," the hooded monk said twisting the screw lever forcing the metal cap down even further on the dead man's cranium. Brains infested with maggots oozed through the ruptured eye sockets and the jaw disintegrated from the teeth being driven through their sockets crushing the surrounding bone.

"Please, I must have water," the voice barely whispered.

"Certainly, certainly," the hooded man replied. "but first I must let you down."

An emaciated body hung from a strappado about twelve feet off the floor. His hands tightly bound with a rope that ran through a pulley and was attached to the wall.

"Let me lower you," the monk said releasing the rope allowing the body to freefall for several feet. Before the body hit the floor, the monk pulled the rope tight."

"Ahhh, ahhh," the victim screamed as both shoulders dislocated and his wrists snapped.

"I thought you were thirsty?" the monk said but the victim had passed out and did not reply. He released the rope allowing the body to drop to the floor. He dragged the body across the floor to the rack, lifted him up and attached his ankles and broken wrists to the rollers at either end. He took a dirty rag and stuffed it partially down the victim's throat then began to pour water onto the rag. Instantly the man awoke believing that he was drowning.

The victim tried to scream but only a muffled moan escaped his mouth.

"Still thirsty? Try a little of this," the monk said and poured vinegar into the man's mouth. The gagging reflex pushed the rag further down his throat till it reached his stomach and the victim again fell unconscious.

The monk continued to pour vinegar down the man's throat until his stomach was distended and hard. The man never regained consciousness and died from a ruptured stomach. Death had done him a favor.

The victims of these malicious acts were not worthy to forfeit their skin for one of the monk's crosses. The men he brought here to torture and kill were the impure. The so called marranos and mariscos, those converts from Judaism and Islam who now claimed to be Christians. A claim of convenience that allowed them to profit and prosper as the Spanish empire declined.

The hooded man's thigh began to throb; blood ran down his leg and seeped between the sole of his foot and his leather sandal. The sandal squished with every step.

"No more time to play," he said to the two corpses that lay before him. "Perhaps in two or three days I will return and bring you a new friend."

He extinguished the torches as he limped back up the stairs. When he reached the pivoting wall, he need only to tap next to the spring-loaded iron bars to release them. He slipped back into the catacomb and waited until the wall closed and he heard the click of the bars falling back into place. He walked back down the main catacomb past the cells where he worked and through a narrow passage that led to a smaller cavern behind the burial crypts of the original templo before it was rebuilt. Here he had to move carefully and quietly. If someone was in the new crypt area, it was possible he could be detected. He climbed a stack of stones he had piled to allow him to reach the uppermost level of crypts. He had removed the body that once occupied this particular crypt. He crawled into the burial space and listened. Hearing no one inside he silently slid back a panel allowing him to see into the antechamber.

"It's gone," he gasped. "They've removed the acolyte's body."

With all the chaos that was taking place at the templo he had not expected anyone to venture into the crypts and discover the body until the morning. He was tempted to enter the antechamber and investigate. He had created a secret entrance through yet another crypt after the remodeling was completed, but he feared someone may be watching the stairs.

It was almost morning and soon the monks would be up and around. He needed to sneak out through the secret passage in the stable before the blacksmith or groomsman arrived for the day. The hooded monk moved silently until he stood behind the tool cabinet in the storage room below the blacksmith shop. He listened carefully to insure the room was empty then slid the latch that allowed the cabinet to swing forward. As the cabinet moved, several of the tools inside shifted nosily startling the monk. He stood momentarily frozen grasping the iron frame cross in case he needed it as a weapon. When no one spoke or moved he slowly entered the room and as quiet as possible closed the cabinet that concealed the hidden passageway. He heard no one in the room above so he opened the cabinet and replaced the tools that were not placed in the proper compartments.

"That should quiet things down a bit," he said not noticing that a saw was missing. As he turned to climb the steps the smell of death filled his nostrils. When he reached the stables, he knew from where the smell came.

"Oh, my goodness," he said looking at his two murder-victim's laying side by side on the table. "It appears that someone has taken more than a passing interest in my work." He saw that both the witch's and the acolyte's skulls had been sawn open. He quickly looked around the room for the cross he had left behind in the witch's head but did not see it. He carefully slipped out of the stable so as not to be seen and started on his journey home.

"Sorry master, I should have done this sooner," he said as he reached the outskirts of the city. "As my god Satan commands, I have sacrificed a body so his servant can return and his will be done." He only hoped he hadn't waited too long since her death to perform the prayer of summons.

He knew he would have to be careful. No ordinary monk had undertaken such an investigation. Someone outside the templo had to be behind this, someone who had done this type of work before.

"Perhaps God has sent me a worthy adversary," the hooded man said.

In fact, God had.

Chapter Eight

"Secrecy"

"How did you know to go directly to the medical building, and why didn't you call me?" Kevin demanded answers.

"Carlo wasn't the only one keeping an eye on the medical building. Interpol knew the doctors were out of the country on vacation and that Lucienne would undoubtedly go to the radiologist's office to destroy all evidence and kill the radiologist," Liz explained.

"Why didn't you tell us that at the airport?" Carlo asked.

"I didn't know about it until my driver picked me up and briefed me on the case," Liz replied. "Besides, I was sure the FBI would've known that information."

Kevin looked at Carlo, who looked away.

"Sounds to me like you are trying very hard to divert the attention away from yourself and your actions," Francois chimed in.

"I'm not the one who shot a man for no reason," Liz snapped back.

"As I was saying," Francois continued, "if what you're saying is true, where are these Interpol agents that were watching the medical office and tipped you off to Lucienne's presence and why is it they didn't join in the fight?"

"And why didn't your friend in the Mercedes stick around to help you out?" Carlo added.

"I never said Interpol had agents watching the medical offices," Liz corrected.

"Then why did you go to the medical office when you did?" Kevin asked.

"Because I knew Lucienne would be there. I've been tracking her for years and she has always been just a step ahead of me. When I heard you had men watching the building, I knew she hadn't reached there yet. I deduced, based on our past history, that she was either on her way or your men weren't doing their job and missed her," Liz added. "I wasn't going to call you based on my intuition."

"But what about the man in the Mercedes, why didn't he stay to help?" Carlo asked again.

"Mr. Donner is merely a driver hired by Interpol. I'd never put a civilian in harm's way," Liz explained.

"A driver, a civilian as you put it, who also briefs you?" Francois said incredulously.

"Just who is this Lucienne?" Kevin asked. "Why have you been chasing her for years?"

"I think we deserve to hear the truth Ms. Purdue. Something up until now you've skirted around," Carlo added.

"I don't mean to be so elusive," Liz began.

"Then don't be," Francois interrupted.

"Give her a chance to explain," Kevin said glaring at Francois.

"You more than anyone should be able to understand why I hesitate in telling the facts," Liz said to Kevin. "Carlo and Francois will think I'm crazy if I tell you the truth."

"Do you really work for Interpol or are you also working with the Vatican?" Carlo asked.

"The Vatican, goodness gracious, no! I've been with Interpol for almost twelve years," Liz began. "However, like what Mr. Bridges does for the Vatican, I investigate some of Interpol's more delicate cases. And from what you witnessed today, I'm sure you agree that this falls into the category of delicate cases."

"I think bizarre is a better descriptor," Carlo replied.

"Bizarre is not the half of it," Liz said. "Lucienne is a Nephilim."

"A what?" Carlo asked.

"A Nephilim, a type of fallen angel," Kevin explained.

"Preposterous!" Francois exclaimed.

"Actually, a demon or disembodied spirit of a Nephilim, left on Earth to lead the human race astray," Liz said.

"And I suppose it's Satan who put her on Earth to kill all of these people," Francois said sarcastically.

"No, God granted a small percentage of these disembodied spirits to remain on Earth, although, Lucienne is no doubt doing the devil's work," Liz replied.

"And killing one of my agents was part of the devil's plan?" Carlo asked.

"No, I believe that the death of your agent was collateral damage. Lucienne was sent here to kill the radiologist and the two doctors who made the claim of a miracle having taken place. Just like she did in Poland and Paris," Liz explained. "The difference here is that a miracle really did take place. The ones in Paris and Poland were fabrications."

"Then why did she kill all those involved in the two false miracle claims? Wouldn't it make more sense to kill the people involved in the real miracle?" Kevin asked.

"By killing everyone in all three claims, it would lead to doubt if one of the miracles was declared to be real by the Vatican," Liz said.

"Why does it matter if the Vatican declares that something that happened was a miracle?" Carlo asked.

"One of the requirements for sainthood is that the candidate for beatification performs a miracle after his death," Kevin explained.

"That's sounds a little tricky," Carlo said.

"Usually this is some kind of medical miracle that can be documented with x-rays, MRI, surgery, things like that," Kevin explained.

"So that's why this Lucienne went to the medical office, so she could destroy the proof," Carlo said.

"Just because this Lucienne is fanatical about stopping this beatification process and is willing to murder to do so, doesn't mean she's supernatural," Francois said.

"Faithful people understand," Kevin said.

"Even some of us without a whole lot of faith are willing to believe some of this mumbo-jumbo after what I saw today," Carlo replied.

"So, tell me, Liz, where do these so-called demons come from and why would God grant them permission to do this?" Francois challenged.

"Most of what we know about the Nephilim comes from the Book of Enoch," Liz began.

"Is that part of the bible? I've never heard of it," Carlo said.

"It's part of the Ethiopian biblical canon," Kevin explained. "It was one of the Dead Sea scrolls and in the original canon, but even before the First Council of Nicaea in 325 A.D. the Church Fathers had denounced and banned it. It was lost for over a thousand years."

"Why was it banned?" Francois asked.

"It is a little difficult for the average person to understand and to believe with all the talk about fallen angels and Nephilim," Liz said.

"Had they included it in the bible it would make it even more difficult for people to believe than it already is," Kevin said.

"These fallen angels had come to Earth to instruct humans about righteousness. Before long they were teaching them about war and pretty soon after that they took a liking to human women. First, they instructed them in magic and conjuring, but their lust overcame their own righteousness and before long these hybrid offspring, or Nephilim, were running around," Liz explained.

"I'm sure your God wasn't too pleased about that," Francois said sarcastically.

"No, he wasn't. In fact, these fallen angels who had lusted after the human women were cast into a place of 'total darkness' called Tartarus. Then God flooded the Earth to remove the Nephilim," Liz continued.

"But then, why would God allow some of them to remain if he wanted them removed bad enough to flood the Earth?" Carlo asked.

"That is something you'll have to ask God when you see him," Liz replied.

"If what you say about why Lucienne is here is true, then we can expect her to show up next in Spain when she tries to take out those two doctors," Kevin said.

"I think we can pretty much count on that," Liz replied.

"And just how will she get there?" Francois asked. "Does she disappear in a puff of smoke and reappear in Spain?"

"No, I would imagine she will take a jet just like I intend to do," Liz replied.

"Then she will be easy to catch," Carlo said. "I have all the airports being watched."

"She is good at disguising herself. Interpol has been watching airports for her for years and she somehow has always managed to elude us," Liz explained. "She probably won't fly directly to Spain from here. She may take a domestic flight somewhere else and fly to Spain from there. Or even fly to some other international destination before she moves on to Spain. No matter how she does it, I assure you, Spain is where she will show up."

"I still don't understand how she got away," Francois said. "You said she was instructed in some magical powers, just what kind of magical powers does she have? Does she hypnotize us or use mirrors or something?"

"Hypnosis and mirrors are tools of Vegas magicians," Kevin interjected. "I saw how she froze the guard's heart in Paris and tried to do it to the radiologist." Kevin looked at the burn mark on his own hand.

"Is that where your burn came from?" Carlo asked. "Why didn't she kill you when she had the chance?"

"She needs Kevin. Or at least she needed him at one time," Liz said. "He's the one that the Vatican listens to when they decide whether to publicize a miracle or not."

"Besides her freezing burning touch, what else can this Lucienne do?" Francois asked. "She seems to be able to just disappear."

"She doesn't disappear, she transmogrifies," Liz started to explain.

"What the hell does that mean?" Carlo asked.

"It means she has the ability to transform her body completely in some strange or grotesque way. Like in the medical office when she changed into that swarm of insects," Liz explained.

"She did what?" Carlo asked

"I was in that office and saw no such thing," Francois said. "There was only you leaning over the radiologist with your hand on his chest. The window was broken open, Carlo's agent was unconscious on the floor and that man was coming at you with a knife. How do we know Lucienne was ever really there?"

"Are you accusing me of something?" Liz said angrily getting in Francois' face.

"We know Lucienne was there because when my agent came in he saw two women, one standing over the radiologist, and one holding what turned out to be a jar of blood in her hand," Carlo reminded Francois.

"Did your agent see this alleged swarm of insects?" Francois asked.

"He never mentioned it. He said after he knocked the jar from the one woman's hand, the other one picked it up and he flew backwards against the wall as if he was hit by a bus. He remembers nothing after that," Carlo explained.

"No one saw this swarm of insects," Francois reiterated. "That is no one besides you, Liz."

"I saw them," Kevin said. "As did you Carlo. Remember after the window exploded and those razor-sharp needles flew down at us. We ducked inside, but your other agent never made it. We went out to try to pull him to safety, but first looked up to make sure no more needles were falling."

"Yeah, that's right, and I saw that cloud that looked like a swarm of locusts flying away from the window. I thought the window breaking busted a beehive or something," Carlo said.

"So, you see Francois, Liz wasn't the only one to see Lucienne transmogrify," Kevin said.

"You two may have seen insects, but only Liz claims to have seen this Lucienne transform, and I personally don't believe in such fanciful theories. I believe in the facts. And the fact is Liz allowed this murderess to escape," Francois said.

"Well the facts don't add up," Carlo replied, "but there's no way I'm going to tell my boss what you just told me. I'd be put on psychiatric medical leave."

"I'd suggest you continue to watch the airports, maybe you will get lucky and catch Lucienne," Kevin suggested.

"Well if what Liz said is true, we're gonna need to have an exterminator along with us if we do find her," Carlo joked.

"Where did the jar of blood come from?" Kevin asked.

"My driver picked up two jars from the grotto for me," Liz answered.

"What did you plan on doing with the blood?" Francois asked.

"The blood of Jesus cleans us from all unrighteousness," Liz replied. "I was going to use it to fight Lucienne."

"Are you telling me that the blood coming from the Our Lady of Lourdes grotto is, or was, the blood of Jesus?" Kevin asked.

"Open your eyes to see what is really happening here, Kevin," Liz said. "America has watered down the bible to make it politically and socially correct. Just because someone is sincere in their beliefs doesn't make a difference. Jesus said 'there is only one way to heaven and that is through me'. God is reminding America that the power of the blood of Christ gives us power over Satan. Satan sent his demon Lucienne to America, but gave you the power to fight her."

"Yes, but the blood no longer runs from the grotto," Carlo said.

"Then the danger of Satan's demon no longer troubles New York. I would suggest we head to Spain as quickly as possible," Liz explained.

"Spain's a large country to search," Francois noted.

"Yes, but we know she'll go after the two doctors and they'll be at the medical convention in Madrid," Kevin added.

"I'm sure the FBI will have more questions to ask all of you, but it won't be me who keeps you from leaving. I'd suggest you do so as quickly as possible before the state department puts departure holds on your passports," Carlo advised.

"I do need to go back to St. Lucy's and speak with the priest to tell him what I discovered. That is why the Vatican sent me here in the first place," Kevin said.

"Well we have no luggage to worry about thanks to Lucienne, so I'm ready to go whenever you all are," Francois said.

"I will need to call Interpol to advise them of my plans," Liz said, "but I can do that on the way to the airport."

"Then why don't both of you come with me to St. Lucy's. It will only take a few minutes, and then we can head directly to the papal jet. I'll call and have it gassed and ready to fly."

"The sooner the better," Carlo said. "I need to get back to the medical building to see how the investigation is going, but from what I learned here, I think I know how it's going."

"No problem" Kevin said "We can take a cab. And thanks for all your help."

"I'm sorry about the loss of your agent," Francois said. "I'm not as convinced as everyone else seems to be that Lucienne is already on her way to Spain. I think more investigating needs to be done here, but there's no way I'm going to let Kevin and Liz out of my sight."

"Thanks for all your help, and I'll pray for your agent," Liz said.

"I better call a cab," Kevin said.

"No need," Liz replied. "My driver is already on his way."

No sooner were the words out of Liz's mouth did the sleek new Mercedes pull up in front of the hotel lobby.

"How'd you do that?" Kevin asked. "I never heard you call anyone"

"I still have a few secrets," Liz said

"More than a few I'm sure," Francois replied cynically.

Chapter Nine

"Obligation"

"Monsignor, it is time to rise," Raul said, slightly shaking Bruno. The sun hung dirty in the early morning sky and the heat was already oppressive. The absenta from the night before had taken its toll with Bruno's head and a thickness clouded his mind.

"I've brought breakfast," Raul replied.

Bruno looked at the breakfast then reached for the flask with the absenta.

"Helps clear my mind," Bruno explained pushing the food aside.

"We must dispose of the bodies soon, Monsignor. Several of the monks are already complaining of the odor and Father..."

"Yes, yes, yes," Bruno interrupted, "we do have a busy schedule today and with this heat it is no wonder the monks complain. Have you completed the drawings of the cross?"

"Drawings? I did complete one," Raul replied.

"Well, I needed two! Didn't I tell you I needed two drawings of both sides of the cross? One for the archbishop to take back to Rome and one to keep with the journal," Bruno said sharply.

"Yes, monsignor, I had forgotten," Raul lied.

"You can make a second copy while I clean up the stables," Bruno said. "Here," Bruno said passing the absenta to Raul, "you will need this before we enter the stable."

"No thank you, Monsignor," Raul replied politely. His head ached as well from the anise flavored elixir's bite.

"Have you been by the sanctuary this morning? Does the Virgin still shed the tears of blood?" Bruno asked.

"Yes, monsignor. Morning prayers were held before the Madonna and her tears continue to fall," Raul replied.

"Are the tears still being collected as I instructed?"

"Of course, and they have completed the walls separating the Madonna from the sanctuary," Raul explained. "Father Santorio asked me to inform you that the archbishop has changed his travel plans. He will be leaving this evening to return to Rome."

"That doesn't give me much time to write up my report. Perhaps we'll have to postpone our trek to the tanneries," Bruno suggested.

"I know of a blacksmith that does work with leather whose shop is not far from the city walls," Raul suggested. "He is familiar with most of the tanners and blacksmiths in the region. The problem is he doesn't care much for the Church and may refuse to speak with us," Raul explained.

"Why does he not care for the Church? Is this man a heretic?" Bruno asked.

"No, he is a godly man, or at least he used to be. He believes that the church has become too elitist and that the monks focus on improving their academic and intellectual skills rather than their spiritual skills," Raul explained.

"A very astute observation I'd say," Bruno replied. "There are those at the Vatican who believe that intellectualism will lead to the demise of the Church. Of course, that same type of thinking is what brought on the Inquisition."

"And there are those who believe the Inquisition ended too soon in Spain," Raul replied.

"And there are those who believe the Inquisition was a mistake," Bruno quipped in response.

The two men walked in silence the rest of the way to the stables.

"Are you sure you don't want another sip before we enter?" Bruno said holding out the flask.

"No, I'll be fine," Raul replied opening the door to the stable.

The smell hit Raul's nasal passages like a hammer, causing him to gag. He struggled to keep from retching. "Please," he finally managed to say reaching out to Bruno for the flask of absenta.

"Bodies do turn quickly in this heat," Bruno replied passing him the elixir.

"Thank you, monsignor," Raul replied in-between swigs.

"Stop, walk no further," Bruno ordered. "Have you been in here this morning?"

"Of course not, Monsignor," Raul replied.

"Well someone has been in here," Bruno replied. "Things have been moved around. That's not where I left the saw, and the bucket with the witch's brains was closer to the door."

The two men were startled by a pounding on the stable door. "I'm here to collect the body," a voice called from outside.

Bruno pulled back the two large bolts that secured the door. Two toothless men waited to load the witch's body into a horse-drawn wagon and carry it away to a mass grave outside the city.

"Shouldn't we have the acolyte's body buried in holy ground?" Raul whispered to Bruno.

"His spirit is already with the Lord," Bruno replied, "but his body has been marked by Satan. Such a body cannot receive the sacraments of the Church."

"I was told we were to pick up one body, a woman named Lucia," one of the toothless men said.

"Then you were misinformed," Bruno replied. "As you can see there are two bodies that need to be taken away."

"That will cost you more," the man replied.

Bruno reached into his satchel and pulled out a silver coin. "This should be more than enough to cover the expense."

The man snatched the coin from Bruno's hand and smiled a toothless grin. In less than a minute both bodies were in the wagon and on their way to the pauper's graveyard.

"The smell will linger but by tomorrow it will be tolerable, especially if we remove the bucket," Bruno explained.

"I thought we were going to try to tan the skin you cut from both of their backs," Raul replied.

"I for one don't plan on sticking my hands in that ungodly slime and I very much doubt if you desire to do so either," Bruno said. "We'll see if this blacksmith will tan the skins for us, we'll offer to pay him well."

"I wouldn't count on it," Raul replied.

"Write down the woman's name in the journal, Lucia I believe he said.

"Yes, that is correct, Lucia de la Cruz. I remember it from the auto de fe," Raul replied.

"How ironic that her surname meant 'of the cross' and it was a cross that took her life," Bruno noted.

"Maybe not ironic at all, maybe that was God's plan all along," Raul replied.

"If not God's, then possibly someone else," Bruno surmised.

Bruno picked up the saw he had used on the skulls and returned it to the cabinet in the storage room below the workshop. Raul began copying the drawing of the cross trying to ignore the smell.

"I know someone has been here," Bruno shouted from below. "The contents of this cabinet have been straightened." He began to look around the room to see if anything else had been changed but nothing seemed out of the ordinary. As he climbed the ladder leading out of the storage room Bruno looked back. The sun's morning rays shone through the trap door and reflected off the brick floor. In front of the cabinet, Bruno noticed curved parallel lines faintly etched into the brick.

"Monsignor, I've completed the drawing, I would very much like to leave this place, the smell is overbearing," Raul called out.

Bruno hesitated momentarily wanting to investigate further but decided it could wait until later. "I'm coming, I'm coming," he called back to Raul.

"Find a covering for this bucket unless you don't mind it splashing all over you on our journey," Bruno advised. "Better yet, find an acolyte to carry it; I want your hands free to take notes."

"Yes, Monsignor," Raul replied, feeling relieved.

ꙮ   ꙮ   ꙮ

"The blacksmith's shop is just beyond that stream up ahead," Raul said. "As I had told you, less than an hour's journey."

"Good, I was beginning to tire," Bruno replied. He reached into his satchel, removed his flask and took a long drawl of the pungent elixir.

"Does the smell of the bucket bother you Brother Bruno?" Raul asked.

"No, the absenta helps my stamina on these long journeys," Bruno laughed.

Even before they could see the workshop, they heard the pounding, as the blacksmith formed the metal with mighty hammer blows. As they drew closer, they could see him toiling over a hot fire and see the sparks fly from the glowing metal with each successive blow.

The blacksmith didn't see the men until they were almost upon him. He sat his hammer on the table next to the fire and tossed the piece of metal he was working back into the oven and buried it beneath the glowing embers.

"Hello friend," Raul called out but received only a cold stare in return. "Brother Bruno had some questions about tanning skins and I thought you might be able to answer his questions or possibly be interested in tanning them for him."

The acolyte sat the uncovered bucket on the ground near the blacksmith.

"I don't work leather anymore," the blacksmith replied, "but if you'd like I'll piss and crap in the bucket for you."

"Your hands tell a different story," Bruno challenged. "They look like the hands of a man who has recently worked leather."

"Then you are unfamiliar with the hands of a tanner, for these are the hands of a blacksmith," the man replied holding his hands high.

"Perhaps you could recommend a tanner who could help us out," Raul said.

"Depends," the smith replied.

"Depends on what?" Bruno asked as he looked around the workshop. Bruno picked up the hammer from the table and began to study the hammer's head.

"Depends on what kind of hides you want tanned," the man replied snatching the hammer from Bruno's hands.

"Human hides. Actually, just small pieces of human skin," Bruno replied waiting for a reaction while he continued to explore the workshop.

"I'd appreciate it if you'd step outside and leave me be," the smith said irritated by Bruno's reply.

"I think you'd better take that piece out of the fire before it is ruined," Bruno suggested, wanting to get a look at what the smith had been working on.

"It'll keep," the blacksmith replied staring back at Bruno.

"I have something I'd like you to have a look at," Bruno said pulling the cross from his satchel. "Do you recognize the workmanship of the metal?" He tried to hand the cross to the blacksmith but the smith backed away. "Take it, have a close look."

Hesitantly the smith took the cross in his hands.

"Feels strangely warm, doesn't it," Bruno said staring at the smith's eyes.

"This is human skin," the smith replied.

"Yes, it is. Human skin that has been preserved and stuffed with human hair, then sewn around the metal framed cross. And if you notice it is more than just a cross, it is a weapon, a dagger. A dagger designed to pierce a human skull and rip the brains right out. See this design on the point. It provides a channel to allow the blood to be drained from the body, an intricate piece of craftsmanship. Do you know who is skilled enough to have made such a cross?" Bruno demanded. "Do you know who would be capable of such a horrendous deed?"

"I'm sorry I can't help you," the smith said handing the cross back to Bruno.

"Can't or won't?" Bruno replied.

"Take your bucket of evil and leave here, I've no use for men of the Church," the blacksmith replied turning away.

"Fetch the bucket, boy," Bruno said to the acolyte.

"Perhaps we can find someone who'll be of more help out by the river," Raul suggested.

"No, I believe I have all the information I need," Bruno replied. "Let's go back to the templo."

Suddenly, Bruno spun around. He had felt the touch of a cold hand on his back. So cold it made his heart skip a beat.

"What is it Monsignor, you look ill?" Raul cried.

Bruno continued to stare back towards the blacksmith shop.

"An evil I have not known lurks very near. God has sent me a warning to prepare for spiritual warfare with this unknown demon."

As the trio headed back into the city Bruno took another swig of his elixir. "Are you sure you don't want some?" Bruno said offering the flask to Raul. "It may make the pain of seeing your brother easier to deal with."

"How did you know he was my brother?" Raul asked taking the flask.

"You told me your brother was a blacksmith," Bruno replied, "but you were hesitant to discuss him. Logically, who else would you take me to see?"

"I must apologize for my brother's behavior. He is an unhappy man," Raul replied.

"Why do you believe he is unhappy?" Bruno asked

"He wasn't happy having to take up our father's trade. He has always been angry that I was the one allowed to serve the Church. He believed it was he who God called," Raul explained.

"Perhaps God called both of you into his service," Bruno suggested. "It's never too late to serve our Lord."

"That's what I told Jayro as well," Raul replied. "I offered him a chance to join the brotherhood at the templo, but he refused."

"He never considered it?" Bruno asked.

"Oh, he considered it," Raul said. "He came and lived at the templo for over a year as it was being rebuilt. He did much of the ironwork for the new building, but he never found a heart for our Lord."

"I thought you said that he believed God called him to serve? Did something happen at the templo that shattered his faith?" Bruno asked.

"He thought that the Church had lost its spiritual focus. He was very bothered by this," Raul explained.

"But there was no individual incident that you can think of that may have caused his disillusionment?" Bruno asked.

"No. He gradually withdrew spiritually, emotionally, and physically. About a year before the construction was complete, he had moved away from the templo monastery. He continued to show up to work everyday, but as to where he stayed, I have no idea," Raul explained.

"Be sure to write down this conversation in the journal," Bruno ordered. "And of course, try to recall all that was said at your brother's shop."

"Yes Monsignor," Raul replied. "Monsignor Mancini, is my brother this demon God has warned you about?"

"No, your brother is a man, not a spirit. Nor do I believe a spirit dwell within him. I'm troubled that he has chosen not to serve our Lord but even troubled more that he worships a false god," Bruno replied.

"How do you know this?" Raul asked.

"God has told me as much," Bruno replied. "Your brother is hiding something, something that tortures him inside. Let us pray that God will lift this veil of darkness and free your brother's soul to worship the one true God."

"Boy," Bruno called to the acolyte, "pour the contents of that bucket over that cliff, I no longer have a need for it."

The acolyte did as he was told, pouring the bucket of urine containing the witch's brain down into the ravine below. It was there that he saw the dead horse lying bloated in the burning sun still harnessed to a smashed wagon.

"Master," the acolyte yelled excitedly running back to where Bruno and Raul waited on the road. "Master, there's a wagon and dead horse in the ravine below. I saw it through the trees. Perhaps it broke free from its owner and plunged off the cliff."

"Perhaps," Bruno replied, seeming uninterested.

"Shouldn't we investigate, Brother Bruno? What if someone there needs our help?" Raul said.

"Boy, did you see anyone down there?" Bruno said.

"No, my Grace," the acolyte replied.

"See," Bruno said to Raul, "the boy saw no one else. Further investigation would be a waste of our time."

"Forgive me for disagreeing, Brother Bruno, but horses pulling wagons don't just run off of cliffs by themselves. I think it warrants further investigation." Raul insisted.

"Very well," Bruno huffed, "but don't expect me to climb down that cliff. Just be quick with it, the archbishop leaves for Rome today and I must speak with him." Bruno pulled out his flask and drank deeply from its contents.

"I'll climb down with the boy," Raul replied.

Bruno waited impatiently; constantly nipping at his flask while Raul and the acolyte descended the treacherous cliff and disappeared into a clump of shrubs and dense trees.

"Well, was it worth the effort?" Bruno shouted.

"It is the gravedigger's wagon," Raul called up to Bruno. "They both are dead."

"The witch," Bruno cried down, "Are the acolyte and witch's body still in the wagon?"

"No," Raul yelled back, "I don't see them anywhere."

"Thank God," Bruno whispered to himself. "The bodies were already buried."

"Wait," Raul called, "I see the acolyte's body caught in the tree limbs."

Bruno remembered the cold touch he had felt as he left the blacksmith shop. "What about the witch, do you see her body?"

"It's not here," Raul replied, "we're coming back up."

Bruno knew there was no need to search further for the witch's body, but as to where it went or who might have taken it, he was unwilling or possibly afraid to speculate.

"What should we do?" Raul asked when he reached the top of the cliff.

"What is there to do but to notify the authorities when we reach the city? I presume you prayed for the Lord to safely deliver their souls," Bruno said.

"Forgive me Brother Bruno, but I was too afraid and didn't think to do so," Raul replied feeling ashamed.

"Then you must do so when you return to the templo," Bruno ordered. "Their souls have waited this long; another hour will make little difference to the Lord."

"What do you believe happened?" Raul asked.

"It seems obvious that something must have startled their horse causing the steed to charge over the cliff before the gravediggers could safely jump clear," Bruno explained.

"But why is the witch's body not at the foot of the cliff with the others?" Raul continued.

Bruno took another swig from his flask. "Just make sure you write all of this down," Bruno said, not answering the question. "Come, we must hurry."

"I'll miss your company my friend," the archbishop said to Bruno as he prepared to leave.

"And I'll miss seeing Rome," Bruno laughed, "and of course, I'll miss you as well my Grace."

"Are you sure you can't join me?" the archbishop asked.

"No, my investigation into the acolyte's death is not yet complete," Bruno replied. "And the Madonna continues to cry. Do you have the containers of the Virgin's tears?"

"Yes, my friend. They're safely locked in my trunk along with the drawings of the cross taken from the witch's head."

"Make sure you give them to Father Moretti so they can be catalogued and stored."

"You needn't worry, Brother Mancini," replied the archbishop.

"I've one more request my friend," Bruno said in a serious tone. From his satchel he pulled out a sealed envelope and handed it to the archbishop.

"What is this?" the archbishop asked.

"It is my will and letters of instructions to be opened upon my death," Bruno responded.

"Why do you give me these?" the archbishop asked.

"God has spoken to me. He has warned me that I'm about to enter a great spiritual battle, a battle I may not survive," Bruno explained. "A powerful adversary lurks in Madrid. I've already felt her cold touch."

"This demon is a woman, you've seen her?" the archbishop asked.

"No, I've only felt her icy touch upon my back and that almost froze my heart. It's been a long time, but I still remember the feel of a woman's touch," Bruno explained.

"Is this demon responsible for the acolyte or the witch's death?" the archbishop asked.

"Not responsible, but somehow involved, I'm sure of that," Bruno replied. "And it quite possibly could be Satan himself who caused the death of the gravediggers and stole the witch's body."

"Has Satan commanded this witch to serve as one of his demons?" the archbishop asked. "Was it her cold touch that you felt?"

"There's much I need to learn about this witch before I know for certain, but I fear it may be more than just a demon Satan has cast before me," Bruno replied.

"I wish you'd reconsider and come with me to Rome," the archbishop said. "I'd order it so if I didn't already know you'd disobey me."

"God has brought me to this place for this battle. I cannot turn from what God has destined for me."

"I'll pray for you daily," the archbishop said. "Be careful my friend. I don't want to have to wait until we both reach heaven to see you again."

"God will protect me," Bruno replied. "Remember your Grace, pray in Latin; Satan hates to hear prayers in Latin."

"It shall be done.

CHAPTER TEN

"Jubilation"

"Would you look at that mess?" Kevin said as the Mercedes approached St. Lucy's.

"They're tearing the metal 'St. Lucy's' letters off the side of the church," Francois noted.

As the car pulled to a stop, Liz jumped out into the mêlée

"Liz, wait!" Kevin called out but she was already lost in the crowd.

"Francois you go and find Liz, I'll be inside speaking with the Reverend Father," Kevin instructed.

Francois headed into the crowd as Kevin pushed his way to the main entrance of the church.

"Mr. Bridges, the Reverend Father is going to be very glad to see you," the deacon, who had helped Kevin earlier, said trying to be heard over the yelling and arguing.

"How long has it been like this?" Kevin asked.

"What?" the deacon replied.

"How long has it been like this?" Kevin asked again, shouting this time.

"It's been building ever since blood started running from the beneath the Virgin, but it didn't turn ugly until we sealed off the grotto," he replied.

"Has the blood started to flow again?" Kevin said.

"No, but the water is running from the spring like it did fifty years ago. We don't need to turn on the tap water," he explained.

The police presence had increased significantly and the scene was close to becoming a full-scale riot. Several people were trying to shove their way into the church and the church security was struggling to keep them out. Suddenly, it became noticeably quieter around the entrance.

"Kevin," Liz said. "Tell the Reverend Father that he needs to open the church and the grotto."

"The crowd will rip the place apart if he does that," the deacon interrupted.

"The curtains need to come down at once," Liz continued. "You are playing into Satan's hands by keeping the believers in the dark. We must bring light into the darkness."

"I will ask him," Kevin replied as Francois caught up to Liz.

"Don't ask him, tell him," Liz demanded. "You're the expert from the Vatican. That's why the Pope sent you here in the first place."

"Did I miss anything?" Francois said as the three were ushered inside the church.

"No, but you can be a big help," Liz replied. "You and the deacon go tell those men to take down the curtains blocking the view of the grotto."

"What did you say?" the Reverend Father huffed as he met the entering trio.

Liz looked at Kevin.

"We need to remove the curtains and allow the people access to the grotto and church in their time of need," Kevin spoke up.

"They will tear my church apart," the Reverend Father insisted.

"God's church," Liz corrected touching him on his arm. "This is merely a building; the church are those people outside desperately seeking Christ. You must allow them to do so."

"You're right," the Reverend Father replied without hesitation. "Open the doors."

"Francois and I will assist out here," Liz said. "I know you need to speak with the Reverend Father in private."

"Thank you," Kevin said to Liz as she and Francois headed for the grotto. It didn't escape Kevin's attention that the demeanor of the Reverend Father dramatically shifted when Liz touched his arm.

"Reverend Father, my name is Kevin Bridges, I was sent here by the Vatican."

"No, I believe you were sent here by God to remind me of my place and purpose," the Reverend Father replied. "Who is that remarkable woman? Is she also from the Vatican?"

"Her name is Elizabeth Purdue, and no, she is not from the Vatican. She works for Interpol. She came here to investigate a series of murders that relate to some of the miracles I've been investigating."

"Are these murders related to the blood flowing from the Virgin in our grotto?" Reverend Father asked.

"I don't know, but I really don't think so," Kevin replied.

"But you just said they are related to the miracle. Are you saying that the blood flowing in the grotto was not a miracle?" Reverend Father asked.

"No, that is yet to be determined, but the grotto was not the only miracle I was here to investigate. There have been several murders associated with the alleged miracles to support beatification of John Paul II," Kevin explained. "That's why Liz and Francois are here with me."

"I know of the miracle of which you speak," Reverend Father replied. "One of our local doctors had a brain tumor healed. How is this man, Francois involved?"

"He is with the French prefecture. I was in Paris investigating a similar miracle when several people involved were killed. Liz had also come to Paris from Poland where other murders had occurred. We deduced that New York would be the next target of the murderer."

"Just who is this murderer you speak of?" Reverend Father asked.

"Her name is Lucienne. We don't know her last name or where she is from, but I do know without a doubt that she's doing Satan's bidding and I know she's not human."

"Not human! Then what is she, some sort of demon?" Reverend Father asked.

"According to Liz, who has been after her for years, she is a Nephilim," Kevin explained.

"Lord protect us all," Reverend Father replied crossing himself.

"There was an attempt earlier today on the lives of some of those involved in that miracle healing of the doctor. An FBI agent was killed, as was one of the associates of Lucienne," Kevin said. "Liz confronted Lucienne in one of the offices. She had brought with her some of the blood from the grotto. Before she could use it, Lucienne escaped through a shattered window by changing into a swarm of insects."

"How did she acquire the blood? I told the vendor not to distribute it until I heard from the Vatican," Reverend Father replied.

"That is what I wanted to ask you. She says you gave two jars to her driver early this morning," Kevin said.

"I did give two jars to a man. I thought he was from the Vatican."

"Did he say he was from the Vatican?" Kevin asked.

"No, but I knew giving him the blood was the right thing to do. I felt it in my heart," Reverend Father replied. "Was I wrong in doing so?"

"I don't think so, but I'm still a little unsure about Liz and who she really works for," Kevin replied. "She seems to be a devout woman of God, yet I know she's not been completely honest with me."

"You must look to God for his guidance," Reverend Father replied. "Let him be your light."

"Thank you, Father," Kevin replied. "I believe I have all the information I need about the grotto to write my report. I wish I could stay longer, but we believe this Lucienne is on her way to Spain. That's where the two doctors she came here to kill are vacationing. If we don't leave soon, we may not be able to. The FBI will want us to stay for questioning and we cannot afford to give Lucienne such a head start."

"I understand completely," Reverend Father replied opening the door from his office to the sanctuary.

Hundreds of parishioners were in the pews praying and all evidence of the near riot had disappeared.

"She's a very wise woman," Reverend Father said. "All they ever wanted was to be closer to God."

The doors leading from the sanctuary to the grotto were wide open allowing the light to stream in. It also allowed Kevin to see Francois and Liz sitting on the benches facing the grotto.

"You look almost melancholy, Francois. Are you feeling well?" Kevin joked.

"Francois was telling me about a trip he made to the real Our Lady of Lourdes when he was younger," Liz said.

"Much younger," Francois corrected. "I'd just entered secondary school."

Kevin looked at his watch, but Liz nodded for him to sit down on the bench. He got the message.

"My mother had terminal cancer. At least that's what my father told me the doctors had said. What he didn't tell me was that they had given her only weeks to live. Like most Frenchmen my father viewed Christianity as little more than a cult. That's why I was so surprised when he announced we were going to Our Lady of Lourdes. I couldn't understand what my father was thinking. Now I know he was desperate and grasping at any straw that might keep his beloved wife alive a little longer."

"Perhaps it was more than that," Liz suggested. "Maybe God spoke to him…"

"Like God has spoken to all these desperate people?" Francois interrupted sarcastically as he acknowledged the hundreds that crowded the grotto area.

"These people are desperate, just like your father was desperate," Liz replied. "Look around Francois, some of these people are seeking the same thing your father was seeking. They are trying to keep a loved one alive. Others are here desperate to break an addiction, others seeking guidance for their future, others seeking hope. All of them praying for a miracle, just as your father prayed for a miracle."

"Were your father's prayers answered?" Kevin asked.

"If you're asking if my mom was cured from cancer, the answer is no. She did live for almost another year which seemed to amaze the doctors. I remember my father telling me it was the happiest year of their lives even though my mom was in quite a bit of pain," Francois said.

"Maybe your father's prayers were answered," Liz suggested.

"So he claimed, and so I thought," Francois said. "When the boys at school heard of my father's story that Our Lady of the Lourdes had answered his prayers and allowed my mom to live, I bore the brunt of their ridicule. Then when my mother died the teasing was relentless."

"Is that when you turned your back on God?" Liz asked.

"There has never been a God in my life to turn my back on," Francois quipped. "My father died less than a year after my mother passed away. It seemed fairly clear to me that my father had been fooled into believing in God by his own desperation. He was convinced they would one day be together again in heaven. I swore I'd never allow myself to be fooled the way my father had been."

"I'm sorry you feel that way," Liz said.

"We need to get to the airport," Kevin said trying to lighten the mood.

"Still," Francois continued, "it is a beautiful place, even though it isn't the real Our Lady of Lourdes."

"Kevin's right," Liz agreed, "we'd better be leaving before it's too late. Soon, someone in the FBI is going to want to know where the Frenchman who killed that man in the medical office ran off to."

"And where the Interpol agent who fought this alleged Lucienne disappeared to," Francois replied.

"And Carlo can hold them off for only so long, so we need to go," Kevin said emphatically.

Lost in their own thoughts, they all quietly headed for the Mercedes.

The silence in the car was shattered when Kevin's Blackberry began to chime.

"Mr. Bridges?" the voice said. "This is Captain Reynolds at the airport."

"Yes Captain, what can I do for you?" Kevin replied.

"Just thought you should know that the plane is fueled and the flight plan to Madrid has been filed. We're ready to go but there may be a slight problem with our departure."

"What might that be?" Kevin asked.

"There are two black Suburbans parked next to us, with a half-a-dozen armed men with jackets that say ICE on them," the captain explained.

"Immigration and Customs Enforcement," Kevin replied.

"Yes sir. They said they are waiting to talk to you and your friends," the captain replied.

"Do they know you are making this call?" Kevin asked.

"No sir, they've already searched the plane and are waiting outside. At least three of them are. One of the Suburbans is pulling away right now and appears to be headed for the international passenger terminal. Now, one of the agents is walking towards the hangar. He probably is headed for the bathroom. These guys have been here for a while drinking lots of coffee."

"Good, the fewer we have to deal with the better," Kevin replied. "We'll still be leaving as scheduled. Once my friends get on board, they'll be safe. I'll claim diplomatic immunity and then ICE legally cannot board the plane."

"That may be true," the pilot replied, "but they can still keep us on the ground. They could try to wait us out."

"The Vatican could get us cleared for take-off, but that could take several hours," Kevin said.

"We don't have several hours," Liz interrupted comprehending the gist of the conversation.

"I'll think of something," Kevin said, "just be ready to go."

"Yes sir," Captain Reynolds replied.

"It seems Carlo held back the hounds as long as he could," Kevin said. "There are several ICE agents waiting to keep us from departing this great land."

"But you have a diplomatic passport," Francois said, "they cannot keep you here."

"That's true, but my diplomatic credentials will do neither of you any good. However, once you're on the plane we may have a valid argument for not allowing them to take you back off," Kevin explained.

"I'm not so sure," Liz replied. "From what I know about ICE, they wouldn't think twice about forcibly removing us from the plane and letting the lawyers sort through the entire mess. We cannot afford to let that happen."

"Somehow, we're going to have to sneak you on that plane," Kevin said pushing send on his phone.

"This is Captain Reynolds," the pilot answered.

"Captain, this is Kevin, is there anyone besides you, the co-pilot, and the ICE agents around the plane?"

"Not right now, but a few minutes ago two men from airline catering refreshed our supplies," the pilot said.

"Good, be ready for two more of the catering personnel to visit the jet," Kevin advised.

"I understand," the pilot replied.

Kevin explained his plan to Liz and Francois.

"A Mercedes headed for the Vatican jet was just cleared through the general aviation security gate," the ICE agent seated in the Suburban called to his two partners standing near the wing of the jet.

"How many passengers?" the senior of the two agents called back.

"He didn't say," the driver replied, "but here comes the Mercedes, so you'll know in a minute."

As the Mercedes approached the jet it stopped at least fifty yards away from the plane. Immediately the Suburban sped to where it stopped and pulled in front of it. The two agents jogged over to join the driver who had now exited and stood with his hand on his weapon just outside the driver's door. The tinted windows hid the occupants from view.

"I'd like everyone to step outside of the vehicle," the ICE agent demanded.

The Mercedes driver stepped out holding his Interpol credentials in his hand.

"What seems to be the problem," Kevin said exiting the back seat holding his diplomatic passport.

"What happened to your two friends?" one of the agents asked while the other looked inside the car.

"You know you're violating international law by searching a diplomat's car," Kevin reminded the agents. He was about to add or a diplomat's airplane, but stopped when he saw Liz and Francois dressed as catering workers carrying supplies to the waiting jet. He didn't want to direct the agent's attention to the plane.

"We're aware of your diplomatic status Mr. Bridges and don't wish to delay your flight any longer than necessary," the agent replied. "However, we'd appreciate your help in locating the Frenchman and the female Interpol agent."

"I assume you're referring to Liz and Francois," Kevin replied. "Have you tried the hotel where they are staying?"

"Mr. Bridges we're not here to play guessing games with you. We're sent to pick up your two friends and since they're not with you I see no reason we should keep you from departing any longer."

"Of course, before you go, that is if you want to go, would you please ask your two friends to exit the jet. Did you really think we would be fooled by the catering…?" Before the agent could finish his sentence two people exited the jet and started back towards the hangar.

"Hold up there," the agent called out but neither person stopped or turned to look.

"Am I free to leave now?" Kevin asked.

"Now that your friends have left, of course," the agent replied smiling. Two of the ICE agents were jogging after the two caterers. The third now jumped into the Suburban and sped off towards the hangar as Kevin hurried onto the plane.

Kevin wasn't sure what to do. His plan had failed. Francois and Liz must have realized they had been seen and chose to sacrifice themselves so Kevin could get away. He felt obligated to leave so their gesture wouldn't be in vain. Besides there wasn't much he could do to get them released. Liz should have no problem and should be able to leave the next day, but Francois may be stuck in New York for several days. Someone had to get to Spain to try to stop Lucienne.

"Let's get out of here," Kevin shouted to Captain Reynolds as he shut the cabin door.

"Roger that," the pilot replied, "the tower says ICE has cleared us for departure."

"Thank God for that," Kevin heard Francois say behind him.

"Now you're thanking God," Liz replied cynically.

"It's only an expression," Francois replied.

"Where did you two come from?" Kevin gasped.

"What do you mean? It was your idea to use these uniforms to sneak onto the plane," Francois replied.

"I know, but…, but, I just saw the two of you get out of the plane and head for the hangar," Kevin replied.

"No one got out of the plane," Liz said. "We've been waiting here praying that the plan would work. And from what I have heard about that Apostle serial killer case, you, if anybody, understands the power of prayer."

"You were praying," Francois interjected, "I was enjoying a glass of wine."

"Then who were the two people dressed as caterers who left here," Kevin asked again.

"If you ask every question twice, we'll never get out of here," Francois joked.

"Please take your seats and prepare for take-off," the pilot said as the plane taxied towards the runway.

ೀ   ೀ   ೀ

"I ordered you to stop," one of the agents said drawing his weapon just as the two caterers reached the hangar door.

The two stepped through the doorway just as the Suburban screeched to a halt. The bright sunlight made it impossible to see inside the hangar. Before the caterers cleared the doorway, it appeared that one of them finally heard the ICE agents command to stop and turned to come out. All three agents drew their guns expecting trouble.

"Hands in the air, now!" the senior agent yelled.

"Whoa, what the hell are you guys doing," a voice replied doing as commanded.

The fourth ICE agent was standing in the hangar doorway with his hands raised.

"Where'd you come from? Where'd the other two go?" the agent barked.

"I went to the bathroom, you know that. The coffee went right through me," the agent explained. "And what other two are you talking about?"

The senior agent shoved him out of the way. The hangar was empty.

"There were two caterers who walked in just as you were walking out," one of the other agents said.

"Man, nobody came walking into this hangar," the agent replied.

"Call the tower, have them stop that jet from taking off," the senior agent ordered.

"My radio is not working."

"Neither is mine."

The senior agent climbed in the Suburban but the radio inside it was dead as well.

"Jump in, we'll try to head them off," he ordered, but when he turned the key the car was dead.

"What the hell is going on here?" one of the other agents asked.

"I don't think hell has anything to do with it," the senior agent replied.

"God must be on their side," one of the agents commented.

"Well duh, it is a Vatican jet," one of the others replied.

All four agents could do nothing more than watch as the papal jet took off and turned towards the ocean.

"With God on your side, who can stand against you?" one of the agents said.

"Certainly not us," the senior agent replied.

CHAPTER ELEVEN

"Patience"

"**...Yea, though I walk** through the valley of the shadow of death, I will fear no evil; thy rod and thy staff they comfort me. Thou preparest a table before me in the presence of mine enemies: thou preparest...," suddenly Bruno's prayer was interrupted.

"You know not how great and powerful your enemies be." A woman's voice spoke.

"Who said that?" Bruno said standing and looking behind him. No one was there. Several monks who had been praying nearby stopped their prayers and looked at Bruno.

"Is something wrong Brother Bruno?" Raul asked.

"Didn't you hear her voice?" Bruno roared.

"I heard no woman's voice, only the murmur of our prayers," Raul replied. "Perhaps it was God answering your prayer."

"God has never spoken out loud to me in the past and I very much doubt that if he did his voice would be that of a woman," Bruno snapped back.

"One should never presume how..."

"I never presume anything," Bruno interrupted. "I analyze the facts and formulate a hypothesis. And the fact is I heard a voice, a woman's voice, so therefore my supposition is that there is a woman present."

Several of the monks could be heard snickering at Bruno's blusterous outburst.

"What did this woman say?" Raul asked trying to calm Bruno down and diffuse his anger.

"It matters not what she said, it only matters that she said it," Bruno insisted, growing even more irate.

"I'll help you search for this woman," Raul said as he began to look between the pews.

"Come, we have important work to do," Bruno said storming down the aisle towards the crypts.

It didn't go unnoticed by Raul that Bruno once again drank from his flask of absenta.

"Be gone witch," Jayro yelled, "your place is not of this earth."

"But it was you who released me unto this place," the witch replied. "I believed I was but a mortal until you freed my spirit to work for Satan, our god, and he revealed to me my forgotten past."

"You speak nonsense, leave this place." Jayro threw his hammer at the spirit that stood before him, but before it struck the witch it dropped harmlessly to the ground. "You're nothing more than a ghost sent by God to torment me for what I have done. Go back and tell God that I have forsaken Him as he has forsaken me."

"No, you have forsaken Him, that's why you were chosen," she replied.

"Chosen? Chosen by whom and for what?" Jayro said.

"Actually, it was you who did the choosing. You chose Satan and Satan has rewarded you for your faithfulness," the witch replied.

"Rewarded me how?" Jayro replied.

"It was Satan who guided you to the catacombs and torture chamber. It was also Satan who showed you the vision of the cross in your dreams. The cross you used to release me and the cross that is the key to your adyctum. He is pleased with what you have created but displeased with your carelessness," the witch explained.

"I don't understand," Jayro replied.

"You were careless when you failed to remove the cross from my head. This monk, the one who came with your brother, he knows it's you who made the cross and he suspects it's you who murdered the acolyte. This displeases our master. You must retrieve the cross and kill this monk. The Inquisition must never end," she warned.

"I've made other crosses to replace the one I lost," Jayro replied.

"No doubt made from the skin you stole from my back," the witch hissed.

"No, but once your skin is prepared it will be used," he replied. "There have been others before you whose skin was the penance paid for their sins."

"And I'd hope there are others who now languish in your adyctum awaiting their penance as well," she laughed, but suddenly turned ominously serious. "Heed my warning, you must be careful for this monk is smart and dangerous but he is human and, like all humans, he is weak. Find that weakness and use it to destroy him. Don't forget for a moment that he is capable of undoing all the evil that Satan has wrought in Madrid."

"If Satan is so great why doesn't he kill this monk himself if he poses such a danger?" Jayro asked.

"Because he has loyal followers like you and I to do it for him," she replied. "Our numbers are many and grow larger as each day passes. One day all of Madrid will owe their souls to Satan. We must make sure nothing happens to change that."

"I'll consider all that you've told me today, witch," Jayro replied, "but there's much I don't understand. I care not about how many souls belong to Satan, but I won't have this monk destroy all I've built beneath the Templo. I assure you, this monk will die, as will my own brother if he interferes. As for you, I've killed you once and shall do so again if you don't leave here immediately."

The witch laughed as she turned to leave, "You never killed me, you released me."

Jayro pulled the cross from beneath his robe to spear the witch again, but she was gone.

Raul stood quietly while Bruno scurried from crypt to crypt trying to read the inscriptions. "I need more light, I can't see anything. Who's responsible for replacing these candles?"

"The abbot has not yet assigned an acolyte to the task," Raul replied, as he replaced the burned-out candles with new ones.

"That's better," Bruno snarled, "but where are the blood droplets and where is the pool of blood from the acolyte?"

"It was scrubbed away by two of our brother monks. Father Santorio ordered it done before he opened the crypts for visitations," Raul explained.

"Then how am I to find what I'm looking for," Bruno replied.

"What is it you seek," Raul calmly replied.

"The blood droplets led to a certain crypt. The inscription may hold a clue as to the murderer, but I can't remember what it said or where it was," Bruno complained. "Do you remember where I stood when the archbishop called for us?"

"I'm afraid my memory is not that well-trained," Raul replied.

"Well then, look at your notes. I told you to write down exactly how we found the acolyte's body and his tunic," Bruno ordered, staring at Raul waiting for a reply.

Raul thumbed quickly through the pages, stopped, then walked to where his drawing showed the body was found. "The body was here and the tunic would have been over here," Raul motioned.

"The blood droplets, where were the blood droplets?" Bruno demanded.

Raul had not written down the exact location where Bruno had followed the droplets but he was afraid to admit as much to Bruno. "You followed a trail of blood into this hallway," Raul sheepishly replied.

"Is that what you had written down, or is that your best recollection?" Bruno asked.

"It's my best recollection. I'm sorry but I didn't notate the location of the blood drops," Raul replied.

"Nor would I have expected you to do so," Bruno said. "However, I believe your memory is better that you think, for I too believe this is the hallway where I found the blood smudge."

Raul held a candelabra as Bruno read the inscriptions on several of the crypts. "It appears that several different stonecutters carved the inscriptions on these crypts," Bruno noted.

"Many of the burial crypts in this hallway came from the old templo. They were moved here when the templo was remodeled. This hallway was once part of the catacombs where the monks were all laid to rest," Raul explained. Some of these crypts were constructed to hold the remains of several generations of monks."

"That must be why some are so much larger than others and are labeled only with bible passages," Raul replied. "You say this hallway was once part of the catacombs that lay beneath the Templo? Are there more catacombs?"

"The catacombs became the new crypt. As far as I know this is all there were," Raul replied.

Bruno suddenly started knocking on several of the crypts.

"I don't believe anyone will answer," Raul joked.

"I may have found the clue we've been looking for" Bruno replied. "This passage inscribed on this crypt is one of the few with the chapter and verse listed below it. *'Ask and it will be given to you; seek and you will find; knock and the door will be opened to you.'*"

"Those are the words of Jesus in the book of Matthew," Raul replied.

"Matthew 7:7, I believe," Bruno responded. But that is not what is inscribed here. The stonecutter wrote 'Matthew' and then this odd symbol. Looks a bit like a Y. Have a look."

Raul looked at the inscription.

> Ask and it will be given to you;
> seek and you will find;
> knock and the door will be opened to you.
>
> Matthew [7:✝]

"Perhaps the stonecutter wasn't aware of the chapter and verse number of the passage," Raul suggested.

"Perhaps," Bruno replied, "but the same cutter seemed to inscribe this other crypt and it is labeled with the proper chapter and verse."

"Maybe it was a mistake and he created a symbol trying to cover his error," Raul said.

"I too thought that may be what had occurred, but upon further inspection, you can see that it has been cut deep into the stone with much precision. This symbol was not cut by mistake," Bruno declared.

"That's why you believe it to be a clue to the murders?" Raul asked.

"Murder, singular not plural. I believe it's a clue to the acolyte's murder only," Bruno corrected.

"But I thought you said the same person killed both the witch and the acolyte?" Raul replied.

"No, I believe I said they were both killed in the same way and that they are somehow connected. It's probable that the same person killed them both, but that must still be proven," Bruno explained. "But to answer your question, I believe that this is a clue to how the murderer escaped without being seen after killing the acolyte."

"I don't understand," Raul said.

"The blood trail led me to this hallway and to this particular crypt. I believe this is not a crypt but a doorway into other catacombs. The inscription is a clue as to how the door is to be opened. A clue I do not yet fully understand but, in time, I will," Bruno explained.

"If it is a door, we should just break it down," Raul suggested.

"If it is not a door, we would be desecrating the resting place of several monks and do great damage to the crypt room. Something I'm sure the Reverend Father would not be pleased about." Bruno replied. "And if I were smart enough to create such an elaborate escape route, I would be smart enough to ensure that whoever tried to breach my door would suffer dire consequences for doing so."

"Then what shall we do?" Raul asked.

Bruno took another swig from his flask. "You'll write down all we have just said and learned. I'll return to my cell to ponder the clue to unlock the passage and take a much needed and deserved rest." Bruno replied.

Anxiousness tore at Raul's mind. The two monks were on the verge of discovering the murderer and Bruno now needed to rest. Raul knew that the absenta was beginning to interfere with Bruno's reasoning. "But Brother Bruno..."

Bruno raised his hand, interrupting Raul. "It's late. We'll continue our investigation in the morning," Bruno said as he climbed the stairs out of the crypt.

"Yes, my Grace." Raul began to copy the inscription from the crypt into the journal. As he carefully copied the design, he realized he'd seen it before.

"It can't be," he said, even though he knew it to be true. The design was the same as the design his brother wore on his ring. He knew he should tell Bruno, but he had to be sure before he accused his own brother of murder.

It would take Raul most of the night to write down all they had discovered and discussed, even longer now that he had begun to make a second copy for himself. And with each sentence written thoughts of his brother tore at his mind.

CHAPTER TWELVE

"Intimidation"

"The FBI must've called ahead," the pilot announced as the papal jet taxied into the private hangar. "Looks like the Cuerpo Nacional de Policía has sent representatives to discuss our arrival."

"Or our eminent departure," Francois commented.

"You know coming here is exactly what Lucienne wanted you to do," Liz said to Kevin.

"What do you mean?" Kevin asked.

"She wants to destroy you by destroying your reputation. You were supposed to be blamed for the murders in Paris," Liz explained.

"She was almost successful. I along with several of my colleagues thought you were behind the deaths of those two henchmen and the medical office fire. I even suspected you were somehow involved in the hotel security guard's death. I was still suspicious until I witnessed what happened in New York," Francois said.

"Thanks for your vote of confidence," Kevin replied, sarcastically.

"In New York she almost succeeded in ruining your reputation as well, Francois. It was you who killed Lucienne's accomplice," Liz reminded him. "In fact, I believe it is probably you that the Cuerpo Nacional is most interested in speaking with."

"We'll see," Francois said, as the Captain opened the door and lowered the steps.

"Welcome to Spain," a man said, offering his hand to Liz as she stepped from the steps to the hangar floor. "You must be Ms. Purdue. I have heard so much about you."

"All good I hope," Liz replied.

"Not entirely," he replied. "My name is Inspector Romero. I'm with the Cuerpo Nacional de Policía."

"And I'm Kevin Bridges," Kevin said stepping in between Liz and the inspector, "how can I help you, inspector?"

"And you must be Francois Bontecou of the Paris Prefecture of Police," the inspector said ignoring Kevin's brusque attitude, as he turned to greet Francois.

"A pleasure to meet a colleague," Francois replied, making sure Kevin was aware of the slight he just received.

"Let's hope you still feel that way after our discussion," the inspector replied. Now it was Kevin's turn to gloat. "May I see your passports," the inspector demanded.

Standing about fifty feet behind the inspector was a petite woman dressed in a business suit speaking into a cell phone. Even dressed as she was, her beauty did not escape either Kevin or Francois' notice.

All three passengers handed their passports to the inspector.

"Now if you will all follow me, I'll have one of my men gather your baggage for a search," the inspector said.

This brought a smile to the three passengers' faces. "I'm afraid we have no luggage. It was all destroyed in an accident before we left New York and we didn't have time to shop before our plane departed," Liz explained.

"Perhaps you could recommend a good clothier here in Madrid," Francois added, managing to anger the inspector even more.

"Your luggage was destroyed in the explosion at the medical building," Romero replied smugly. "Wasn't that where you shot that man?" He said to Francois. "And I believe you were found standing over a body with no one else in the room," he added, speaking now to Liz.

"Are we supposed to be impressed or something," Kevin replied. "Obviously you have spoken with the FBI, but apparently, they only told you, or you only heard, part of the story."

"Then I guess we need to spend a little time together so you can tell me the whole story," Romero retorted.

"Guess again. As you can see, that is a diplomatic passport and unless your state department decides to deport me, which isn't going to happen, you have no right to detain me," Kevin insisted.

"I can and I will keep you and your friends here as long as it takes," the inspector snapped.

"As long as it takes for what?" Liz asked.

"As long as it takes for me to find out what happened in New York and what the three of you are doing here," he replied.

"I believe what happened in New York is out of your jurisdiction, so unless you have an extradition request from the United States government, you have no right to hold or even question us," Kevin replied. "As to why I'm here, it's none of your damn business."

"And as to what we are doing here," Liz interrupted, pointing to Francois. "We're chasing an international murder suspect who has killed several people in Poland, Paris, and New York, whom I believe is now in Spain to kill two more people, and it's you who are interfering in our Interpol investigation."

"Then you should have notified Cuerpo Nacional de Policía," Romero insisted.

"Your agency was notified over eight hours ago by Interpol," Liz quickly replied.

"I'm sure if that was the case my comisario would have informed me as such when he instructed me to meet your plane and question you. And as for your diplomatic immunity," Romero said, turning to Kevin, "You can file a complaint with my government when I'm through questioning you."

Kevin pulled his cell phone from his belt and began to dial. Romero nodded to one of the uniformed officers standing behind Kevin who grabbed the cell phone from Kevin's hand.

"You have no right," Kevin shouted.

"No, we have every right," Inspector Romero replied.

"Excuse me," the woman in the business suit said delaying what was close to becoming an international incident. "I've been sent by the Templo Eucarístico to collect Mr. Bridges and his friends."

"I'm afraid that won't be possible," Inspector Romero began to explain when his cell phone began to ring.

"This is Inspector Romero," he replied politely after seeing the name of the caller. "Yes, sir…, but… yes, sir… no… no, sir… yes, sir, …Comisario Diaz, sir, … I know, sir… yes, sir…I understand, sir…at once, sir." Romero stood quietly holding the phone even after the caller disconnected.

"You can reach Mr. Bridges and his party at the Hotel Atlantico on Gran Via. Or you can call me at the templo. Here is my number," the petite woman handed her card to Inspector Romero.

"Don't think this is the end of this," Romero growled. "My comisario will not be happy about this when I inform him."

"I believe Comisario Diaz has already been informed," the woman replied.

Almost immediately Romero's phone began to ring again. "Yes Comisario Diaz? Yes, sir…, yes, sir, …At the Hotel Atlantico on Gran Via…"

"Not me," Liz interrupted, knowing what the superintendent was asking Romero. "I'll be staying with friends and can be reached at the Interpol office."

"Or through the templo number I gave you," the woman added. "Forgive me, I haven't introduced myself," she said turning to the three passengers. "My name is Oralia Toribio, I work as a part-time secretary, part-time do-everything-else for the templo," she laughed.

"Well I must say you are excellent at the do-everything-else part," Francois complimented, trying to be the charming Frenchman. "How did you get the inspector called off so easily?"

"The Chief Superintendent of Cuerpo Nacional here in Madrid is a devout Catholic and a good friend of Bishop Castillo. I told him Kevin was here with two Interpol investigators to help search for the bishop and that he was being kept from doing so by this Inspector Romero. He said he'd handle it, and like always, he did."

"Did you say the bishop is missing?" Kevin asked. "Why wasn't I told of this before? I thought I was originally called here because of the crying Madonna?" Kevin said.

"You were called about the tears of blood. In fact, it was me who called the Vatican. They told me you'd be coming to investigate. It was shortly after that when it became obvious that the bishop had indeed disappeared. The Vatican appointed an acting bishop who decided it would be best if you didn't come so as not to interfere in the investigation to find the bishop. When I got the call from the pilot to expect you and two friends, I was quite surprised,"

Oralia explained. "Usually it's the Vatican who informs me of such things."

"I may have forgotten to let the Vatican know we were on our way here," Kevin admitted.

"Well they know now. Right after I heard from the pilot the bloody tears from the Madonna turned into a heavy stream. I called the Vatican to tell them of the seriousness of the situation at the templo and thanked them for deciding to send you after all. They didn't know what I was talking about so I called the acting bishop. That was even a bigger blow-it than calling the Vatican. He seemed genuinely upset to hear that you were on your way. So, I called the Reverend Father at St. Lucy's back in New York. He told me all that had happened there and he was surprised to hear that your plane made it safely away. He said not two minutes after you left his church a half-a-dozen FBI showed up looking for the three of you. I can't wait to here your version of the story," Oralia said.

"I can't tell you how happy we are you came to meet us," Liz said.

"I was pleased to hear you had no luggage. I didn't know how I was going to fit the four of us and your luggage into my Citroën Picasso."

"Thank you," Liz replied," but Interpol has already sent a car to pick me up."

No sooner were the words out of her mouth did a new Mercedes CLS 550 identical to the one in New York turn next to the hangar. A tall smartly dressed man exited and opened the back door for Liz.

"How do you do that?" Kevin asked.

"I guess we are working for the wrong organizations, my friend," Francois said to Kevin.

"Really, how did they know to come at this exact time and place? I never heard you call anyone to tell them when and where we would be arriving," Kevin asked Liz again.

"My little secret," Liz smiled. "Mine and millions of others who know about text messaging. I'll meet you at the templo in two hours. From what Oralia said about the Madonna, I think we can safely assume Lucienne has already arrived in Spain."

"You think the crying Madonna is related to Lucienne and these murders?" Kevin asked.

"I've no doubt they're related," Liz replied.

"If that is true, why is it no such miracle of a Madonna crying in France was reported?" Francois asked.

"Not all incidents are immediately reported," Kevin replied. "Before the Vatican gets a report about a suspected miracle, the bishop whose region the miracle occurred in must observe it and form his own opinion. This can take some time, especially if it occurs in some remote church or village," Kevin explained.

"And unless the press gets a hold of the story, the Vatican doesn't always make such events public knowledge," Liz added.

"I'm afraid I'm still not convinced. This Lucienne is nothing more than a murderess that we need to stop before anyone else ends up dead," Francois said.

"We need to find the two American doctors before she does," Kevin said, having forgotten about how Liz contacted Interpol.

"Do we know where they are staying?" Francois asked.

"Interpol should have that information by now," Liz said.

"Perhaps we should inform the local police," Francois suggested.

"After what just happened with Inspector Romero? I think not," Liz warned. "I believe the police would hinder our investigation more than they would help."

"Yes, but they may have information about the missing bishop that may be relevant to our investigation," Kevin said.

"I'll have my contacts at Interpol see what they can find out about the bishop," Liz said.

"I don't think I like you leaving us again," Kevin said to Liz. "Last time you almost got yourself killed when you tried to take on Lucienne by yourself."

"Trust me, I wasn't alone," she replied, "and don't worry, I'll meet you at the Church in two hours and I assure you that I've no plans on trying to catch Lucienne before then."

"Yes, but what if things just happen, like you said they did in New York?" Francois asked.

"It won't, not this time," Liz assured them.

"How can you be so sure?" Kevin asked.

"God has told me so," Liz replied and climbed into the Mercedes. Francois and Kevin both had their doubts.

"Mr. Bridges, a warning before you leave," Inspector Romero said as he hurried over to the departing group, but not before the Mercedes raced off. "It would be foolish to try to keep the Cuerpo Nacional out of your investigation here in Spain."

"We wouldn't want to be made to look foolish, now would we," Francois chided.

"Don't you hate it when your boss hangs you out on a limb and then walks away like he had nothing to do with it?" Kevin said to Romero.

"A common practice in our profession, wouldn't you agree?" the Inspector replied, trying to ingratiate himself into their favor. "I apologize for my behavior, I'm only sorry Ms. Purdue is already gone."

"I'm sure you'll get the chance to apologize in person," Francois said, "For I suspect we'll be seeing more of you in the near future."

"My comisario has made that very clear to me," Romero replied.

"You know where to find us," Kevin replied climbing into the Citroën. "Stop by in an hour and I'll tell you what we know, but chances are you won't believe a word of it."

CHAPTER THIRTEEN

"Repentance"

Father Adega had been praying and fasting since his release from the processional. It was the penance Reverend Father Santorio had assigned. Father Adega had solicited the young prostitute who had come to confession, but knew he wasn't the first clergy to do so and wouldn't be the last. Never-the-less, what he did was wrong and he needed to atone himself for his transgression. He had been ordered to pray before the Madonna for two days without stopping and was doing as ordered. It was almost 2:00 a.m. and he had been at it for over twenty-eight hours. Consequently, his legs had gone numb from kneeling and his bladder felt like it was about to burst. He prayed God would ease his discomfort, but he knew not to follow the Reverend Father's penance could mean excommunication.

"Father Adega," the monk interrupted. "His Reverence has sent me to inform you that this portion of your penance is complete."

Father Adega looked up slowly. "What do you mean this portion?"

"His Reverence believes he was too harsh. He now wants you to mop the floor of the crypt room," the monk replied, holding Father Adega's arm as he tried to stand.

"I must thank the Reverend Father for his mercy," Adega replied.

"You can do so in the morning, he has retired to his cell for the night," the monk replied. "Hold my arm until the blood begins to flow in your legs, it will be difficult for you to walk for a few minutes after being on your knees for so long."

"You talk like you have had a similar experience," Adega replied. "First you must help me outside so I can relieve the pressure of my bladder."

"Of course," Jayro replied, keeping his hood pulled down over his face.

Even at this early hour several parishioners, as well as several monks from both the templo monastery and neighboring abbeys were praying before the Madonna. Two monks had been assigned to continually collect the bloody tears and wipe excess blood off the marble sculpture. It was also their job to keep an eye on the continuous queue of visitors making sure they didn't approach the Madonna too closely and attempt to steal some of those precious tears.

"I believe I can stand alone to do this job," Father Adega laughed, as he finally relieved the pressure on this bladder. "I know I should be grateful that Reverend Father has shortened my penance, but isn't it one of the acolyte's duties to mop the crypt floor each evening?"

"Did you not hear that the acolyte who was responsible for that task was found murdered two nights ago?" the monk asked.

"I've heard nothing about this, but that was the night of the auto de fe and, as I am ashamed to admit, I was part of the accused in the processional and didn't arrive back to the templo until after the miracle was discovered," Adega confessed.

"Perhaps it is better you didn't know. It may have distracted you from your penance. Your focus needed to be on seeking forgiveness for what you have done," Jayro replied.

"I don't believe it is a monk's place to judge my morality or behavior," Adega snapped back.

"Nor is it a priest's place to act in such a sinful way by seeking pleasures of the flesh from a confessor. You were tried and convicted by the tribunal, you deserve to be punished for what you did," Jayro scolded.

"I'll let God be my judge when the time comes," Adega replied.

"Follow me to the crypt and I'll show you what needs to be done," the monk explained, knowing that judgment was closer than the priest could ever had imagined.

"Wake up," Bruno roared, as he shook the sleeping monk who had fallen asleep at the table. "I see you never made it to bed last night.

"It appears I fell asleep while writing in the journal," Raul replied.

"Well I hope you are current because we have much to investigate this morning and you'll have much writing to do," Bruno warned. "I brought you some breakfast."

Bruno sat two bowls of broth on the table with some dark bread.

"The bread is still warm," Raul said.

"It should be, I paid a young boy to fetch it fresh from the bakery," Bruno replied.

"Are we returning to the crypt this morning?" Raul asked.

"No, I've already been there. I found some fresh blood on the crypt floor," Bruno said nonchalantly.

"Fresh blood! Does that mean the murderer has struck again?" Raul gasped.

"There wasn't that much blood," Bruno replied, "and it wasn't near the crypt where we found the acolyte.

Someone possibly lost their balance and struck their head while walking down the stairs."

"If that were the case the brother in charge of watching over the visitors would have mentioned it to the abbot," Raul replied.

"No such report was made," I already checked with the abbot. "And if you recall, we were there after the crypts closed and the acolyte had cleaned up for the night."

"Then where did the blood come from?" Raul asked.

"I thought you might have hit your head after I left you last night, but I saw no wound on your head when I woke you."

"No, I didn't injure myself in the crypt," Raul replied.

"I'm troubled by something the abbot did tell me," Bruno said. "Do you know Father Adega?"

"Of course, he was the priest found guilty by the tribunal. The Reverend Father ordered his penance be two days of continual prayer before the Madonna," Raul explained

"Only he ended his prayers early last night," Bruno replied.

"That's in direct defiance of his Reverence. Adega risks excommunication by doing so," Raul exclaimed.

"Several witnesses report a monk interrupted his prayers and Adega left with the aid of this monk."

"I don't understand why he needed the monk's aid?" Raul said.

"Apparently you haven't spent enough time on your knees praying. If the priest had been there for over twenty-four hours, his legs wouldn't function well and he'd need some help to stand, let alone walk. They said the priest looked very relieved when he left the cathedral."

"I know Adega, there's no way he would defy the Reverend Father's penance. His Reverence must have decided the punishment was too harsh," Raul responded.

"The abbot spoke with the Reverend Father and that wasn't the case. And now Father Adega seems to be missing. He didn't return to his cell nor has a search of the church and monastery turned up any results as to his whereabouts," Bruno explained.

"Do you believe the blood in the crypt may be Adega's?" Raul asked.

"Very good," Bruno replied, "you are starting to think like an investigator. Here, have a drink of this, it will help wake you up."

Without thinking Raul took the flask from Bruno and took a strong draw of the absenta. The sting of the acrid liquid made him wince.

"I know, this batch isn't quite as delicate as the last, but it will suffice," Bruno said, taking an even larger swig of the green liquid.

Raul could never imagine the green tonic as delicate. "Do we search for the priest?" Raul asked.

"Not yet, I'm going to finish breakfast while you write down this conversation. Then we'll start our search for Father Adega," Bruno explained.

"But what about the hidden door in the crypt and the murder investigation? We can't just forget about all that," Raul insisted.

"The alleged hidden door," Bruno replied. "And you forgot to mention the crying Madonna. Of course, we'll continue our investigation, but as you theorized earlier, perhaps we'll find that all of this is connected," Bruno replied, then took another drink from his flask and seemed to momentarily weave as if he were about to blackout.

"One more thing," Bruno remembered. "Collect two containers of the bloody tears from the Madonna."

"For what reason?" Raul asked, but Bruno did not seem to hear him. Then almost trance-like Bruno spoke.

"But now in Christ Jesus you who once were far away have been brought near through the blood of Christ."

Bruno dropped his chin to his chest and closed his eyes as if he were praying.

"Be sure to write that down," Bruno whispered. "It's from Ephesians."

Raul desperately wanted to tell Bruno about his brother's ring but couldn't bring himself to do so. Even more disconcerting was Bruno's excessive drinking and how Raul believed it was beginning to affect Bruno's investigation. He wanted to speak to Bruno of this but thought better of it. For who was he to judge?

୨ ୨ ୨

When Father Adega awoke he immediately reached for his aching head, but a feeling of vertigo overwhelmed him as he lost his balance. It was pitch-black and he seemed to be leaning against a wall, as he reached out groping for a way to catch his fall, his hand found a metal bar which he used to steady himself, but the feeling of falling didn't subside. It was then he realized he wasn't falling, but swinging in a cage.

"What's happening here? Is anyone there?" Adega called out, but no answer came.

"What's that smell, where am I? Someone please help me." Still there was no answer, just the creaking of the chain that held the cage and the pungent odor of death rising upward.

୨ ୨ ୨

"Why have we returned to the stables?" Raul asked Bruno.

"As you no doubt recall, because I know you wrote it down," Bruno said inferring the precision he demanded in Raul's recording of the facts, "I told you someone had disturbed the bodies when we left for the night. The saw had been moved, as had been several tools in the cabinet in the storage room below."

"You never told me about the storage room," Raul interrupted.

"That's why I'm telling you now," Bruno replied. "As I was saying, I noticed the tools in the cabinet weren't as I had left them. As I was climbing the ladder out of the room the sun's rays were just coming through that window and illuminated the storage room. I noticed parallel arcs in the dust in front of the cabinet, lines I'd never have seen if not for the morning sun. This leads me to believe the cabinet is concealing a hidden passageway."

"A passageway to where?" Raul asked, scribbling furiously in the journal.

"That, my friend, is what we're about to find out," Bruno replied as he lit a wall lamp in the dingy room. "Grab hold and help me pull."

"But what if there is no passageway?" Raul asked.

"Then we'll push it back into place, of course," Bruno answered.

With a loud crack the cabinet swung free from the wall and the two men tumbled backwards.

CHAPTER FOURTEEN

"Knowledge"

"**I didn't know prostitution** was legal in Spain," Kevin remarked as they drove past the templo.

"It's not," Oralia remarked. "Here prostitution doesn't have the stigma attached to it that one would find in your country. The local police ignore it as if it wasn't there."

"Pretty hard to ignore if you ask me," Francois said. "There must be at least twenty prostitutes per block in this neighborhood."

"The Gran Via is known as the location to find female companionship," Oralia replied.

"It's too bad it is so near the templo," Kevin remarked. "Hasn't the Reverend Father complained to the police? I mean, look at this, there are prostitutes lining the street in front of the church."

"And many of them confess their sins and attend Mass here regularly," Oralia replied. "Of course, the Reverend Father wishes it wasn't like this, but it is, so we make the best of it. We only wish more of them would visit us, for God welcomes all who enter his house."

"Aren't we going to stop here?" Kevin asked.

"No, I just wanted to show you where the templo was so you can walk over here after I drop you at your hotel, which is right here," Oralia said pulling to the curb and jumping out. "The templo is directly behind the hotel."

"We just have to run the gauntlet of prostitutes to get there," Francois added.

"You get used to it," Oralia said. "The Reverend Father is very anxious to speak with you Mr. Bridges, but I did overhear that your luggage was destroyed in New York so I'm sure you'd like to freshen up and perhaps buy a change of clothes before you meet him. There are several clothiers in this area, as you can see. However, I would recommend El Corte Inglés, it's the high-rise just across the street, behind the theater. It's one of Spain's premiere department stores. I'm sure there you will find clothes to suit your taste," she explained, staring at Francois' caterer's outfit.

"El Corte Inglés is an excellent suggestion," Inspector Romero said joining the group on the sidewalk.

"It's not quite been an hour," Kevin said.

"I was so curious to hear your story I just couldn't wait," Romero replied.

"Then by all means join us as we shop," Kevin replied.

"Here are your room keys," Oralia replied. "I picked them up before I came to the airport. I guess we won't need the third room now that Ms. Purdue has decided not to join us."

"Don't cancel the room quite yet," Kevin replied. "I've got a feeling Liz may be joining us here soon."

"Then you hold on to it," Oralia said. "I'll see you gentleman at the church, say, in one hour?"

"Better make it an hour-and-a-half," Kevin suggested.

"More like two hours," Francois offered.

"I like the hour-and-a-half better and I'm sure the Reverend Father will also," Oralia replied.

"An hour-and-a-half it will be then," Kevin replied.

"Then we best begin shopping," Francois said. "I'm a little picky about what I wear."

"I can see that," Oralia said, and everyone but Romero got the joke.

"We believe Lucienne arrived in Spain a little over five hours ago. That was when the Madonna's tears began to flow heavily."

"Is she here in Madrid?" Liz asked.

"We don't know that for sure, but it seems logical since the medical convention is here."

"Do we know where the two doctors are?" Liz asked.

"One of them is staying at the Emperador Hotel with his girlfriend. The hotel is under surveillance. The other doctor and his wife checked out of their room yesterday and rented a car. The clerk at the rental agency wasn't sure where they were headed, but they did have golf clubs and asked for a map of Andalucía. They don't plan on returning the car for a week, which is when their flight is scheduled to return to New York."

"Well that narrows it down to about a third of the country," Liz replied.

"Yes, but the golf clubs would leave us to believe that they are headed somewhere between San Roque and Málaga."

"Why do you say that?" Liz asked.

"There are over twenty-five golf courses along that section of the coast. That area is a very popular golf destination."

"Have you asked the police to search for the car?" Liz asked.

"Not yet. We know agents of our enemy work in all levels of law enforcement. The fewer people who know, the better chance we have of reaching the doctor first."

"Do we know why the Madonna began crying in the first place?" Liz asked.

"Jesus weeps for the great evil that now flourishes in Madrid."

"Just as planned," Liz replied.

ం ం ం

"You're right," Romero said to Kevin, "As a police officer I don't believe a word of it."

"Neither did I at first," Francois reminded him.

"However, as a lifelong Catholic and believer in God and the Holy Word, how can I not believe what you've told me? What troubles me most is the role Ms. Purdue plays in your story," Romero said.

"What do you mean? Don't you trust Liz?" Kevin asked.

"She's an Interpol agent," Francois added, stepping off the escalator. "I see the sports coats over there."

"Do you know that for sure? Just how much do you really know about Ms. Purdue? From what you've told me she suddenly appeared in Paris the evening of the murders there. In New York she arranged to arrive at the medical building before you and was found standing over the agent's body," Romero explained.

"Yes, but what about the man who tried to kill her?" Francois asked.

"The one you killed before he could be questioned?" Romero remarked. "Do you know for sure that he was trying to kill her? The FBI isn't so sure. And what about her answer to your question before she left you at the airport. When you asked her how she could be so sure things wouldn't happen here as they had in New York she responded because God told her so."

"You just told us that you too are a man of God, doesn't God tell you things?" Kevin asked.

"Not in so many words and nothing that specific," Romero replied, "but I…" Romero suddenly paused and looked back at the escalator they had just left.

"Do you think this would look good on me," Francois asked, holding up an Armani sports coat.

"Something wrong?" Kevin asked Romero.

"No, I thought I recognized someone."

"Your mistress with another man," Francois teased.

"Actually, I thought it was my boss, Comisario Diaz, but that seems most unlikely," Romero replied.

"I've no doubt that Liz is who she says she is, an Interpol agent and a servant of God," Kevin said.

"…*Satan himself masquerades as an angel of light. It is not surprising, then, if his servants masquerade as servants of righteousness.* That's from 2nd Corinthians," Romero recited.

"You're telling us that you think Liz is a servant of Satan?" Francois said.

"No, I'm just trying to make a point," Romero replied.

"And that point is…" Kevin said.

"And that point is that the two of you are caught up in an international multiple murder investigation and, as I see it, one of the most obvious prime suspects is assisting in the investigation. I think you need to step back and take a good look at what's going on around you," Romero suggested.

"And I think if you'd been through what we've been through, this conversation wouldn't be taking place," Kevin replied, as again Romero's attention was drawn to the escalators.

"Afraid your boss is checking up on you again?" Francois laughed.

"No, but see the man with his back to us getting on the escalator? He is on the Council of Ministers and a very powerful man in Spanish politics. In fact, he was close to being the President of Spain, but King Juan Carlos preferred Zapatero," Romero explained. "I wonder what he's doing here."

"Probably buying a new suit," Francois replied.

"Or having lunch," Kevin added.

"Not likely," Romero replied. "It's very unusual to see one of the ministers out-and-around without bodyguards. Especially, in such a public place as this."

"Not exactly the kind of store the ruling class frequents I would venture to guess," Francois said.

"Are you sure it was him?" Kevin asked.

"Almost certain," Romero replied, continuing to watch as the man slowly disappeared from sight.

"Francois, we're out of time. I've barely enough time to shower and change before our meeting with the Reverend Father," Kevin said. "You can buy a coat later."

"I feel so underdressed without a jacket," Francois replied.

"Then stay and pick one out, but I'm leaving," Kevin replied.

"You Americans have no sense of style," Francois replied, hanging the Armani jacket back on the kiosk.

"Are you coming, Inspector?" Kevin asked.

"I'll meet you in the hotel lobby after you freshen up. I think I'll look around here a little longer," Romero replied.

"Shopping or investigating?" Francois replied.

"Maybe a little of both," Inspector Romero replied.

Romero walked over to the escalator and looked up. "Should I, or shouldn't I?" he asked himself, but he answered his own question when he stepped on the moving steps.

His police instincts paid off as he saw two other men, who not only looked vaguely familiar, but seemed to look out of place in the department store. Both were wearing expensive designer suits and walked with an affected air that reflected their superior manners and graces.

Romero was on the top floor of the store where the restaurants were located, but these men had not come from the public area. They were walking from an unmarked door on the far wall. A door Romero headed directly to. He grabbed the handle to see if it was unlocked when it suddenly turned. He quickly jumped behind the door and pretended to be looking at a painting on the wall as another man impeccably dressed exited and glanced towards him. Before the door closed completely, Romero grabbed the handle and disappeared behind the door. He stood at the bottom of a plush carpeted staircase.

"I guess this wasn't the top floor," Romero said to himself, as he headed up the stairs.

He moved slowly listening for any others that could be headed his way, but heard nothing. When he reached the top, he was in what had to be the executive dining room. It had an incredible view of most of Old Madrid including the Plaza Mayor and the Prado, and a direct view down the Gran Via. There were seven place settings on the inlaid walnut table where a luncheon had apparently just ended.

"How do you get an invite here?" Romero whistled.

There were two other doors at the opposite end of the room in the only wall without a floor-to-ceiling window. On the north wall there was a window, but also two elevator doors. One had a typical display showing all the floors but required a key to call for the car. The second elevator had no display, only a small panel with a strange opening.

"This one must be special," Romero thought. "I've never seen a key like that before."

Suddenly, one of the back doors flew open and several workers entered and began clearing the table. None of them paid any attention to Romero who stood frozen trying to decide what to do.

"Can't find your key?" a voice called from behind him. "It's okay, you can use mine."

A man came over who was dressed much nicer than the workers cleaning the table.

"I must have left it on the table and someone else picked it up," Romero said, playing along.

"You'd better check with security. You know how Señor Guidino gets when someone misplaces his keys," the man said.

"Boy, do I," Romero replied as he stood in front of the elevator waiting for the man to insert his key.

"Wrong elevator," the man said curiously, as he put his key in the elevator with the display.

"What was I thinking," Romero replied, laughing. "It's no wonder I always lose my keys."

"Yeah," the man replied suspiciously, "no wonder."

"Saved by the bell," Romero thought as the elevator chimed and the door opened.

"Thanks for your help," Romero said as he entered and pushed the button for the basement.

"My pleasure, Señor…, I'm sorry I didn't get your name," the man said.

"Carlos, Juan Carlos," Romero replied as the elevator door shut.

Romero held his finger on the close door button just in case the man realized he had been made a fool, but as the elevator began to move, he could hear the man calling security.

When the elevator door opened to the basement parking garage two security guards were waiting. Fortunately, Romero got off at the top floor restaurant and blended into the early lunch crowd on the escalator.

CHAPTER FIFTEEN

"Truth"

The cracking of the metal bolt ripping the wooden frame of the cabinet echoed through the catacombs startling Jayro.

"The witch was right," he wheezed. "They've found the entrance, and so much sooner than I expected." He quickly doused the flame of the candles that provided his working light. In the blackness he could no longer see the table before him and groped wildly until he found the metal cross. He slipped the twine attached to the cross around his neck and slid the cross beneath his robe. The cold iron against his bare skin sent chills down his spine yet warmed his heart.

"Those who dare to invade my adyctum shall dearly pay," he whispered touching the cross. Quickly the hooded monk moved into the main catacomb keeping his hand against the wall feeling his way towards the secret entrance to the torture chamber. He had yet to hear any voices signifying that someone had entered the catacomb, nor was the blackness disturbed by the glow of a lamp or candle. He pulled the cross from beneath his robe and lifted it to where his fingers could feel the indentation in the wall. He had built the secret entrance years before and had carved the scripture on the wall just as he had on the hidden entrance in the crypt room. However, unlike the crypt, the design on the point of the cross and not the design on his ring was the key to opening the secret passage. He heard the click as he pushed the cross into the first seven and then came the clanking of the two iron bars as he pressed the cross point into the second seven. He stood silently before opening the door listening to see if the noise alerted his intruders, but still no one came, so he quickly pivoted the door and ducked behind it, partially shutting it as he continued to watch for the glow of an approaching light.

"Help me," the weak voice of Father Adega whispered. "Water, I need water. Please, I know someone is there."

As no answer came, he used what little energy he had left to begin to swing the cage in which he was suspended. The rusty chain grated against the metal cage creating considerable noise.

"No, no, stop that noise," the hooded monk ordered, in a hushed voice, but Father Adega couldn't hear him above the racket he had created.

The monk hurried down the stairs as quickly as the darkness would allow him to do safely. When he reached the bottom of the steps his leg smashed into the rack tearing the scab from his wound. Immediately blood began to ooze from the savage wound.

"Curse you, Adega," the monk wheezed. He felt for the rope connected to the pulley system that raised and lowered the cage. The cage containing Father Adega hung at least ten feet off the floor of the chamber, but it was not floor that was directly below the heavy iron cage. A deep pit had been built into the floor. The pit at one time was filled with hot oil and used for dipping the caged victims of the inquisition. It was a guaranteed means of extracting a confession and removing the skin. Fortunately, for Adega, the pit was now nothing more than a sewer, less than two-thirds full of water and human waste.

"This will teach you to obey when I tell you to be quiet," the monk hissed as he released the rope. The cage plunged into the vile mixture with a sickening thump and slowly settled to the bottom. Adega's head hit one of the bars knocking him unconscious but, since the cage was designed to keep him upright, his head remained just above the muck.

Without even checking on Adega, the monk hobbled back up the stairs and took his position behind the door to await his intruders.

"Now it is your turn," the hooded monk hissed.

"Help me up," Bruno ordered

"Shouldn't we go for help?" Raul asked, pulling the larger man to his feet.

"Help for what?" Bruno said. "I believe the two of us are very capable of exploring the catacombs on our own."

Raul wasn't so sure but was not going to challenge Bruno. Raul walked up and peered into the tunnel behind the cabinet while Bruno took another strong draw from his flask.

"I think you've had enough of that this morning," Raul warned.

"And I think you should mind your own affairs," Bruno retorted.

"What if the murderer is hiding inside?" Raul asked.

"If we discover evidence that leads us to that conclusion, then I will immediately send you for the alguacil," Bruno promised. "Now light these candles." Bruno pulled two large candles from his satchel along with the cross taken from the witch's head. "Perhaps you should grab that hammer," Bruno said to Raul.

"But I thought you said…"

"Shhh…," Bruno interrupted. "Did you hear that?"

"I didn't hear anything," Raul replied. "I think I should go for help now."

"We've already discussed that," Bruno replied. "Did you collect the bloody tears as I requested?"

"I have them here," Raul replied, handing the two containers to Bruno, who carefully placed them in his satchel.

"Follow me," he said as he headed into the catacombs.

Reluctantly, Raul lit his candle and followed. "Do you smell that?" Raul asked.

"I smell nothing. What is it you think you smell?" Bruno barked.

"Two days ago, I wouldn't have known, but now I know the unmistakable odor of death," Raul said solemnly.

"Death doesn't smell. Putrefying corpses, now they smell. Here, have some absenta. It will disguise the odor," Bruno explained.

Raul took the flask just to keep Bruno from drinking further.

They walked slowly for several yards down a long narrow passageway. "There are scriptures written on all of these walls. Perhaps these too are crypts where the former monks were laid to rest," Raul said.

"Perhaps," Bruno replied, "but it is more likely we'll find the remains of former monks stacked in recesses along one of those side corridors up ahead."

In the flickering candle light, Raul could make out at least four openings leading from the main catacomb. "What if someone is hiding in there?" Raul asked nervously.

'That's why you brought the hammer. You did remember to pick up the hammer?" Bruno said.

Raul raised it into a striking position for Bruno to see and so he could defend himself as they approached the first opening.

"Good, you go first," Bruno ordered, getting the startled reaction he had hoped for from Raul. "Just kidding," he laughed, trying to ease the tension. "Stay behind me."

Without hesitation Bruno darted into the first side hallway only to find it filled with skeletons as he had expected.

All the while the hooded monk peered through a crack above the torture chamber doorway plotting how to destroy the two intruders. Bruno and Raul passed by the secret entrance completely unaware of the danger that loomed so near.

"Be careful," Raul whispered as Bruno burst into the second side hallway, only to find another burial chamber. "I'll go first on the next one, it's only fair," Raul said.

"Nonsense," Bruno boomed, "I'm the investigator and I'll assume the risks."

"Yes, my Lord," Raul replied. "I'm not the bishop, call me Bruno."

"Sorry, Brother Bruno," Raul replied.

The third chamber was the same as the first two but was in great disarray with bones scattered haphazardly.

"Looks like somebody tossed in a few extra parts," Bruno joked, moving less carefully from the third and into the final chamber.
"And now I see why."

"What is it?" Raul asked, hurrying to catch up.

Inside the fourth chamber was the hooded monk's work table with the tanned human skins stretched out to dry.

"This wax is soft," Raul noted, touching one of the candles on the table. "These candles were just snuffed out moments ago."

Suddenly Raul realized what that meant and tensed, lifting the hammer as if preparing to strike. Bruno turned serious as the turned to face the corridor they had just left.

"We must move cautiously," Bruno warned. With his fingers he instructed Raul to face the left while he would face the right when they reentered the corridor. He counted down with his fingers and the two intrepid monks dashed back into the corridor ready to do battle, but no opponent waited.

"Let's keep going," Bruno said.

"Shouldn't we go for help?" Raul asked.

"Not until we've finished our search," Bruno insisted.

Very carefully the two continued down the catacomb, Bruno looking forward and Raul keeping watch behind, their vision limited by the dim light of the candles.

Behind them, just out of range of the soft glow, the hooded monk slid quietly along towards them, his back pressed against the catacomb wall.

"Looks like the catacomb is coming to an end," Bruno announced as the narrow passageway gave way to a larger cavern. "I believe we have reached the back of the crypt room."

"There is no back on that crypt," Raul said, pointing up high.

"And I would venture to guess it is empty," Bruno replied, pointing to a pile of bones lying on the floor next to dozens of stones stacked as a staircase to the opening.

"I'll have a look," Raul said.

As he climbed up and into the empty crypt Bruno continued to look around at the back of some of the other crypts.

"It's empty," Raul called down, his voice echoing in the empty chamber. "It looks like there is a sliver of light at the far end. I'll have a look."

Hesitantly, Raul crawled into the crypt. As he did so, Bruno who had discovered that one of the lower crypts had a latch, opened the back and finding it empty also crawled in. Had he not seen the latching mechanism at the far end to release the other door, he wouldn't have been so bold.

"Very ingenious," Bruno said pushing the lever that allowed the front of the crypt to open.

He quickly climbed through and into the templo's crypt room. "Just as I thought," he said looking at the inscription on the crypt he had just exited.

"Brother Bruno, what…where…how did you get in there?" Raul asked in amazement.

"This is how our murderer escaped," Bruno explained. "Remember that strange symbol after the scripture quotation of Matthew 7:7 we had looked at earlier? You know, the one where the blood trail ended."

"Yes, of course," Raul replied, backing out of the crypt he was in.

"It is a lock that requires an identical key to unlock the crypt door. Whoever built the crypts must have installed it and holds the key," Bruno surmised.

"That would be Jayro, my brother," Raul finally admitted to both Bruno and himself, as he climbed through the passage and joined Bruno in the crypt room. "He was in charge of building these crypts. He also wears a ring that bears that symbol."

"I've known since we visited him that your brother was the murderer we seek," Bruno said.

"Why didn't you tell me? Why didn't you have him arrested? Raul demanded.

"It was something you had to realize on your own," Bruno replied. "I also needed more than my suspicions to have him arrested. Now that we have discovered the secret passageway into the catacombs, along with your realization that the symbol on his ring is the key to that passageway, we've more than enough proof to have him arrested."

"I have long been suspicious of my brother but was afraid to face the truth. I feel partially responsible for why he turned out the way he did," Raul confessed.

"God gave us all the ability to choose our own paths," Bruno replied.

"My concern is that Jayro may be responsible for Father Adega going missing," Raul admitted.

"Perhaps now you should go seek help. Tell Reverend Father what we have discovered and then…"

"You're not coming with me?"

"No, I intend to continue to search the catacombs," Bruno replied. "There may be clues we overlooked that could lead us to Father Adega."

"You shouldn't do so alone," Raul insisted.

"I'll be fine. I'm sure Jayro left as soon as he heard the cabinet break open. Besides, as I was explaining, after you inform his Reverence, have the abbot send one monk for the alguacil and you bring three or four back with you to help in the search."

"I'll leave you the hammer," Raul said, sitting it and Bruno's journal on the floor next to the crypt.

"That won't be necessary, but if it makes you feel better go ahead," Bruno replied. "And don't forget to leave my absenta".

"Just be careful," Raul instructed, handing Bruno the flask.

"Your brother is a man just like you and I and, I fear no man. But there is another who serves Satan whom we do need to fear," Bruno said.

Raul didn't want to hear anymore, he wanted to get out of the crypt room and find help. As he turned to leave, he could hear Bruno guzzling the intoxicating mixture.

∽ ∽ ∽

Lurking in the cavern shadows on the opposite side of the crypts, Jayro listened intently. As soon as he heard Bruno's plan he headed for the stable entrance. He had to stop his brother before he could sound the warning. The throbbing of the wound on his leg made the task even more difficult and blood dripped steadily from his robe onto the catacomb floor.

CHAPTER SIXTEEN

"Understanding"

"Surprised to see me?" Liz asked, as Kevin and Francois stepped out of the elevator and into the lobby.

"No, you said you'd meet us here in two hours," Kevin replied.

"No, I said I'd meet you at the templo in two hours, which was exactly fifteen minutes ago. You weren't there, so I walked here. I don't think the Reverend Father is too happy to be kept waiting. Perhaps we should go."

"Inspector," Francois called out, seeing Romero sitting in the lobby. "Did you find what you were looking for in the store? I don't see any parcels."

"No, I bought nothing, but I did have a good look around."

"Did you find the Cabinet Minister?" Kevin asked.

"No, but I did see…"

"Forgive me for interrupting, but I do think we should hurry to the templo. His Reverence is expecting you and we do have some rather urgent business to discuss," Liz suggested.

"What kind of urgent business?" Romero asked as the group headed out the door.

Liz looked for approval before she answered.

"Inspector Romero will be assisting us while we are here in Madrid," Kevin explained to Liz. "Francois and I told him about Paris and New York. Of course, he didn't believe a word of it, but he claims to be a devout Catholic…"

"I am a devout Catholic," Romero interrupted.

"And he does believe in Satan, angels, and demons," Kevin continued, "so, I don't think we could find a better

176

intermediary to work with here in Madrid. Now having said all that, if what you found out can wait till after my meeting with the Reverend Father, you can tell us all at the same time."

"Of course," Liz replied.

"Is that okay with you inspector?" Kevin asked.

"Most certainly. I wouldn't…"

"You police inspector?" A scantily-clad African woman asked, stepping in front of the group.

"Excuse me?" Romero replied.

"I heard 'im call you inspector," she said pointing to Kevin. "You wit' da police?"

"I'm with the Cuerpo Nacional," Romero replied.

"You hea 'bout da miss'n work'n girls?" she asked.

"I'm afraid I don't know anything about any missing working girls," Romero responded.

"Working girls?" Francois asked.

"She's talking about prostitutes," Romero explained. "If some of your working girl friends are missing you should report it to the local police," he said, turning back to the woman.

"Like hell," she snapped. "Three day 'go Misty went do just that and that night she up and disappeared. Shawna say it police who take her."

"How many of your friends are missing," Liz asked.

"Five girls that work this neighborhood gone in the pas' three week. Pimps say they ain't in jail. Say they know nuttin'. Some of us think'n 'bout finding a new street."

"I think that would be an excellent idea," Liz recommended.

"I'll look into it," Romero replied.

"Yeah, you look into it. Dat wat police always say, 'we look into it'," she said mockingly, as she eyed a prospective client and crossed the street.

"As you can obviously see, my country still has much it needs to improve," Romero replied sheepishly.

"As does the rest of the world," Kevin replied, "As does the rest of the world," he repeated, this time under his breath.

୨ଚ ୨ଚ ୨ଚ

"It began slowly about two weeks ago," the Reverend Father explained. "One of our parishioners, who cleans the sanctuary in the evenings, found droplets of blood on the feet of the Madonna. He wiped them up thinking nothing of it, but when he walked by an hour later, there were more droplets."

"Is this the first time this has ever happened?" Kevin asked.

The reverend looked at Oralia. "No, we know of it happening one other time," Oralia said. "There are church records that report a similar miracle occurring when the templo was rebuilt and dedicated in 1725."

"I wonder why the Vatican didn't inform me of that fact," Kevin said.

"There's been no lack of misinformation on everyone's part concerning this miracle as far as I'm concerned," Oralia said sounding exasperated.

"Almost a week ago the bishop declared this a probable miracle. He sent samples of the blood to the Vatican and requested an investigator be sent here. Two days later the bishop disappeared and the acting-bishop canceled the request. The very next day blood began to flow heavily from the Madonna. Several times I tried to contact the acting-bishop but was unable to reach him. So, two days ago, I took it upon myself to forward the request again. That's when we were told by the bishop at the Doctrinal Office that you would be coming. He also sent a fax he thought might help in your investigation. It arrived this morning."

Oralia picked up the paper on her desk and handed it to Kevin, who sat it down next to him.

"Well aren't you going to read it?" Francois asked.

"I hadn't planned to do so. At least not in front of everybody," Kevin replied. "There might be some classified material not appropriate for a secular audience in here."

"Oh, for the love of God," Oralia groaned. "The Reverend Father and I already read it. After all, it was addressed to His Reverence. All it contains are the DNA results from the sample of bloody tears we sent them along with three other sets of results. It also tells you where you can find out the details about the first time the Madonna cried."

"And where might that be?" Kevin asked.

"At the Archdiocese in Toledo," his Reverence replied.

"But you won't find them there. I already looked," Oralia replied.

"Where will I find it?" Kevin asked.

"Cardinal Cañizares Llovera knew nothing about the papers, so I tracked down the former cardinal, Francisco Álvarez Martínez."

"Is he still alive?" Liz asked.

"He was when I spoke to him about the papers, but that was right after he participated in the last papal conclave to select the Pope. He was about to turn eighty," Oralia explained.

"That was over three years ago. What were you doing looking for these documents back then?" Kevin asked.

"Oralia has a personal interest in those papers or rather journals," Reverend Father said. "It was an ancestor of hers who documented the 1725 investigation in those journals. He was a monk here at the templo. The actual investigator recruited him to write the notes about the investigation."

"So, if this journal is no longer at the archdiocese in Toledo, where is it?" Kevin asked.

"Cardinal Martinez said it was loaned to the Museo del Prado for inclusion in their research library, but when I checked they could find no record of it in their files," Oralia explained.

"Well that sounds like a dead end," Francois said.

"Not quite," Oralia replied. "The archdiocese still had their copy of the shipping invoice. It was sent to Carlos Hernandez, director of the research library."

"Did you speak to him?" Liz asked.

"He has since retired from the Museo del Prado and hasn't or won't return my calls," Oralia explained.

"I'm confused," Romero spoke up. "Just what does this journal and these DNA results have to do with the murders in Paris and New York?"

"And Poland," Liz added.

"I'm not sure that they do," Kevin replied.

"Of course they do," Liz responded. "Jesus cries because of the evil that has come to Spain."

"Then why didn't a Madonna cry someplace in France when Lucienne came there?" Francois asked.

"According to the DNA results it did," Kevin replied, scanning the paper in his hand. "We just didn't hear about it. It seems the original Our Lady of Lourdes had a similar experience with blood running from the grotto starting two days before Lucienne committed her murders in Paris."

"Anything else we should know about the blood?" Francois asked.

"Only that the blood samples from the grotto in New York, from Lourdes in France, and from here at the templo all have identical DNA, and came from a man. A man of Jewish descent," Kevin told the group.

"Well that seems a little far-fetched," Romero replied.

"You said there were four samples," Francois said, "what about the fourth sample?"

"The fourth sample was from blood sent to the Vatican when the Madonna first cried here at the templo in 1725," Kevin said. "It too is identical to the others."

"That's impossible," Francois insisted.

"No, that's miraculous," Liz corrected. "It's God showing us he's here and cares about what is happening."

"If he cares so much, why doesn't he do something about it and get rid of this Lucienne," Francois said.

"That's not how God works, my son," the Reverend Father said to Francois. "God has given us free will, the power to choose our own destinies."

"Yes, but I do know the bible also tells us that God wants to rid the world of evil and that he is capable of doing so, so in cases like this, why doesn't he?" Francois persisted.

"If God were to judge and remove all those who do evil acts, who would be left, for we all have sinned," Reverend Father replied.

"Okay, back to my original question, how does all this relate to these murders?" Romero asked.

"And to the disappearance of the bishop," the Reverend Father added.

"I've no idea," Kevin admitted, "but there's no doubt in my mind that they somehow all are related. I believe when we stop Lucienne the Madonna will stop crying."

"And how do you plan to find her," Reverend Father asked.

"We believe she's here in Madrid to kill the two doctors she failed to kill in New York. They're here in Madrid attending a medical convention," Kevin explained.

"One of them is," Liz added. "He is at the Emperador Hotel, just a short way down the Gran Via near the Royal Palace. I've several people watching the hotel. The other has left Madrid to do some sightseeing by car."

"Interpol usually contacts my office when they are operating in Madrid. I've heard nothing about a stake-out at the Emperador," Romero huffed.

"Do you know where the second doctor went?" Kevin asked.

"No, but I've people working on finding that information out," Liz replied hesitantly.

"I can help with that," Romero offered, still miffed about Liz's last announcement. "All I need is the doctor's name. He'll have to present his passport at every hotel and when he does so it is entered into a database."

"What if he's camping," Francois said, just to be obstinate.

"Then we'll use the police to track down his car. A very simple matter," Romero insisted.

"Why are you so interested in this journal anyway?" Kevin said to Oralia.

"Because of the shame it has brought to my family for generations," she replied softly.

"I don't understand?" Kevin replied.

"Bruno Mancini was a prelate assigned by the Vatican to investigate the Madonna's tears in 1725," Oralia began.

"Your predecessor, Kevin," Francois commented.

"However, it wasn't just the tears he was investigating, but a series of gruesome murders. Raul Toribio was the monk assigned to assist Bruno and record all that was said and that he witnessed."

"That would be your ancestor," Liz added.

"Yes, of course. Three days after the investigation began the tears ceased to flow," Oralia explained.

"What happened," Romero asked.

"That's what I'm hoping the journal will tell me."

CHAPTER SEVENTEEN

"Deliverance"

Bruno picked up the journal Raul had left alongside the hammer and opened it to the last entry. From his satchel he pulled out a pen and ink and began to write.

Never does a man feel more distant from God, but in reality, is closer than ever before, than when he admits a truth he has long known but feared to admit. These are times when God enters the heart and forgives a man's sins. In time Brother Raul will come to realize this and forgive his brother's sins. Yet a greater evil than that of a deranged murderer seethes from within these walls, for that is why the tears of Jesus flow from the Madonna. I have felt her icy touch and...

A soft thud resonated in the cavern behind the crypt room startling Bruno from his writing. He sat down the journal and started to pick up the hammer but remembered the deadly cross still in his satchel. He glanced at the staircase leading up to the church, hoping to see Raul returning with several more monks, but knew it was much to soon for that, so he quietly crawled back into the crypt that served as the secret passage into the catacombs. He paused once inside and listened to see if he could detect movement in the cavern, but hearing no sound and seeing no glow from a candle, he risked reentering the catacombs.

꙳   ꙳   ꙳

As he hobbled through the catacomb Jayro came to the secret door that led to the torture chamber. He paused, glanced back towards where he had just come and then pulled the cross from beneath his robe and used the point to relock the door. The bolts sounded like gunshots as they slammed back into place securing the door. Without further hesitation he continued towards the storage room entrance praying he would be in time to stop his brother from revealing the truth. He entered the storage room through the still open cabinet and grabbed a wheelwright's chisel off of the floor that had fallen when the cabinet broke free. He climbed the ladder and hurried across the yard towards the abbey. Just as he was about to enter a monk stepped from the doorway.

"Good morning, brother," Brother Ignacio said, waiting for a reply but receiving none. Jayro didn't look up and pushed his way past the monk.

It was still early and most of the abbey monks were still in prayer. Brother Ignacio didn't recognize the monk who had just pushed by him, but knew no monk should be entering at this time or be acting that way.

Jayro recognized his brother hurrying from the crypt room staircase and was about to call him when a hand grabbed Jayro's shoulder. "Brother why did you push…," but before the monk could finish Jayro spun around and thrust the chisel into the monk's throat.

"Help me, our brother has been hurt," Jayro called out to Raul, trying to disguise his voice.

Raul paused trying to decide what to do.

"Hurry, he's getting away," Jayro called out, knowing that if Raul didn't come to help, he'd never be able to catch him.

Raul took another step towards the sanctuary door then turned and ran to help the monk in distress, fearful that it may be his brother who was escaping yet again.

༄ ༄ ༄

Bruno relit his candle and headed down the long catacomb. About twenty feet past the cavern he saw a torch projecting out from the wall.

"Smart, real smart," Bruno commented. Jayro knew to place the first torch far enough from the cavern so there would be no chance of light escaping through a crack into the crypt room. Bruno admired a well thought out plan even though it was an evil plan. Bruno took the torch from the wall and used his candle to light it. The sudden brightness momentarily blinded him but, as his eyes adjusted, the increase of light revealed something he had either missed or that wasn't there when he and Raul first explored the catacombs.

"Blood," Bruno said, reaching down and touching the droplets. He scanned the catacomb and could see that some of the drops were smeared, having been stepped on.

His head jerked upward as he peered down the darkened corridor before him. "You were here," Bruno said.

Bruno could see that the smeared droplets headed away from the cavern and crypts. Had the droplets been there when he and Raul first searched the catacombs the blood droplets would have been smeared and tracked towards the crypt room.

"How much did you hear?" Bruno whispered, suddenly concerned about Raul's safety. He pulled the cross from his satchel and slowly continued down the corridor, following the blood trail and at the ready for any surprise attack.

He could see that the droplets led past the side chambers and on towards the storage room exit. Still, he took no chances and approached each chamber with caution.

"What have we here?" Bruno said, as he reached a place in the catacomb where several drops of blood had collected and had been smeared in several directions along the floor by the side wall.

"What made you stop here?" Bruno asked himself, but decided it best to continue following the trail of droplets.

He reached the cabinet and entered the storage room. The trail of blood continued up into the stable and then out into the yard, but there was no one around. "You may have gotten away for now, but we know where to find you," Bruno said and headed back to the catacombs, confident that Raul would soon return with help.

"I'm coming," Raul called, as he ran to the two monks.

Just as he arrived, Jayro dropped Brother Ignacio's limp body, turned, and plunged the chisel into his brother's chest. "You fool," Jayro chided. "You thought you could stop me? Your God is no match for the powers of the great Satan. What have you to say now?" Jayro said, as he twisted the chisel.

Raul grabbed the chisel with both hands trying to keep his brother from pushing it further into his chest. "You're mad," Raul wheezed, "Stop before it is too late. God, open his eyes and turn him from darkness to light, and from the power of Satan to God, so that he may receive forgiveness of sins and a place among those who are sanctified by faith in you."

"Your God, forgive me? Forgive me for what? For recognizing him as the imposter he is? For allowing men like you to destroy the Church and what it once stood for? No brother, my eyes are open and I have seen the 'Light' and have felt her icy touch. Sanctified by faith? I have been sanctified by my faith in Satan. Your God is dead. Your Church is dead. And now, brother, so are you," Jayro ranted, as he drove the chisel into his brother's heart.

❧ ❧ ❧

"Why did you linger at this exact spot?" Bruno said, as he stood directly on the cluster of blood drops. The walls of the catacomb were covered in scripture verses and as Bruno held the torch up to read the verse directly above the collected blood a smile spread across his face.

> Ask and it will be given to you;
> seek and you will find;
> knock and the door will be opened to you.
>
> Matthew 7:†

"At least you got the chapter and verse right this time," Bruno said. Since he had discovered that the symbol on the crypt was actually a lock that protected the catacombs from unwanted intruders, it was only logical this verse was also a lock. Bruno ran his fingers over the letters carved to create the verse. When he reached the first seven signifying the chapter, he immediately could feel that the edges were worn and rounded, unlike the sharp edges of the letters carved for the verse. The second seven, the one designating the chapter, was also considerably more worn than the verse letters.

"The sevens must be the lock," Bruno said, "but how do I find the key?"

Bruno looked for a crack in the wall that would show where the door and the wall met. There were several possibilities but no obvious separation. He next felt along the bottom but the wall revealed nothing. He was still holding the cross in his hand that he was prepared to use as a weapon. He stuck the point of the cross into the first seven to see if anything moved, but nothing happened. He next poked and prodded the second seven with the cross tip, still without success.

Frustrated, Bruno pulled the flask from his satchel and took a deep draw of the emerald liquid. "A clear mind, I must have a clear mind to see," Bruno roared.

Bruno lifted the cross to try the poking at the first seven again when God opened his eyes. "Thank you, Lord."

Bruno touched the emblem on the outer edge of the spear point. It was a perfect seven, identical to the sevens carved into the wall. "And I thought you made it that way to speed up the draining of the blood." He lifted the cross and inserted the raised seven into the first carved seven.

"A perfect fit," Bruno announced. He pushed lightly and heard a soft click. He repeated the process with the second seven, but instead of a click, two loud clanks echoed through the catacomb as the iron bars securing the door released.

"Knock and the door will be opened to you," Bruno recited, as he pushed on the door. Silently, the door pivoted on its axis and swung open.

"Perhaps Raul was correct, that is the smell of death," Bruno commented, as the overwhelming putrid odor drifted into the catacomb and filled his nostrils. He took one more swig from his flask then stepped through the threshold and into the darkness.

He stood on a narrow stone walkway that seemed to extend several feet to his left paralleling the catacomb but, of course, separated by the massive side wall. A low parapet skirted the opposite edge of the walkway and beyond that was blackness even the torch could not penetrate.

Bruno found the staircase leading down into the dark nothingness and began his descent. "You could've at least replaced the torches," Bruno complained, as he passed several empty and used up torches.

With each step, more horrors of the room he was entering came into view. "The inquisitor's chamber, no doubt," Bruno said. "And from the smell of things, it's still in use."

The absenta which usually does a good job making the smell tolerable wasn't even sufficient to conceal the cacophony of acrid odors. As Bruno approached the bottom of the stairs the aroma of vinegar mixed with the putrid smell of decomposing bodies was overwhelming.

"I hope that's just bad wine I smell," Bruno remarked. As he reached the bottom of the steps he found from where the odor emanated. Stretched on the rack was a body lying in a pool vinegar that seemed to be flowing from all the dead man's orifices. Bruno made the sign of the cross. "*Ave Maria purisima*. No wonder the Virgin cries the blood of Jesus."

"Lord, whoever did this, repay them for their deeds and for their evil work; repay them for what their hands have done and bring back upon them what they deserve," Bruno prayed, reciting part of Psalm 28.

As he continued around the outskirts of the large room he came to the table where another victim sat shackled to a chair, his head, inserted in a device attached to the table, completely crushed and now separating from the spine that was sticking out from the torso. This time Bruno only made the sign of the cross, unable to find the words to speak.

"Help me," a voice whispered. "The rats, the rats!"

Bruno turned quickly at the sound of the voice coming from across the room.

"Please, help me," the voice could barely be heard.

Bruno could see the top of the iron cage sticking out of a pit filled with the vilest muck imaginable. Across the top of this muck dozens of rats scurried about.

"They're eating me alive," the hoarse voice whispered.

"It was then that Bruno realized a body lay below the frenzy of rats inside the cage. "Father Adega, is that you?" Bruno asked.

"Help me," was the only answer.

Bruno waved the burning torch trying to scare the rats away from their meal, Father Adega. It worked momentarily, but within seconds some of the braver vermin, or hungrier vermin, were already attacking. Bruno lifted his torch to find the rope and pulley to raise the cage. He saw that the rope hung freely from the pulley attached to a large rafter, grabbed it, and pulled. Despite his size and great strength, the cage was firmly stuck in the quagmire of disgust and refused to even budge. Bruno knew he needed help and prayed that Raul would appear at any moment.

"Help me," Father Adega called again.

"I cannot do this alone; I'll have to go for help," Bruno said, in as soothing a tone as possible.

"The rats," Adega whispered.

"I'll light a fire to try to keep them at bay until I return," Bruno explained. He laid down the cross he still held as a weapon and began searching the chamber for something that would burn. He found three other torches, lit them and laid them around the pit. Shadows danced on the walls and for the moment the rats all seemed to vanish.

"Thank you, Lord," Adega whispered, then screamed, "No!" louder than ever before.

"What is it?" Bruno asked.

Bruno heard a swishing sound and turned just as the giant pendulum whizzed by his head ripping through his robe and slashing his shoulder.

Jayro had returned to the catacomb, closing and locking the cabinet in the storage room. He was enraged to find that Bruno had entered his torture chamber. He quietly slipped through the door and had eased down the stairs, noticed only by Adega who thought it was the help Bruno had promised. At least he thought that until he saw the monk release the pendulum.

"How dare you enter my adyctum," Jayro growled, grabbing a 'cat's paw' from the wall and then rushing towards Bruno.

"This is no holy place," Bruno replied, "this is hell on earth." Bruno held the torch in front of him to fight off Jayro.

Bruno heard the swishing of air just in time and dove to the floor as the pendulum swung out of the darkness just missing him. What didn't miss, were the slashing claws of the 'tickler' that shredded through Bruno's robe and ripped deep gouges in his forearm. Had it not been for the pendulum once again swinging past and keeping Jayro momentarily at bay, Bruno would surely have been torn to pieces. As Bruno rolled across the floor trying to escape Jayro's slashing attack, he knocked the three torches into the pit of muck extinguishing them.

"Deliver me from my enemies, O God; protect me from those who rise up against me. Deliver me from evildoers and save me from bloodthirsty men," Bruno prayed, reciting another verse from Psalms.

"Your God has no power here," Jayro yelled. "Satan has delivered to me the power to strike down his enemies." Jayro swung the 'cat's paw', but Bruno rolled away causing Jayro to miss, barely catching Bruno's back and leaving small scratches.

Again, the pendulum swished the air as it flew across the room in its downward arc several feet from where Bruno struggled to avoid death.

Bruno tossed his only weapon, the torch, to the far corner of the chamber; hoping darkness would afford him more protection.

"My eyes are used to the darkness of this place," Jayro chortled, pausing for a moment to allow his eyes to adjust. It was just enough time for Bruno to crawl beneath the table where the crushed head rotted. Bruno kicked the chair holding the decapitated body towards Jayro who believed it was Bruno rushing towards him. He lashed out viciously with the 'cat's paw', shredding the decomposing flesh and ripping the bones from the arm. It was just enough of a distraction for Bruno to grab the cross he had laid on the table earlier and circle behind Jayro. A perfect plan, had not the excessive amount of absenta Bruno consumed earlier caught up to him, causing him to lose his balance and tumble onto the floor within easy reach of Jayro's deadly weapon.

"You fool," Jayro said, standing above him. "Satan's powers are too great for a mere mortal such as you. You were doomed from the beginning. I promise you, it won't be a quick death," Jayro smiled a twisted evil grin.

"I don't fear you, for my God will come. He'll come with vengeance; with divine retribution he'll come to save me," Bruno prayed

"He better hurry," Jayro laughed, as he raised the 'cat's paw' to begin the barbaric flailing of Bruno. Suddenly, the swishing of the pendulum startled him. Jayro turned just as the pendulum swung back in its lower arc, smashing the sharpened edge attached to the heavy ball directly through his forehead and skull. The impact threw his body towards Bruno who instinctively held up the cross as protection. As Jayro's body collapsed atop Bruno the point of the cross pierced Jayro's back impaling the already silenced heart.

"Thank you, Lord, but next time, please don't wait so long," Bruno said pushing away the limp body.

"Thank you, God," Father Adega whispered.

"I'll get help," Bruno assured him, as he staggered to his feet.

"Please hurry," Adega begged.

Bruno pulled the cross from Jayro's back. He grabbed the torch still burning in the far corner of the chamber and relit the other three torches before he hurried up the stairs.

"Have faith," Bruno shouted to Adega, who could only nod in response.

When he reached the catacomb, Bruno turned and headed for the passage that led to the crypt room. He didn't think he would be able to climb the ladder that led from the storage room with the injuries to his shoulder and forearm.

When he reached the cavern behind the crypt room he called out but no one responded. With some difficulty he climbed into the crypt that served as the secret passage and slithered through dropping onto the crypt room floor. The room was much colder than he remembered. He pulled the nearly empty flask of absenta from his satchel, lifted it to his lips, and tilted his head back to drain the last remnants of the bottle. When he lowered his head, the dead witch stood before him.

"You killed the man who set me free," Lucia said.

"Be gone witch, you've no place in God's house," Bruno replied.

"I agree, a witch does not belong in such a sanctified place as this. But as I said, I was set free, free to do what my lord Satan has destined for me. I'm not a witch, I'm a Nephilim, born of the sons of God and the daughters of man," Lucia replied.

"That's impossible," Bruno replied. "God destroyed all the Nephilim in the Great Flood."

"Yes, and he cast my father into Tartarus, the place of darkness, but he allowed our spirits to remain as demons to lead the human race astray," Lucia explained. "What kind of god would do such a thing?" She walked slowly behind Bruno and shut the crypt door that served as the secret passage.

"God's plan is perfect. I'm not one to question it," Bruno replied. "I'm just his servant and as his servant I call upon the Lord to rebuke you. Be gone demon."

Bruno reached into his satchel for the blood Raul had collected from the Madonna.

"It is said that men's hearts will fail at the sight of a Nephilim," Lucia said. "Do you think it's true?"

Suddenly, Bruno became extremely cold and could feel his heart slowing down. "What are you doing to me?" Bruno gasped, unable to move.

"I'm delivering you to your Lord. Isn't that what you want?" Lucia laughed. Lucia took the cross from Bruno's stiff hand and placed it around his neck.

"Why do you do this?" Bruno could barely speak.

"Because I'm the Lucia de la Cruz, Satan's 'light of the cross', and in spiritual warfare, someone must die," she replied. "And since I already died, it's now your turn," she replied, placing her hand on Bruno's robe. The coldness of her hand burned through the material and left a perfect handprint burned into Bruno's chest. "But don't worry, I won't saw off the top of your head."

୭   ୭   ୭

"He must have gone completely mad," the abbot explained to Reverend Father.

"Perhaps it was that foul-smelling elixir Bruno forced him to drink that caused him to snap," Reverend Father suggested.

"Only God will ever know," the abbot replied. "We believe he first killed Brother Bruno in the crypt room. Brother Ignacio must have seen him leaving the crypt room and in his panic, Raul stabbed Brother Ignacio in the neck killing him."

"But why would he then kill himself? God could forgive him for his sins of murder, but never will a man who takes his own life enter the Kingdom of Heaven," Reverend Father replied.

"Do you think this has anything to do with the Madonna's bloody tears ending?" the abbot asked.

"I think it has everything to do with it," Reverend Father replied. "The power of the blood of Christ gives us power over Satan. When the tears ended, Satan took advantage."

"I've sent someone to inform the alguacil about what has happened," the abbot said. "After he's finished here, I'll have Raul's body and belongings returned to his family. We cannot bury him in sanctified ground after what he has done."

"Telling the bishop that his good friend, Bruno, is dead isn't a task I look forward to. How did Raul kill Brother Bruno? I'm sure the bishop will want to know," Reverend Father said.

"They appear to have struggled. Brother Bruno had several deep cuts on his arm and his shoulder had a deep gash, but none of these wounds would have killed him. When we found him, his body was extremely cold and there was an imprint of a hand burned into his chest," the abbot explained.

"Sounds like the work of Satan," Reverend Father replied.

"I shudder to think that Brother Raul was a servant of Satan," replied the abbot. "We found Brother Bruno's journal next to his body. Perhaps you should give it to the bishop."

"An excellent suggestion, but before I send it to him, I want you to record in it what you believe happened. Be sure and include that information about the handprint. Do you know what Bruno was doing in the crypt room?" Reverend Father asked.

"No, but perhaps if we read his journal it may tell us," the abbot suggested.

"No, I'll leave that decision up to the bishop. Just write what you have told me and give it to me as soon as possible," Reverend Father ordered. "We'll inter Brother Bruno here at the church. I'll perform the sacraments, but I'm sure the bishop will want to do so also when he returns."

"What about the rest of his possessions?" the abbot asked. "We'll save them for the bishop, but if there is any religious jewelry or sacred items, place them with the body before he is interred. And get one of the acolytes to clean up this blood. I've seen drops everywhere."

"Lord, help me, please, help me." Adega's whisper grew softer, though his faith stayed strong.

The rats now had another source of fresh food and they lapped at the fresh blood pouring from Jayro's skull. It would be another day before Father Adega died, but not before the rats had chewed off and eaten his lips, nose, ears, and eyeballs.

CHAPTER EIGHTEEN

"Vengeance"

"**This Bruno Mancini**, is he buried here at the templo?" Kevin asked.

"He is interred here, yes," the Reverend Father replied. "He entered heaven in the summer of 1725, according to records.

"What about your ancestor, Raul Toribio, is he interred here also?" Kevin asked Oralia.

"No, and that's why I need to find out what happened. According to family records, he was buried in a common grave outside the city sometime in 1725, as well."

"You said Raul was one of the monks at the abbey, shouldn't he be interred here?" Liz asked.

"One would think that to be the case, but it didn't happen," Oralia answered.

"Do we know how either of them died?" Francois asked.

"No, Oralia has done much research to try to discover exactly what happened, but so far has met with limited success," Reverend Father explained.

"Limited success? That must mean you have discovered some things."

"I do know Bruno Mancini believed that he was about to die in a great spiritual battle," Oralia said. "Besides the samples of the bloody tears and the drawings, Bruno sent his will and letters of instruction for the disposal of his estate back to Rome with the archbishop, but he also shared some information with the archbishop who wrote it in his own journal. The archbishop tells how he tried to talk Bruno into leaving with him, but Bruno explained that God had destined him for this great battle with one of Satan's demons."

"Did this demon have a name," Liz asked.

"Not that I can recall, but it was described as a she, with an icy touch that could freeze a heart, and was possibly the reincarnation of some murdered witch whose death he was investigating." Oralia explained.

Liz, Kevin, and Francois all looked at each other.

"Why would he be investigating a witch's death?" Romero asked.

"I've no idea," Oralia replied. "But she…"

"Tell me more about this demon with the icy touch," Liz interrupted.

"There's nothing more to tell," Oralia replied.

"You mentioned some drawings that the archbishop took to Rome along with the Madonna's bloody tears. Drawings of what?" Kevin asked.

"Drawings of some sort of cross if I remember correctly," Oralia replied.

"Can you describe it to us," Kevin asked.

"Oh no, I didn't pay that close of attention, but I'd recognize it if I saw a picture of it. However, I'm sure the Vatican still has the drawing filed away somewhere. It should be fairly easy to find since they just tested the blood sample that was sent with it. I could call and find out if you'd like?" Oralia offered.

"I'm not sure it's important," Kevin replied, "but perhaps you should do so. Is there anything else you think we should know?"

"The cross was used in the murders…," Oralia began to explain.

"Ahem." Oralia looked at the Reverend Father. "Oralia is somewhat of a conspiracy theorist," Reverend Father said.

"She has some unproven notions which I have asked her not to share."

"I love conspiracy theories," Francois piped up. "I'd like to here what you think."

"We all would, but I don't think now is the proper time," Liz added. "We need to go warn the doctor that he is in danger."

"I thought you said you had people watching his hotel," Romero replied.

"I do, but something tells me we need to get over there soon," Liz replied.

"Reverend Father, Oralia, thank you for the information. I'm not sure when we'll return, but I don't imagine it will be too very long. Oralia, perhaps you can see if the Vatican can fax those drawings," Kevin instructed.

"I'll see what I can do," Oralia replied.

"I've an emergency meeting with the acting-bishop this afternoon, something about tonight's processional, so I'm not sure if I'll see you again until after the ceremony," Reverend Father said to Kevin. "Inspector Romero, I certainly hope your men are successful in finding the bishop. There seems to be a lot of evil in Madrid these days."

"I'm sure the local police are doing everything possible to find him," Romero replied.

"Like they are in finding the disappearing prostitutes," Liz interjected.

Romero ignored the slight. "I'll have some uniformed officers meet us there," Romero suggested, "they can help control access to the hotel."

"That's a good idea," Kevin replied, "but just make sure no one does anything till we get there."

"As long as this Lucienne doesn't try anything, then that shouldn't be a problem," Romero replied. "We can take my car."

"Thank you, but I think we would be more comfortable in my car," Liz replied. No sooner were the words out of her mouth was the Mercedes pulling up in front of the templo.

"How do you do that?" Francois asked.

Liz just smiled and opened the car door for him and Kevin. "Will you be joining us, Inspector?" Liz asked.

"No thank you. I don't think my boss would approve, but mind you, I'll be right behind you so don't go breaking any laws on your way there," Romero teased.

"We wouldn't dream of it," Liz replied.

୨ ୨ ୨

"Adela, could you answer the phone while I pick up this Sunday's program from the printer. The delivery boy is home ill and no one can drop them by," Oralia explained.

"Sure," Adela replied, "my first counseling session isn't for another hour."

"Thanks, I really appreciate it," Oralia replied. "I shouldn't be more than fifteen minutes. Oh, and if Elisa comes in looking for her candle, it's on the table where she left it."

"No need to rush," Adela assured her.

Oralia had been out of the office for less than a minute when there was a soft knock and a stranger entered.

"Good afternoon, how can I help you?" Adela asked, as she looked up from the desk.

"I've an appointment with Reverend Father," the formally dressed man replied.

"I'm sorry the Reverend Father had to leave unexpectedly," Adela said searching for Oralia's desk calendar. "Perhaps you'd like to reschedule Mr…, I'm sorry I don't seem to find the calendar anywhere, what time was your appointment?"

"You are the Reverend Father's secretary?" the man asked.

But before Adela could answer, the office door opened. "Oralia, have you seen the bishop's Paschal candle for the processional tonight?" a rather exasperated plump woman wailed. "Oh, I'm sorry to interrupt, I didn't know Ora…"

"It's quite alright, Elisa. The candle is right there on the table, where you left it," Adela replied. "And remember, he's only the acting-bishop, Reverend Father wouldn't be pleased to hear you refer to him as the bishop."

"Goodness gracious, if my head wasn't attached I'd probably lose it too," she laughed as she picked up the long candle.

At no time did the dapper gentleman turn to see who had barged in. The intruder had answered his question, at least he thought she had. He was convinced the woman before him was Oralia Toribio.

As the plump woman left, she looked at Adela and mouthed the words "he's cute" then shrugged holding up her free hand and mouthed questioningly "white gloves", causing Adela to smile and shoo her friend away.

"I'm sorry for the interruption," Adela apologized "Now, where were we?"

"You were about to reschedule my appointment," the gentleman said.

"Oh yes, and you were about to tell me your name," Adela replied.

"No, I was about to...," the man paused and looked up at the video monitor that showed the front of the church.

Adela looked up to see what the man was looking at. In that split-second the man pulled a cross from beneath his suit coat and smashed it through Adela's forehead crushing her skull and burying the tip deep within her brain. He caught her as she collapsed trying not to get any of the blood on his clothing.

"I guess it wasn't a theory after all," the man smiled.

The fax machine suddenly came to life startling the man. He quickly laid Adela's body across the desk with her head hanging over the trash can, allowing her blood to drain. As he headed for the door, the fax spit out a drawing of a cross just like the one he had buried in the secretary's head.

He pulled the drawing from the machine with his bloody glove. "Now that you've got the real thing, you won't need this, Mr. Kevin Bridges." He laughed wadding the paper into a ball and tossing it into the corner of the room.

He opened the door and walked directly to the stairs leading to the mausoleum, ignoring the two monks who stood talking at the opposite end of the lobby. It was still two hours before the public would have access to the crypts so he knew he would be alone. He walked directly to the crypt with a verse from Matthew on it. He pulled the gloves from his hand revealing the ring. On the ring was a unique design that fit perfectly into the matching symbol carved into the marble. He heard a soft click then pounded twice on the corner of the crypt. The door silently swung open, but before he entered, he touched his chest to assure the golden chain with the seal of the seven, remained secure.

"As our Lord Satan commands, I have sacrificed a body so his servant can return and his will be done," the man prayed. He then looked up at the verse written on the crypt and began to recite. *"Ask and it will be given to you; seek and you will find; knock and the door will be opened to you,"* the man laughed and climbed through into the catacombs, locking the secret passage behind him.

༄ ༄ ༄

"Hon, someone's hea to see ya," the woman said in a thick southern drawl, knocking on the bathroom door.

"What?" a voice called from inside.

This time the woman opened the bathroom door slightly. "I said, there's someone hea to see ya."

"I didn't order any damn paella," the man replied.

This time she went all the way into the bathroom. "I said there's a policeman hea to see ya."

"Well, what's he want?" the man replied.

"I don't know what he wants, you all just hurry on outta there," she ordered.

"Tell him I'll be right out."

"He'll be right out," the woman said, passing on the message that all four of them had already heard.

"The doctor turned the shower handle to off, but nothing happened.

"What the hell," he said, turning his face as the spray started coming out much quicker, harder, and colder. The pressure of water spray was really starting to hurt. He raised his hand to block the spray from his face and screamed. The water was like needles and ripped into and through his hand.

"Ahhh, help me," the doctor screamed trying to get out of the shower's jammed door.

Kevin and Romero were the first through the bathroom door, just as the doctor came crashing through the glass enclosure landing on the floor in front of them.

"Call an ambulance," Kevin yelled. The doctor lay on the floor, his arm looked as if it had been run through a meat grinder and his hand was shredded. There were several other cuts to his body but most had occurred when he broke through the glass.

"Inspector," Liz called. "Contact your men, Lucienne must be nearby. I'm going to look for her."

"Stay here," Kevin ordered, but Liz was already gone by the time Kevin looked up to respond. "Francois, don't let her out of your sight," Kevin called, but Francois was on the phone calling for assistance and didn't hear Kevin's command.

The inspector started to turn off the shower. "Don't touch that," Kevin yelled, but Romero had already turned the water off.

"Water was getting all over the floor," Romero explained.

"It was the water that did this to him," Kevin said.

"That's impossible," Romero replied

"Welcome to my world," Kevin responded.

"Pass me that towel," the doctor's girlfriend ordered. "We need to slow down the blood loss."

"Are you a nurse?" Romero asked.

"No suh, I'm a neurosurgeon," the petite southern-belle replied, as she continued to evaluate the doctor's mangled arm. "No bones seem to be broken, that's good. Massive tissue and arterial damage, though," she said with no trace of an accent, as she continued her preliminary examination. "We have a good chance of saving the arm."

"Francois, where's Liz? I told you to follow her," Kevin shouted.

Francois tried to open the door but the safety lock was in place. He unhooked the mechanism and rushed into the hallway but Liz was nowhere to be seen. He ran to the staircase and listened but heard no echoing from footsteps.

"She must've taken the elevator," Francois said, reentering the room. "There was no sign of her on this floor or on the staircase. What's even weirder," Francois continued, "is the room door was locked on the inside when I tried to get out."

"Damn," Kevin muttered, "I got a bad feeling about this."

CHAPTER NINETEEN

"Abomination"

She knew she was taking a risk, but she was willing to deal with the consequences. When she reached the doors of the elevator, she passed right through them and dropped in a freefall. She tumbled over and over, her skin feeling as if it were being torn from her body. But as she plunged through that veiled pellicle into the pit of total darkness, she was unafraid. She had been here before.

"At last you've returned," Lucienne said. "I didn't think you had the courage to return here."

Lucienne stood alone, illuminated in the total darkness.

"You've no right to interfere in my work," Liz challenged. "It was my task to spread doubt of the miracle claims attributed to John Paul II."

"Yes, but that was before Christ took such an interest in the matter. And be honest, you were doing such a poor job of it. But, why must we argue about it?" Lucienne said. "There are so few of our kind left we should work together. Look, your light is coming back."

"I'll never work with you," Liz replied.

"Do you still believe God may have mercy on your Nephilim soul if you behave here in Tartarus and display righteous behavior on Earth?" Lucienne laughed.

"I didn't choose to be a Nephilim," Liz replied.

"No one chooses to be born who they are. God chooses. And God chose you to be born the daughter of a lustful rebel angel and a human woman," Lucienne said.

"If God doesn't believe we can be redeemed, why did he allow so many of us to remain after the flood?" Liz replied.

"God didn't allow us to remain in this form. He allowed our disembodied spirits to remain, as demons, to try to tempt the human race and lead them astray. You forget that it was our lord, Satan, who showed us how to take human form. Speaking of which," Lucienne cackled, "How does such a righteous Nephilim as you plan to return to the human realm. If I recall it's been several decades since you last visited Tartarus. Did you forget that the only way out of here is for someone on earth to murder another human and summon forth your spirit to take human form?"

"I haven't forgotten," Liz said quietly.

"Either you're not as righteous as you'd like God to believe, or you're planning an extended stay in Tartarus," Lucienne gloated. "As for me, I'll be leaving here any moment now. I've much unfinished business in Madrid."

"How can you be so sure?" Liz asked.

"It's already been arranged. I could never have escaped the hotel in human form with all the police and your associates present, so I knew I'd have to return here. While you and your friends tried to save the doctor at the hotel, one of the 'Seven' was preparing to kill the church secretary to bring me back," Lucienne explained.

"Oralia Toribio, the secretary at the Templo Eucarístico?" Liz gasped.

"Oh, that's right, you know her," Lucienne laughed.

"What do you mean 'one of the Seven'?" Liz asked.

"One of the 'Seven of the Cross', a very powerful and, how should I say it, 'evil', group of men who have found the ways of the Inquisition much to their liking," Lucienne explained.

"Are these 'Seven of the Cross' the great evil that Jesus now weeps for, or is it you that causes the Madonna's bloody tears?" Liz asked.

"Me, I thought it was you. Everywhere you go one of these miracles seem to pop up," Lucienne replied.

"Miracles are authentication of God's Divine Mission," Liz explained.

"Miracles are the fool's gold of modern religion. They serve Satan's cause more than they serve God," Lucienne responded. "You can't imagine how many humans fell from the narrow path when the so-called miracle of Christ appearing on the grilled cheese sandwich sold on Ebay."

"It doesn't have to be that way," Liz replied.

"You need to look around you. All these souls are condemned to languish here until the day of final judgment and believe me, if He has already sent you here, your future doesn't look promising," Lucienne said. "God's divine mission doesn't include our salvation, regardless of what you may believe."

"I'll never allow…" Liz stopped in mid-sentence as Lucienne's luminescence began to fade.

"Looks like I gotta go, better make yourself at home, you may be here for a while. Maybe we'll meet again after I've killed the doctor. Who knows, maybe I'll kill all your friends while I'm at it," Lucienne laughed, as she disappeared into the blackness.

"We'll meet again and it will be sooner than you think," Liz replied to the blackness.

ھ ھ ھ

"My men have searched every floor and room twice now," Romero said to Kevin. "There's no way Liz is anywhere in this building."

"But how could she have gotten past your men so quickly?" Kevin asked.

"She couldn't have. Nor could this Lucienne have gotten past my men. Right now, I'm not convinced this Lucienne actually exists," Romero said.

"Oh, she exists," Francois added. "Of that, I have no doubt."

"What makes you so certain that Liz and Lucienne aren't the same person?" Romero asked. "From what you've told me, they've never been seen together, but catastrophe always seems to strike when one of them is around."

"Is this more of your crazy theory about Liz being a servant of Satan masquerading as the light of God?" Kevin huffed.

"I'm only making a suggestion based on the facts as I know them," Romero replied.

"You believe it's a fact that servants of Satan masquerade as servants of God?" Francois asked.

"I told you I was a devout Catholic, and as a Catholic I believe in the truth of the Bible," Romero replied.

"Well I believe in the truth of what I see, and I saw two different women. One good, one bad," Francois replied. "And Liz is good!"

"And I believe we need to find both of these women as quickly as possible," Kevin said, stepping between the two policemen.

At that moment Kevin's Blackberry began to chime.

"This is Kevin Bridges," he answered.

"Mr. Bridges, something terrible has happened, you must hurry back to the templo," Oralia pleaded.

"What's wrong?" Kevin asked.

"It's...it's Adela," Oralia began to cry. "Someone has murdered Adela."

"Have you notified the police?" Kevin asked.

"No, I thought I should call you first. You see, she was murdered by that cross," Oralia whimpered.

"What cross?"

"The cross I saw in Bruno Mancini's papers at the Vatican," Oralia replied.

"Did anyone see who might have committed the murder?" Kevin asked, worried that Liz might have shown up back at the templo.

"Elisa walked in on Adela and a gentleman talking in my office," Oralia explained. "And that's where I found Adela's body when I returned."

"Your office, what was she doing in your office?" Kevin asked.

"I asked her to answer the phone while I ran to the printers for this Sunday's program," Oralia said beginning to cry again. "My goodness, do you think the murderer was looking for me?

"I doubt it, it was probably just a random act," Kevin lied. "Did Elisa get a good look at the man?"

"Not his face, but she said he was impeccably dressed. He was even wearing those fancy white gloves," Oralia replied.

"Inspector Romero is still with us, I'll tell him what you've told me and we'll come there immediately. Don't touch anything and don't allow anyone in or out of the templo," Kevin ordered.

"I'll keep the office closed, but I cannot guarantee that we'll be able to stop the parishioners from coming to worship," Oralia replied.

"At least keep everyone in the sanctuary," Kevin said.

"That I think we can do," Oralia replied. "Just hurry, please."

"What happened at the templo?" Francois asked.

"Someone was murdered," Kevin replied. "I'll explain on the way."

One of the problems a Nephilim faced when being brought back to Earth after a victim was murdered, was exactly when and where they would materialize. Almost always it would be near where the body of the victim lay, as long as the body was all together. It also could be as long as a day or two after the murder, depending on how aware the disembodied spirit of the Nephilim was that they were being recalled to human form. After several years in Tartarus these demons would forget they could take human form and the transition could be lengthy when the call finally came.

Lucienne knew her call would be coming almost immediately. She had arranged for it before she returned to Tartarus. She also knew Liz would likely follow her there which made it all the better. Liz could be stuck in the dense blackness for decades, but Lucienne had other ideas.

"It's an angel from God," one of the acolytes shouted, pointing to Lucienne who slowly faded into existence in the mausoleum of the templo.

"Not exactly," Lucienne laughed. "You're only half right about the angel part and you got the God thing all wrong."

The two acolytes assigned to polish the mausoleum floor and replace the candles before it opened for the day, dropped to the floor and prostrated themselves before Lucienne.

"Finally, the respect I deserve," she responded. She quickly headed up the steps knowing that Kevin and the others would soon be arriving at the templo. Now wasn't the time to confront Kevin. There would undoubtedly be several police with him and, Lucienne could be overwhelmed, forcing her to escape back to Tartarus and she hadn't prepared for such a necessity.

"Who are you and what are you doing in the mausoleum?" Oralia demanded as she saw Lucienne ascending the stairs.

"Forgive me, but I came to pay my respects. I know it's early, but the door was open and I thought no one would care," Lucienne replied, as a chill seemed to fill the room.

"No, that's not possible," Oralia replied. "The door to the sanctuary is kept locked until it's time for the crypts to open."

"Well it was open when I came in," Lucienne replied heading for the door."

"I think you should wait here until the police arrive," Oralia told the woman. "Someone was murdered in the office and I'm sure they will want to speak with you about it."

"Do you suspect me?" Lucienne laughed. "Don't be absurd, do I look like a man?"

"Oralia, it was a man I saw in the office," Elisa spoke up. Oralia shot her a stern glance.

"Oralia? I thought Oralia was the secretary who was killed?" Lucienne said.

"No one said anything about who was killed or if it was a man who did the killing. Why would you think it was me in the office and how did you know it was a man who did it?" Oralia challenged.

"I've had enough of your insinuations," Lucienne replied, as she tried to open the door to leave.

"It's locked, just like I said it was," Oralia smirked.

Lucienne used her powers to instantly freeze the door handle and lock which seemed to explode in her hand. "No, you're mistaken. It's open just as I said it was," Lucienne replied, quickly passing through the open door pulling it closed behind her and freezing the door in place.

"Don't let her get away," Oralia shouted to the two monks following the conversation. The closest monk ran to pull the door open but jumped back screaming when he touched it.

"It burned me," the monk cried.

The second monk approached more cautiously, slowly bringing his hand to the door. "It's frozen," he said. "It was so cold it burned your hand."

"That's not possible," Oralia replied, as she rushed to the door, but she too could feel the coldness.

Oralia grabbed a large candelabrum, knocking the candles across the room. "Stand back," she cried and smashed the heavy metal base against the door. The ice cracked and the door swung open.

"Be careful not to touch anything," Oralia ordered as she slipped through the opening.

Several people in the sanctuary were staring at her, as she rushed in, but the woman was nowhere in sight.

"Did anyone see where she went?" Oralia yelled as she rushed to the front of the sanctuary, through the door, and out onto the street, but the woman had disappeared.

Both the monks followed her into the sanctuary and began searching.

"Did you see the angel?" one of the acolytes shouted rushing into the sanctuary. "God sent us an angel," he repeated.

"What are you talking about?" Oralia replied.

"While we were cleaning in the crypts, one of God's angels materialized right before our eyes," the acolyte replied, dropping to his knees in front of the crying Madonna.

"It's another miracle from God," the second acolyte cried, as he joined his neophyte brother.

"Let no one in or out of the templo until Mr. Bridges arrives," Oralia ordered. "And I mean no one!"

Oralia believed that it was an angel they had seen, but she knew it wasn't an angel sent by God.

CHAPTER TWENTY

"Forgiveness"

"**I've been in daily contact** with the comisario of the Special Operations Group of the Cuerpo Nacional. He assures me that everything possible is being done to find Bishop Castillo," the acting-bishop explained.

"Is there any truth to the rumor that the ETA has taken him prisoner and are holding him as a means to further their cause?" one of the Reverends asked.

"That's one possibility the comisario told me they are looking into. There are several Basque Separatist terrorist cells operating in Madrid."

"Under the circumstances, don't you think we should scale back the Fiesta de San Martín. Three days of processionals seems a bit excessive," Reverend Father stated.

"It'd be absurd to do so," the acting-bishop snapped back. "The former bishop took much pride in these processionals."

"Bishop Castillo is still the bishop, not the former bishop," the Reverend Father corrected. "The fact that he's missing doesn't change that. He will remain the bishop until the Vatican appoints a new one."

"Yes, but until that time, I'm the acting-bishop, and as such, it's my desire that the processionals continue as scheduled. Now is there any more business to discuss?" The bishop was visibly angered by the Reverend Father's challenge.

"Yes, I think we need to discuss the miracle at the Templo Eucarístico," Reverend Father said. "The Madonna continues to shed the bloody tears, yet you told the Vatican not to send their investigator, even though Bishop Castillo had requested it."

"I'd say that is a moot point since the investigator has arrived and began his investigation," came the harsh reply.

"You are well informed," Reverend Father responded.

"Now, if no one has any important business to discuss, I suggest we all go and prepare for tonight's processional."

Before anyone could raise an objection or concern, the acting-bishop left the conference room and headed to his private office to meet with an expected visitor.

୨୦   ୨୦   ୨୦

"The fool killed the wrong woman," Lucienne complained. "We sent him to silence Oralia and now his incompetence will only make matters worse. What do you intend to do about it?"

"The question is, 'what do you intend to do about it'?" the acting-bishop replied.

"Carlos is one of the 'Seven' and the first of the three processionals is tonight. All members of the "Seven of the Cross' must march in tonight's processional," Lucienne insisted.

"And all seven will march," the acting-bishop replied. "But Carlos Hernandez will not be one of them. He had served us well, but even before this failure, suspicion had fallen upon him. That's why I ordered the secretary of the templo murdered. She found out it was Carlos who has the journal and she shared this knowledge with the Vatican investigator."

"Kevin Bridges, I know him well," Lucienne replied. "He's well-protected by God's grace, although, he doesn't yet realize it."

"My sources tell me that he's already planning on contacting Carlos. He presents a direct danger to the 'Seven'. I trust you will find a way to derail his investigation," the acting-bishop said.

"I'll dispose of Carlos today and I'll make sure we benefit from his murder," Lucienne replied, "but Satan demands that seven must march in the processionals and it was Carlos who carried the Libro de Reglas."

"And I said seven will march. There's another who wishes to join the 'Seven of the Cross'. He is a man of vast political power who can do much to help keep Madrid awash in evil," the acting-bishop explained. "He can bear the Book of Rules. And if all goes as planned, he will be the next él Presidente."

"And is this replacement willing to fulfill the requirements of the Inquisition and all that our lord Satan demands of him?" Lucienne asked.

"Never have I met a man with such an insatiable appetite for sadistic torture," the acting-bishop replied. "Of course, you already know this, but if he fails to fulfill his mandate, he'll suffer an unspeakable painful death."

"And it will be I who administers that pain," Lucienne laughed.

The acting-bishop didn't share her humor. "I'm troubled by something else I've been told," he said. "I know there's a lieutenant with the Paris Prefecture that has joined this Mr. Bridges in his investigation. I've also heard there is a woman who claims to have been chasing after you for some time. It's this woman that concerns me."

"She's an Interpol agent. Why should that concern you?" Lucienne replied.

"My sources tell me that she might be more than just an Interpol agent. They say she might possess a special insight into what is happening, or, that perhaps she has special powers," the acting-bishop probed, trying not to sound too concerned.

"If you are asking if she's an angel of God, the answer is no," Lucienne explained. "She may think she is doing God's bidding but she's no closer to God than you or me. I can assure you of that."

"That's good to hear," the acting-bishop replied, somewhat relieved. "Still, I've heard rumors and even heard Bishop Castillo speak of the guardian angels of Interpol."

"I've no doubt that guardian angels do exist," Lucienne replied, "but I've never heard of them working for Interpol. And like I said, I can tell you for certain that this woman is no angel."

"Nor are you," the acting-bishop replied, "and neither am I."

∾   ∾   ∾

"If he didn't leave by the front door or use the back, then how the hell did he leave here?" Francois asked. "Excuse my French." He added when he saw Elisa's shocked face.

"Watch, in just a couple of seconds the woman will come running out the front," Oralia explained. "Right...now!"

"That's Lucienne, no doubt about it," Kevin said. "Stop the tape, so we can get a better look at her face."

Elisa pushed the pause button.

"Looks a little like Liz to me," Romero suggested.

"Ridiculous," Francois said, "Lucienne looks nothing like Liz. Are you trying to suggest Liz may have something to do with this poor girl's murder?"

"No, I just find it peculiar that once again we have a murder and Liz is unaccounted for," Romero remarked.

"Well I'm very troubled that Liz is missing as well," Kevin agreed, "however, I know for a fact that the woman in this picture is Lucienne and not Liz. When you see the video from the hotel murders in Paris you'll agree."

"So, this Lucienne materialized right in front of you?" Romero asked one of the acolytes.

"Yes sir, we were cleaning in the mausoleum when suddenly she just kind of faded in," one of the boys said.

"Has anyone checked the oxygen level in the mausoleum or smelled those boy's breath. Maybe they found the communion wine stash," Romero joked.

"No sir, we are completely sober. It was another message from God, just like the Madonna's bloody tears," the other acolyte said.

"As a trained investigator what you are telling me is a little hard to believe," Romero replied.

"How do you explain the frozen door," Oralia asked Romero. "Look at the monk's hand. It is burned where he touched the door and see, the lock is shattered."

"You believe this Lucienne murdered Adela?" Romero asked.

"No, it was a man who killed Adela. I saw him," Elisa said.

"You claim to have seen him, yet he doesn't appear to be coming or going on any of the videotapes. We've searched the entire templo and there is no gentleman that fits that description on the premises. Are you sure it wasn't one of the monks who you saw?" Romero asked.

"I've worked here for years and know every one of the monks by name. Besides, this man was a gentleman. He even wore white gloves just like…" Elisa paused. "He was dressed just like those men dress in the processionals. You know, with the fancy coat and trousers. They wear white gloves when they carry the paschal candles. The only thing missing was the hat," Elisa explained.

"The first processional of the Fiesta de San Martín is tonight. Perhaps we can find him there," Oralia suggested.

"Excellent idea Ms. Toribio. Elisa, if I find a safe place on the processional route where you can view the participants would you be willing to try to recognize the man you saw today?" Romero asked.

"I'm willing to give it a try, but remember, I never saw his face," Elisa explained.

"I think it's worth the try and I'll make sure you're safe and protected," Romero replied.

"Don't touch that!" Romero yelled at Kevin. "The forensics team hasn't cleared this room yet."

"I need to have a closer look at that cross," Kevin explained, reaching for it once again.

"Not till we're through with it," Romero ordered, gently pushing Kevin's hand away.

"That could take days," Kevin replied. "I need to examine it now."

"I'm afraid your diplomatic immunity doesn't give you the right to interfere with a murder investigation here in Madrid," Romero sneered. "Why don't you speak to the Pope about it."

"Perhaps I shall," the Reverend Father responded as he walked into the office.

"Your Reverence, please forgive my rudeness," Romero replied, bowing to the Reverend Father.

"I believe under the circumstances we should be working with each other not against one another," Reverend Father suggested. "My driver informed me of the terrible tragedy. I came back as quickly as possible."

"The senseless murder of a human being is always a terrible tragedy," Romero replied. "I'm so sorry it had to happen here in your office. I'll have my people finish up here as quickly as possible. Now if you all would be so kind as to wait in the sanctuary, my team can wrap things up in here."

Neither Kevin nor Francois were accustomed to being ordered out of the murder scene, but it would give them a chance to speak with Oralia and the Reverend Father without Romero listening in.

"I think it's obvious that I was the intended target and not Adela," Oralia explained. "The murderer thought it was me behind the desk."

"And it would have been had you not gone to pick up the church bulletin when you did," Reverend Father added.

"From what you told us earlier, it seems even Lucienne believed it was you who had been murdered. That means the murderer and Lucienne must somehow be working together," Kevin surmised.

"I don't understand why this so-called gentleman didn't appear on any of the videotapes monitoring the entrances to the templo," Francois commented.

"Maybe he left the same way this Lucienne arrived," the Reverend Father suggested. "Perhaps he too was an angel of Satan."

"No, I got a feeling this man was as real as you or me," Kevin replied. "Lucienne likes to use human accomplices in her murders."

"You know he may have gone out the same way she came in," Oralia said.

"Why do you say that?" Francois asked.

"I never told you the whole story about Bruno Mancini's journal," Oralia began. "When I was a little girl my grandfather had a journal that belonged to Raul Toribio, my ancestor and the monk who kept the record of Bruno Mancini's investigation here at the templo. It was a duplicate Raul kept for himself, but with his own notes and comments written in the margins."

"You read the journal?" Kevin asked.

"Yes, parts of it, but honestly I don't remember a whole lot about it. I was only twelve or thirteen at the time. However, there are some things that I do remember," Oralia explained.

For instance," Francois said.

"Well I remember Raul making lots of notes about how much absenta Bruno started drinking right before he was killed. It was as though he knew he was about to die, Raul wrote."

"You said something like 'he may have gone out the way she came in'," Kevin reminded her.

"Oh yes, Raul wrote how Bruno discovered a hidden entrance behind the cabinet in the stable that led into some catacombs beneath the templo," Oralia began.

"Yes, but those stables were torn down more than a century ago and the church and monastery rebuilt and expanded several times since then. No one even remembers exactly where the stables were located," the Reverend Father explained.

"The journal also mentions the crypt room and what he believed to be a secret passageway located in there as well," Oralia continued. "But he never mentions exactly where. He just kept referring to a verse in Matthew."

"Dozens of the crypts are inscribed with verses from Matthew," the Reverend Father added.

"Do you remember the verse?" Kevin asked Oralia.

"I'm afraid I don't. Like I said, there's much I don't remember," Oralia replied.

"Does your grandfather still have the journal?" Francois asked.

Oralia closed her eyes to fight back the tears.

"That's a sensitive subject with Oralia," the Reverend Father spoke up. "You see, her grandfather died when his house caught fire when she was still but a child. She blames her older cousin for the tragedy since he was the last one to see the grandfather. Oralia believes her cousin set the fire to hide the fact that he stole the journal. God forgive me, and you too Oralia, for what I'm about to say but, I loathe your cousin and wouldn't doubt he is capable of such an egregious act."

"You know Oralia's cousin?" Kevin said.

"Of course, her cousin is the acting-bishop, Father Toribio," the Reverend Father replied.

"Why would the acting-bishop want the journal so badly?" Kevin asked.

"Perhaps it holds the secret to the Madonna's bloody tears," Francois suggested.

"Or the secret to Lucienne and how she acquired her remarkable abilities," Kevin said.

"You know I just remembered something else. When the journal talked about that murdered witch, it mentioned something about her release," Oralia said.

"Do you remember her name?" Kevin asked.

"No, but I know the approximate date she would have been killed and I bet I can find it in the historical records at the Prado library," Oralia said.

"That might help, but it's Bruno's journal that we need to get a hold of," Kevin replied.

"Didn't Romero say he found the former librarians address?" Francois remembered. "Perhaps we should pay him a visit this afternoon."

"I'd still like to get a closer look at the cross that was used to murder Adela," Kevin said. "I've got a feeling it could tell us a lot."

"Forget about it," Francois replied, "there's no way Romero will give that up."

"Who knows, maybe God will speak to his heart," Kevin replied.

"God better have a loud voice for that cold heart," Francois snickered.

"If God wants something to happen, it will be done," the Reverend Father added.

"Which brings up another concern," Kevin said, "what do you think happened to Liz?"

"Liz seems to have the ability to show up at the most apropos times," Francois noted. "I wouldn't doubt that we see her before the day is out."

"I can only hope you're right my friend," Kevin replied. "What do you say we go find that librarian?"

"You know Romero will insist on going with us," Francois said.

"Like that hasn't happened to me a couple of times already," Kevin replied with a smile.

"I'll see what I can find out about the witch," Oralia replied.

"I wish I could be more of a help, but I need to notify Adela's husband about her tragic death," the Reverend Father explained. "I will direct the monks to pray for your success and your safety."

"Thank you," Kevin replied.

"I think we should all meet back here before the processional tonight," Oralia suggested.

"That's a good idea," Kevin said. "I think Liz would look for us here first, and besides, I'd like to have a look around, once all of Romero's men are gone. Keep thinking about that journal, Oralia. Anything you can remember could be a big help."

"And I'll pray you are successful in finding Bruno Mancini's copy," Oralia replied. "Good luck!" Oralia leaned over and kissed Kevin on the cheek catching him by surprise then turned and hurried out the door.

"What was that all about?" Francois asked.

"I have no idea, but I thought it was the Frenchmen who always did the kissing," Kevin replied, causing Francois to grin. "What do you say we get Romero and go find that librarian."

"Sounds like a plan to me," Francois replied.

Oralia hid in the confessional until she saw Romero leave with Kevin and Francois.

"Sometimes you have to give God a hand," Oralia said softly.

She walked to the table where the forensics team had laid out the plastic bags containing the evidence they had collected. Without hesitation Oralia slid the bag containing the cross into her purse and headed out the sanctuary door.

"Father, forgive me, for I have sinned," Oralia began to confess.

CHAPTER TWENTY-ONE

"Faith"

"Lucia," Carlos gasped in surprise, as he walked into his living room and saw the Nephilim sitting in his favorite leather chair.

"I go by the name of Lucienne these days. You should know that," Lucienne scolded.

"Forgive me, but being such a student of history, I tend to remember you as the witch Bruno Mancini described in his journal, no offense intended," Carlos explained.

"None taken," Lucienne replied.

"To what do I owe the honor of your presence?" Carlos asked. "Are you here to thank me for recalling you from Tartarus this afternoon?"

"Why should I thank you for what is your sworn duty?" Lucienne replied.

"Forgive my insolence," he beseeched.

"How are the preparations coming for the auto de fe? You know our lord Satan is looking forward to tonight's processional of the guilty as well as their execution," Lucienne continued, ignoring his apology.

"The whores confessed last night while confined in the stocks," Carlos said. "The 'Seven' took pleasure in their suffering; although I regret to say that the confessions came quickly after only a mild blistering of their feet."

"And no doubt the 'Seven' took personal pleasures from the whores in the process," Lucienne smirked.

"This I cannot deny," Carlos replied.

"I certainly hope the guilty will be able to walk in the processional as the regulations demand," Lucienne said.

"The drugs we have given them will dull any pain they may have. They'll be able to walk," Carlos assured her.

"I certainly hope the effect of the painkiller is gone when it is time for the execution of their sentences," Lucienne said.

"You worry too much," Carlos replied. "All will go as planned."

"Will it? Where is the Libro de Reglas you are to carry in tonight's processional?" Lucienne asked.

"There on the table next to my candle. Why do you ask?" Carlos replied, sensing something was not right.

"What does the book of regulations say about a brother of the society failing in his duties?" Lucienne asked.

"You know as well as I that death is the only punishment for any member of the 'Seven of the Cross' found to have harmed the society in any manner," Carlos quipped.

"Wouldn't you agree that revealing oneself as one of the 'Seven' would jeopardize the entire society?" Lucienne asked.

"Of course, but none of the 'Seven' are foolish enough to ever do such a thing," Carlos replied. "It's unthinkable."

"I would've thought so," Lucienne said.

"Stop playing games," Carlos demanded. "What are you getting at?"

"You failed me today," Lucienne accused, "and in failing me you've failed the society."

"How did I fail you? I killed the secretary and left the cross as instructed. I called you back from the darkness just like you taught us to do," Carlos replied, beginning to sound desperate.

"Yes, but you were seen and you weren't seen," Lucienne replied.

"If this is your idea of a joke, I fail to see the humor in it," Carlos replied. "What do you mean I was seen and then not seen?"

"A woman walked in on you while you were in the secretary's office," Lucienne began.

"Yes, but she never saw my face," Carlos said.

"No, but she did recognize your clothing as that of a participant in the processional," Lucienne replied.

"There are hundreds who wear such clothing and who will participate in the processional. That means nothing," Carlos insisted.

"Why did you use the secret passage in the mausoleum rather than the front door when you entered and left?" Lucienne asked.

"Obviously, I didn't want to be seen. We all know there are cameras that monitor the entrances to the Templo Eucarístico," Carlos explained.

"So, you admit that you weren't seen," Lucienne said.

"That's why I used the catacombs," Carlos replied, exasperated by the Lucienne's convoluted logic.

"You see, that's were the problem lies. You were seen in the office but, you weren't seen leaving the templo. Therefore, they now know there is another way in and out of the templo. And by calling me forth into the mausoleum, they are convinced the secret passage is somewhere in there," Lucienne explained.

"It's a simple matter to throw in some old bones and lock the back of the crypt that serves as the passageway. Even if they're able to open the correct crypt, it'll look no different from the rest," Carlos explained.

"That's an excellent idea," Lucienne said. "However, there's one other problem."

"And that is?"

"You failed to kill the secretary, Oralia Toribio," Lucienne replied.

"That's impossible! I buried the cross in her skull and drained her blood into the trashcan. I assure you she was dead. Besides had she not been, I would've been unable to summons you back from Tartarus," Carlos explained.

"That's true. Had you not killed that woman I wouldn't be standing here. Unfortunately, the woman you killed wasn't Oralia Toribio."

Carlos felt his lungs collapse as a freezing chill engulfed his body as though he had plunged into a frozen lake.

"What are you doing to me?" Carlos wheezed.

"I'm fulfilling the regulations, "Lucienne replied. "Your actions betrayed the society and have put the secrecy of the 'Seven of the Cross' in jeopardy. You must die."

"That can't be," Carlos whispered.

"Already the police are on their way to your apartment," Lucienne replied. "But be assured, your death will not be in vain. Your passing will serve me and the society more than you can imagine."

A pounding on the door startled Lucienne.

"Carlos Hernandez, this is the Cuerpo Nacional, we need to speak with you," Inspector Romero's voice boomed.

"You're too early," Lucienne whispered.

Carlos tried to call out but his lungs felt like rocks.

"You won't need this anymore," Lucienne said yanking the key to the torture chamber door from the gold chain around Carlos' neck. Links from the chain scattered across the floor.

"You've served us well in the past," she said, as she placed her hand on his chest, freezing his heart and other organs solid. Her hand print burned through his suit leaving the image of her hand branded into his chest.

Lucienne grabbed the Libro de Reglas from the table.

"As our god Satan commands, I have sacrificed a body so his servant, Elizabeth, can return and his will be done," Lucienne prayed. Lucienne grabbed a Tiffany lamp and hurled it towards the front door where it shattered with a tremendous clamor. By the time the last pieces of the pricey artifact hit the floor, she was out the back door of the apartment.

۶   ۶   ۶

Her eyes had begun to adjust to the darkness, although there was very little to see. The air was stifling and hot. She tried not to move, for with every step came the billowing clouds of the red chalky dust that covered the ground. Her lungs ached from the fine powder that now coated her nasal membranes and throat making breathing nearly impossible. Then again, Liz wondered, was breathing even necessary in such a horrid place?

Liz knew that eventually the guardian would realize something had happened to her and assume she had returned or was taken to Tartarus. At least that was her hope. But then again, what would he do, or for that matter, what could he do? It's not as if a guardian angel will go out and murder someone in order to summon you forth. That's just not going to happen.

"No, if God wants me to intervene on his behalf, then He will provide a way," Liz decided, and began to pray. She got down on her knees and put her hands straight out in front of her, then began. *"Our Father which art in heaven, hallowed be thy name, thy Kingdom come, thy will be done on earth as..."* but before she could finish her hands began to fade into translucency and she could feel every cell of her body being torn apart. Within a few seconds all that remained was a disturbed cloud of dust gently floating in the vastness.

The transition from Tartarus back to Earth left Liz dazed. The brightness of the light temporarily blinded her and she tripped tumbling atop Carlos' frozen body.

"Lucienne," Liz cried. "What evil is this?"

She moved from atop his body and placed her hand on his chest to see if she could possibly save him. At that exact moment, gun in hand, Romero burst through the door with Kevin and Francois right behind.

"Don't move," Romero shouted. "Show me your hands and stand up slowly," he ordered.

"Liz," Kevin shouted rushing towards her, "are you alright? What happened to you at the hotel and how did you get here?"

"Step away from her Mr. Bridges," Romero ordered.

Kevin did. He knew it wasn't wise to argue with anyone holding a gun.

"Now step away from the body, Ms. Purdue," Romero ordered. "Mr. Bridges, see if he's still alive."

Kevin reached for Carlos' neck to check for a pulse, but quickly withdrew his hand.

"What's the problem?" Romero asked.

"He's frozen," Kevin replied. He touched Carlos's hand and found it not nearly as cold. As he tried to find a pulse, the ring on Carlos' finger slipped off. Kevin caught it before it clattered onto the floor and cuffed it in his hand to hide it from Romero.

"He's dead," Kevin said as he gently laid the arm back on the floor.

"I told you Liz couldn't be trusted," Romero said. "This time we caught her in the act."

"Don't be absurd," Kevin responded, "Feel the body. It's frozen solid. There's no way she could've done that."

Romero walked over continuing to keep his gun aimed at Liz's head. He knelt down to feel the body and drew his hand back quickly. "He's so cold it burned my hand. Look at his chest. She was touching his chest when we came in. Her hand print is burned through his suit and onto the skin."

"Listen to what you are saying," Kevin said. "You actually believe Liz used her hand to freeze Carlos solid? How do you plan to write that up in your report?"

"I had nothing to do with his murder," Liz said. "I just arrived and found him on the floor. I was trying to revive him."

"Arrived from where?" Romero asked. We didn't see you come in. Is there a back door?"

"The back door is over here," Francois called out, "and it's open and very cold to the touch."

"Hold up the palms of your hands, I want too see if they have freeze burns," Romero ordered.

Liz raised her hands.

"See," Kevin said, "Had she touched him her hands would have been burned. Someone else had to have done this."

"The mysterious Lucienne, no doubt," Romero replied snidely. "Do you really expect me to believe that?"

"Do you really expect anyone to believe what you see here?" Francois said. "Remember, I too was a skeptic until I saw what happened in New York."

"I thought seeing the video in Paris would've convinced you," Kevin interjected.

"If we don't stop talking and get moving the other doctor will soon be dead," Liz said.

"And how would you know that?" Romero asked.

Liz paused and looked at Kevin. "I know because Lucienne told me," Liz blurted out.

"You talked to Lucienne?" Kevin asked in astonishment. "Where, When?"

"You wouldn't understand," Liz replied.

"If you expect me to believe you're innocent, you better try to make us understand," Romero threatened.

"I can't," Liz said softly.

"Then I'm afraid I'm going to have to place you under arrest," Romero replied. "Turn around slowly and put your hands behind your back."

Liz complied and stood quietly as Romero handcuffed her.

Kevin wandered over to where Francois was standing. "Try to find the journal," Kevin whispered, hoping he could trust Francois.

"Have a seat while we look around," Romero ordered Liz.

"Where do you think these pieces of gold chain are from?" Kevin said picking up several links.

"What are you doing? Put those back where you found them. This is a murder scene, you're not to touch or move anything. Don't you know anything about police work?" Romero ranted.

"They're from a necklace he had on," Liz said. "You can see the marks on his neck from it being ripped off. There must have been something important on that chain for Lucienne to go to all this trouble. Look at those links, that's a very unusual design."

"I said put those down," Romero ordered Kevin.

"All what trouble?" Kevin asked, as he slipped two of the links into his pocket.

"Her setting all this up, so you'd walk in on me standing over the body and think I murdered him. Believe me, she went to a lot of trouble and took a big risk to get me here," Liz explained.

"Look at this picture on the table," Francois said. "Looks like Carlos with a male companion. They are both wearing matching chains."

"Can you see what's on the chains?" Liz asked.

"Who's running this investigation anyway?" Romero said.

"I think I need both of you to clear out of this room until my forensic team arrives," Romero ordered.

Kevin nodded slightly to Francois and walked over to Liz, distracting Romero while Francois removed the picture from the table. He had already found what he believed was the journal and stuck it in his waist line at the small of his back.

"I'll wait in the hallway," Francois said.

"I need you out of here, too," Romero said to Kevin.

"At least let me talk with her for a minute before you take her in. What harm can that do?" Kevin replied.

"All right, but just until my back-up gets here," Romero said.

"What should we do?" Kevin whispered to Liz.

"You have to get me out of here," Liz replied. "If you don't, the doctor will die as will many others."

"How do you know all this? What did Lucienne tell you?" Kevin asked.

"Get me out of here and I'll tell you everything. It has something to do with a group called the 'Seven of the Cross', whatever that may mean."

"You don't know?" Kevin asked.

"I have an idea, but unless you get me out of here, we will all be in danger," Liz implored.

"I can't do it," Kevin replied. "I thought I trusted you, but now, I'm just not sure. When you disappeared at the hotel and then showed up here, with no explanation, my faith in you was shattered."

"You have to get me away from here and back to the templo. If not in me, you must have faith in God. Remember, faith is being sure of what we hope for and certain of what we do not see."

Kevin had never in his life been so flummoxed as to what he should do. He had to make a decision quickly for he could hear the wailing of police sirens approaching.

"Romero, you're a man of faith," Kevin said. "What does God say about faith?"

Romero stared at Kevin for a moment. "It's strange you should ask me that," Romero replied. "Hebrews 11:6, it's one of my favorite verses in the bible. *'Without faith it is impossible to please God, for he who comes to God must believe that He is and that He is a rewarder of those who diligently seek him'.*"

"Do you have that kind of faith?" Kevin asked.

"I told you before that I'm Catholic," Romero replied suspiciously.

"But do you really have the faith to believe that God will reward those who diligently seek him?" Kevin pressed.

"What are you getting at?" Romero asked.

"I'm asking you to have faith and believe in what Liz is telling us," Kevin asked.

"The verse says that we must have faith in God, not in the servants of the evil one," Romero replied, sharply.

"So now you believe that there are supernatural forces involved in this investigation? You admit that this is a battle between good and evil?" Kevin asked.

Romero didn't immediately answer.

"My faith tells me that Liz isn't a servant of Satan," Kevin said.

"I'm sorry but I don't share your faith," Romero asked.

"Then I ask for your forgiveness," Kevin replied.

"My forgive….," but before Romero could answer Kevin smashed his right fist into Romero's nose while using his left hand to twist the gun from his hand.

"Where are the keys to the handcuffs?" Kevin asked.

"I think you broke my nose," Romero yelled.

"We don't need the key," Liz replied moving her arms to allow the handcuffs to slide from her wrists to the floor.

"How did you do that?" Romero asked, while trying to stop the blood pouring from his nose.

"Sorry I had to hit you like that," Kevin said. "I hope someday you'll understand, but I believe in Liz and have faith in her goodness."

"You know you won't get away with this," Romero said.

"Inspector, try to find out all you can about a group called the 'Seven of the Cross'. I think they're behind much of the evil that is taking place here in Madrid," Liz said.

"Now if you'd kindly move into the bathroom," Kevin said. "I'm sure there's something in there to help with the bleeding. I'm afraid it's necessary to lock you in, but it sounds like your back-up is almost here and I'm sure if you yell loud enough Francois will hear you and come let you out."

"You'll never get away with this," Romero warned.

"For everyone's sake, you better pray we do," Liz replied.

CHAPTER TWENTY-TWO

"Loyalty"

"So, where do you think they went?" Oralia asked.

"I've no idea. I was standing in the hallway when suddenly I heard this loud pounding and yelling. I ran into the apartment and unlocked the bathroom door. Inspector Romero was mad as hell, ranting and raving about how Kevin locked him in the bathroom and escaped with Liz," Francois explained to Oralia and the Reverend Father.

"What did Romero do?" Reverend Father asked.

"At first, I thought he was going to handcuff me, but he soon calmed down and realized I had nothing to do with them getting away," Francois continued.

"He did issue a bulletin to all metropolitan police to look for them, but I don't know what good it will do since he had no picture of them. The police aren't going to stop every couple on the street and ask them to identify themselves," Francois said.

"I'm sure it won't be long till they do have a photo to distribute," Oralia added.

"That's true," Francois answered.

"Do you believe Liz killed this librarian?" Reverend Father asked.

"Not a chance," Francois replied. "She was somehow set-up to make it look like she did it, just like what Lucienne tried to do in New York."

"I bet they come back here," Oralia said.

"Romero already has police watching the front and back entrances to the templo and I'm sure the hotel is being watched," Francois said. "But I agree with you, I think they'll try to make it back here."

"I'm almost afraid to ask," Oralia said, "but were you able to find Bruno Mancini's journal?"

"I believe this is what you're looking for," Francois said pulling the journal from his waist.

"I assume Inspector Romero knows you took the journal," Reverend Father said.

Francois didn't reply, he only grinned at the Reverend Father.

"Forgive him, Lord," Reverend Father prayed, then crossed himself.

"Kevin also told me to take this photo that was sitting on a table. It shows the librarian and another man. What's interesting are the identical gold chains they are wearing. Look at the pendant; it looks like a number seven. Does that mean anything to either of you?" Francois asked.

"They both are dressed the same," Reverend Father noted.

Oralia stopped thumbing through the journal and looked at the photograph. "Didn't Elisa say the man she saw today was wearing white gloves and a fancy suit?" Oralia asked. "I'd like to show her this photo."

"I see no reason why she shouldn't see it," Francois replied.

"I'll go find her," Oralia said, handing the journal back to Francois.

"Is it the right journal?" Francois asked.

"It's almost identical to the one I remember looking at as a child," Oralia said, as tears began to fill her eyes.

"I'll go find Elisa," Reverend Father said.

"Thank you," Oralia replied. "It reminds me of the wonderful days I spent with my grandfather when I was young and how angry I was when he died. I can't help but blame my cousin. That man has no right to even call himself a Catholic let alone acting-bishop. He is evil."

"That's a strong statement," Francois replied.

"But a well-deserved one," Oralia responded.

"Reverend Father said you wanted to see me," Elisa said coming through the door. "He said to forgive him for leaving you without saying goodbye, but he just realized how late it was getting and he had to prepare for this evening's Mass and processional."

"I wanted you to have a look at a photo I found," Francois said, handing it to her.

"That's him! That's the man I saw today talking to Adela," Elisa shrieked.

"Which one?" Francois asked. "This one, I recognize the hair and that's the exact suit and gloves he was wearing. Who is he? We should contact the inspector at once."

"He's the librarian from the Prado. He was murdered in his apartment this afternoon," Francois said.

"Goodness gracious," Elisa replied, crossing herself. "I guess I won't need to go with the police and look for him in tonight's processional then."

"No, I think you should still go and see if you recognize this other man in the photo," Oralia explained. "But Inspector Romero doesn't want anyone to know the librarian was murdered. Not even his own officers. He thinks there is a snitch in his department and he is going to use this to try to ferret out the culprit, so you mustn't tell anyone, do you understand?"

"Yes, of course," Elisa said, "I'll not tell a soul."

Francois and Oralia remained quiet until Elisa left the room.

"Lord, forgive me for I have sinned," Oralia prayed.

"I think the Lord can overlook a little white lie," Francois assured her.

"I hope you're right," Oralia replied. "But I'm afraid it's more than just a little white lie."

"What are you talking about?" Francois asked.

"I liberated an item from the crime scene here at the church," Oralia confessed, walking over to her desk drawer.

"I was going to give it to Kevin, but now I'm not sure what to do with it," she explained as she pulled out the cross that had been embedded in Adela's skull.

"Romero will go ballistic when he finds out the cross is missing," Francois said.

"Should I call him and give it back?" Oralia asked.

"Hell, no!" Francois blurted out. "If you did that we'd both end up in jail. Just leave it in the drawer and we can pretend we know nothing about it. Besides, I agree with you, if Kevin returns, he's going to want to have a look at it."

"I know it's not right, but I actually feel better about having taken it now that I know you're guilty of doing the same thing at the librarian's apartment," Oralia confessed.

"Let's hope Kevin and Liz show up so our crimes aren't for naught," Francois replied.

୨୦   ୨୦   ୨୦

"How did you get out of those handcuffs?" Kevin asked as they ran down the steps into the subway tunnel system.

"I haven't been completely honest with you," Liz began. "I'm a Nephilim, the same as Lucienne."

"I thought you said Nephilim were demons that God allowed to live to lead people astray," Kevin replied. "Bad angels who God decided to punish."

"I said fallen angels, not bad angels," Liz replied.

"Is there a difference?" Kevin asked. "Hurry, the train is about to leave." The two rushed on board just as the doors began to close.

"I think there is. My father was a rebel angel who came to earth to tutor the human race in righteousness. Unfortunately, he and many other of these angels became consumed by their desire for human females."

"I remember this from the Book of Genesis," Kevin replied.

"There's very little information in Genesis about what happened," she replied. "The Book of Enoch explains it in detail."

"That's not part of the Bible, at least not the Bible I know. Tell me what happened."

"The unbridled lust of these angels led to a race of hybrid offspring called Nephilim. God was not the least bit pleased by this so he cast these so-called 'fallen angels' into Tartarus to await the final judgment."

"That still doesn't explain how or why you're here now," Kevin said.

"Many Nephilim abused their powers so God flooded the earth destroying them all," Liz continued.

"Noah's flood," Kevin interrupted.

"God's flood," Liz corrected, "And, like I told you before, ten percent of the disembodied spirits of these Nephilim were allowed to remain as demons."

"But you're human," Kevin insisted.

"Satan found a way for some of us to take human form in order to wreak havoc and tempt the human race into doing evil. However, in order to take human form, we had to first agree to go to Tartarus. Once there, we had to convince a demon to coerce a human into murdering another human and summon us forth. We then would be free to wander the earth in the shell of the murdered human to spread the evils of Satan."

"So far you haven't said much to reassure me of your good intentions," Kevin said.

"I think that even a demon, or a Nephilim like myself, is capable of free will. If I choose to live a righteous life perhaps God in his mercy will look kindly upon me at the final judgment."

Kevin wasn't sure what to believe. His heart told him to have faith, but his head told him that Liz was totally out of her mind.

"What happened to you back at the hotel?" Kevin asked. "You just seemed to disappear. Is that one of your 'powers'?"

"A Nephilim cannot disappear and reappear at will. However, we can at anytime choose to return to Tartarus," Liz explained. "When I entered the hallway at the hotel I saw Lucienne. I saw her make the leap to Tartarus and decided to follow and confront her."

"You returned to Tartarus?" Kevin said.

"Yes, it was a difficult decision, but I had to face Lucienne," Liz replied.

"I'm a little confused here," Kevin said. "If you and Lucienne returned to Tartarus, then how did you both get back here. You said someone had to be murdered and that the murderer would have to summon you forth."

"That's correct," Liz said. "I don't know who summoned forth Lucienne, but she left Tartarus only minutes after we arrived," Liz said.

"That means Lucienne had prearranged for someone to be murdered. That's why Adela was killed in the church. When you return, where do you return to?" Kevin asked.

"We return to where we were summoned from. In my case, Lucienne murdered that man in the apartment and then summoned me forth, hoping to place the blame for his murder on me."

"So that's why Lucienne suddenly appeared in the templo's mausoleum. Whoever killed Adela went into the mausoleum before summoning Lucienne forth. Why is it the acolytes didn't see the man who murdered Adela before Lucienne appeared?"

"The passage from Tartarus back to earth takes the same length of time that passes between the murder and the summoning forth. That's if you are expecting it. I was summoned almost immediately after Lucienne killed the man. Her summons may have come several minutes after the murder was committed, giving the murderer plenty of time to get away and to guarantee Lucienne wouldn't suddenly appear at the scene of the murder."

"How did she know we were going to be at the librarian's apartment?" Kevin asked.

"I didn't even know he was a librarian," Liz replied, "but it seems obvious that someone who knew you were coming passed the message along to Lucienne."

"It has to be Inspector Romero," Kevin said. "I can't believe anyone from the church would do such a thing."

"I don't think Romero would do so purposely," Liz replied. "It is more likely his comisario or someone else at the Cuerpo Nacional who passes the information along when the inspector reports to his boss. Why were you there in the first place?"

"The dead man was Carlos Hernandez, former librarian of the Prado. We went there to try to get a journal written by Bruno Mancini. The journal may explain why the Madonna cries the bloody tears, but it also may tell us the significance of the cross we found sticking out of Adela's head," Kevin explained. "We better get off here, Romero will have his men watching the subways before long."

"One more exit," Liz said.

"Where are we going?" Kevin asked.

"I saw an address inscribed on the inside of that ring you slipped off the dead man's finger. I'm guessing whoever made the ring also made that chain and pendant. I think it's worth investigating."

"You were able to see that from clear across the room?"

"Incredible vision, one of the benefits of being a Nephilim," Liz explained.

Kevin wasn't so sure.

"Does this ring have anything to do with the 'Seven of the Cross', you mentioned back at the apartment?" Kevin asked

"It has everything to do with it," Liz replied.

"I thought we needed to go so we could stop Lucienne from murdering the other doctor," Kevin replied.

"We do," Liz replied, "but I have a feeling that we really need to speak to the jeweler. He may prove to be a big help."

"We're going to need more help than that," Kevin replied. "We're going to need a little help from our friend's back at the templo."

"We'll also need to find out exactly where the doctor is," Liz replied.

"Shouldn't Interpol be able to help us with that information?" Kevin asked.

"They can if Romero hasn't already contacted them," Liz replied. "Once we're back above ground, I'll make a call.

Here's our stop. You go first and I'll follow so it doesn't look like we're together."

"Good idea," Kevin replied, "but I think you should go first."

"What, you don't trust me?" Liz said with a smile.

Liz exited the car and Kevin followed a few seconds later, making sure to stay a short distance behind. There were no police at the platform and none waiting when they reached the street. When Kevin caught up to Liz, she was just ending a phone conversation.

"Who was that?" Kevin asked.

"Interpol, they're accessing the Cuerpo Nacional data bases to see what information they have on the doctor's whereabouts. We should know something by this evening," Liz explained.

"That's good news. I'd call the templo, but I'm sure Romero will already have the phone tapped," Kevin said.

"And you can be sure he'll have the templo and your hotel staked out," Liz replied.

"If we're going back to the templo, we're going to have to figure out a way to sneak in," Kevin said.

"I'll leave that part up to you," Liz replied.

"I haven't spent much time in Madrid, where exactly are we headed?" Kevin asked.

"The address on the ring says Calle Bordadores 25. It's near the Plaza Mayor, just a few blocks from your hotel and the Templo Eucarístico. This is old Madrid," Liz explained.

Kevin suddenly stopped in front of an old building with a big sign that said Navaret.

"This is Calle Bordadores 5, we want 25," Liz said.

"Yes, but this store gives me an idea for getting us back into the templo," Kevin explained.

"Give me the ring and the gold chain links. I'll go ahead and see what I can find out from the jeweler while you do what you have to do here," Liz explained.

"I think I'd better go with you," Kevin said.

"No, I think it would be best if I went alone. Not having another man around makes it easier to use my feminine charms to get the information I need," Liz explained.

"I don't like it, but I don't doubt your abilities," Kevin replied, handing her the ring and chain links.

"There's a tapas bar on the opposite side of the plaza. We'll meet there. I could do with a bite to eat and a glass of sangria," Liz said. "And whatever you do, don't use your credit card. Romero would find us in a minute."

"Thanks for the warning. Just be careful," Kevin said.

"Don't worry I'm not planning on leaving you," Liz responded.

"It's never planned," Kevin said, "it just seems to happen."

"Not this time," Liz replied and hurried down the street.

CHAPTER TWENTY-THREE

"Commitment"

"**I'm sorry Miss,** but we are closing early today for the processional," the haggard looking man explained.

"Are you Mr. Jiminez?" Liz asked. "This is Jiminez Jewelers isn't it?"

"Yes, just as the sign says," he replied impatiently, pointing to the sign, "but I'm closed."

"Please, I need to replace a gold chain," Liz said.

"Come back tomorrow, I'll be happy to sell you a chain," he replied, continuing to lock the door.

"Perhaps, if you just have a look at one of the broken links," Liz insisted, and opened her hand revealing the unique link.

"I'm sorry but you'll just…,' the jeweler stopped in mid-sentence when he saw the link.

"I'll just what?" Liz said, seeing the man visibly upset at the sight of the chain link.

"You'll…, maybe…, there is another jeweler just down the street, I'm sure he'll be able to help you with a chain," the jeweler stammered.

"Yes, but can he help me with this ring," Liz said pulling the ring from a pocket.

The jeweler looked around to see if anyone else had seen the ring. "Please, come inside quickly."

The jeweler led Liz into the back room. "Where did you get this?" the jeweler asked.

"It was given to me," Liz replied.

"Don't lie to me," the jeweler said, "Tell me who gave you this ring."

"First you need to answer a few of my questions," Liz ordered.

"I think you had better give me that ring," the jeweler said, "before I call the police."

"I am the police," Liz replied, showing her Interpol identification.

The jeweler turned white. "I've made seven other rings identical to that one," he admitted.

"Seven total or seven others?" Liz asked.

"Seven others counting the one that was picked up this morning," he replied.

What about the gold chain and pendant?" Liz asked.

"It's an amulet, not a pendant. Each contains a very rare emerald. I originally made seven of those as well, but last week, I was asked to make another," the jeweler replied.

"Who ordered...," Liz began, but was interrupted when the bell rang signifying someone had come in the door.

"I thought I'd locked the door," the jeweler said. "Excuse me for a moment," he said as he left the back room.

It took only a few seconds for Liz to realize something wasn't right.

"Mr. Jiminez," Liz called walking out of the backroom.

The room was empty but Liz could sense that something was wrong. When the police cars skidded to a stop in front of the store, she had no doubt.

Kevin had finished his shopping and had just walked out the front door of Navaret carrying his purchase, when a speeding car raced by just missing him. He leaped back into the doorway as a second car followed directly behind the first. It took him a moment to realize that both of these cars were police, as were two others screeching to a halt in front of the jewelry store.

"I should've never let her out of my sight," Kevin swore under his breath.

He watched for a brief moment, just as any curious onlooker would do, then, casually strolled to the tapas bar where he and Liz had agreed to meet. He was relieved to see that none of the police were Romero, but Kevin was sure Romero would be there soon and it would be best if he wasn't around when Romero showed up.

"I hope there's a back door," Kevin said softly.

As Kevin continued to watch, he was encouraged that none of the officers brought out Liz in handcuffs. That encouragement turned to concern when an ambulance pulled up behind the police cars and the attendants appeared to be in no hurry to render aide.

"Your sangria, sir," the waitress said sitting the glass on the table. "Would you like to order now?"

"Not quite yet, thank you," Kevin replied.

The waitress smiled and moved on to the table of American tourists that had just sat down.

"I bet it was a robbery gone bad," one of them conjectured.

"Do you think he was shot?" another asked.

"No, I didn't see any blood, but he sure looked white," the other replied.

Kevin caught the attention of one of the tourists. "What happened over there?"

"Someone robbed the jewelry store," one of them answered.

"We don't know that for sure," another piped in.

"I heard the ambulance driver say that the jeweler was dead, though," another one said.

"Did they catch the murderer?" Kevin asked, but none of the tourists knew or was willing to venture a guess.

It had been almost fifteen minutes since Kevin had entered the tapas bar and still no Liz. He decided he'd better leave before Romero showed up and they began to campus the vicinity looking for witnesses. He put a five Euro note on the table and headed out the door.

"Sir, sir," the waitress called loudly, causing everyone to turn to see what the problem was.

Kevin didn't turn to respond.

"Sir, you forgot your parcel," the waitress yelled.

"Damn," Kevin whispered, then turned around smiling. Everyone in the bar was staring at him. "Thank you," Kevin said, taking the package from the waitress.

"And thank you for the generous tip, sir," the waitress replied.

Kevin just nodded and headed out the door, turning up a side street away from the jewelry store. When he reached the corner, a new black Mercedes CLS 550 pulled in front of him and the driver got out.

"Please get in the car," the driver said mechanically.

Kevin hesitated just for a moment before he realized that Liz must be in the backseat behind the darkened windows.

Kevin opened the door, "I'm so glad…" but he stopped when he saw no one in the back seat and hesitated getting in.

The driver was already behind the wheel. "Please, Mr. Bridges, we must hurry," the driver said in the same mechanical monotone.

Kevin knew he needed to get out of the area fast and realized Liz must have arranged for the car to pick him up, so he climbed into the back.

Before he even closed the door, the driver was speeding away.

"Where's Liz?" Kevin asked, but received no reply.

The car had gone no more than three blocks when it suddenly pulled to the side of the street.

"What's the matter," Kevin said, but immediately the back door opened and Liz jumped in. Before Kevin could react, the car shot off again.

"What happened in the jewelry store?" Kevin asked. "You had me really worried."

"I was set up, again," Liz replied.

"By who?" Kevin asked.

"At first, I suspected you," Liz replied. "I've been watching you in the tapas bar for the last ten minutes, trying to decide if it was you who called Romero."

"Why in the world would you think that?" Kevin asked.

"Who else knew I was in the jewelry store?" Liz replied. "But I couldn't imagine you'd be involved with Lucienne."

"Lucienne, what does she have to do with this?"

"I believe it was Lucienne who killed the jeweler before he could tell me anything," Liz replied. "She must've followed us from the librarian's apartment, guessed that we were heading to the jeweler's shop and contacted the police."

"You really believe Lucienne would go to such extremes?" Kevin asked.

"I know she would go to such extremes just to make me suffer," Liz replied. "My concern was if you were somehow involved."

Kevin was hurt by the distrust Liz obviously had, but realized that he too had distrusted her when he first saw the police cars. He thought she'd once more used a diversion to slip away.

"How did you get away?" Kevin asked.

"There was a back door, I came out on the next street," Liz said, hoping Kevin wouldn't see through her lie.

Kevin knew that if there was a back door it most likely led to a courtyard and not the next block, but he wasn't about to challenge her. They'd gotten away and she hadn't left him as he had feared she would.

"So how do you plan on getting us inside the templo?" Liz asked.

"It won't be a problem," Kevin replied, "but first I think we should find a good spot to watch the processional. Everyone from the templo will either be participating or watching, so there's no need to return there yet."

"That's where the jeweler told me he was headed when I first arrived at the store," Liz said. "Before he was killed, he did say that he had made seven of the rings and seven of the chains and pendants for a customer."

"The "Seven of the Cross'?" Kevin asked.

"I don't know," Liz replied, "but it does make sense. Another thing he did tell me was that he made an eighth ring and amulet just last week."

"I guess someone knew the librarian wasn't going to be around for long," Kevin said.

"It would seem so," Liz replied. "Here take these, I don't need them." She handed the ring and chain link back to Kevin.

"How did Lucienne get mixed up with this group?" Kevin asked.

"I'm not positive, but I think it started right around the time the Madonna of the Templo Eucarístico last cried," Liz speculated, "But at that time she didn't go by Lucienne. She called herself Lucia de la Cruz, Light of the Cross."

"I bet that was the name of the witch Oralia spoke of in her ancestor's journal. Perhaps Bruno's journal will tell us more than we think," Kevin said.

Liz's blackberry chimed softly and she turned away from Kevin to answer.

"I know where we can find the other doctor," Liz replied. "We'll leave first thing in the morning, but for now, I agree that there is much we can learn at the processional."

After all Liz had said and all Kevin had witnessed, he still didn't know quite what to believe. Much of it was too supernatural and unfathonable. He was a very Christian man who believed in miracles and God's unlimited powers, but he also was an investigator who depended on the facts. The trouble was, he wasn't sure what was fact and what was fiction. And the more Liz told him, the more that line blurred.

CHAPTER TWENTY-FOUR

"Corruption"

"It's my duty to report that Señor Hernandez was found to have breached our Libro de Reglas and brought unwanted attention to our society," Toribio explained.

"He must die," the five other men said in unison.

"Our 'Light of the Cross' has already seen to it," Toribio beamed.

"Praise the 'Light'," one of the men replied, as the others mumbled in agreement.

"The 'Light' has given to me the Libro de Reglas which Carlos was to have carried in the auto de fe. In his stead the newest member to the 'Seven of the Cross' the honorable Gabriel Arciga of the Council of Ministers shall carry the book," Bishop Toribio announced.

The five other men gathered in the private El Corte Inglés dining room applauded vigorously as their newest member entered the dining room. They already knew Carlos was to die, the 'Light' had predicted it. They also knew who his replacement was to be. That had been decided during hours of private discussions. There had been several possible candidates. A surprising number of men seemed to share their beliefs, but few possessed what they considered the courage to fulfill the destiny given to them by the "Light".

What they considered courage, most would consider a macabre pleasure derived from sadism.

In an abbreviated ceremony, kept short due to the impending auto de fe, Señor Arciga was presented with his ring and gold chain which held the amulet that was the key to the torture chamber entrance. He was also entrusted with the Libro de Reglas.

"It shall be your duty to carry our sacred book that contains our rules and history as given to us by the 'Light'," Toribio explained.

"When will I meet the 'Light'?" Arciga asked.

"You've already met her," Toribio replied. "It was through her that we first discovered that you possessed fervor for and delighted in the perverse and darker side of human nature."

"I don't understand," Arciga said.

"The 'Light' was once a victim of one of your sadistic rampages," Toribio replied.

"How can that be? I made sure none that pleasured me ever survived," Arciga insisted.

"You cannot extinguish the 'Light'," Toribio replied. "You may have killed the flesh but the 'Light' can always be summoned forth from the darkest reaches of hell. In time you too will learn how to summon her forth."

Toribio turned to the five other members. "It's time to gather the accused, but first a toast."

One of the men opened a cabinet and removed a crystal bottle full of a green liquid and poured it into seven glasses.

Toribio grabbed two glasses and handed one to Arciga. "This absinthe is made from a recipe we found in the journal of Bruno Mancini. Monks created this divine wormwood almost a hundred years before the Swiss made the claim. Gentleman," Toribio said quieting the room. "Tonight, is our night. This night belongs to the 'Light' and the 'Seven of the Cross', but we must remember who has made this possible. Hail Satan!" Toribio shouted.

"Hail Satan," the six other men yelled in return, and they all chugged the glasses full of the emerald liquid.

Immediately following the toast, four of the men entered the private elevator reserved exclusively for the use of the senior manager of El Corte Inglés. One of the men placed his fist against the elevator controls, inserting his ring into the matching indentation which allowed access to a sublevel of the building known only to the "Seven of the Cross" and the two remaining Japanese engineers who designed and built the elevator and secret room.

"Señor Diaz, are the shrines prepared for the execution?" Toribio asked.

"I watched as the laborers we hired to place them in the Plaza Mayor set them up," Diaz replied. "Don't concern yourself. All will go just as we planned."

"Make sure everyone knows their assignments, it must be done just as the Libro de Reglas ordains," Toribio reminded him.

"It will be a spectacular ending to our first auto de fe," Diaz assured him.

"The first of many," Toribio replied, "but I'm somewhat concerned about the investigator from the Vatican and the Interpol agent, I want no surprises."

"And there shall be none. I'm aware that they are still not in custody, but I've ordered Inspector Romero to use all resources necessary to capture them. It's only a matter of time."

I've no reason to believe otherwise," Toribio replied, "I've complete faith in the ability of the Cuerpo Nacional. Now, please forgive me, for I must leave to attend the Mass that precedes the processional and our auto de fe. I'll look for you in the plaza at the end of the processional."

"It shall be a memorable night," Arciga said.

"A night when the 'Seven of the Cross' fulfills its destiny and Satan begins his reign over Madrid," Diaz exclaimed.

"And the 'Light' shall shine upon us all," Toribio replied.

୬ଡ଼   ୬ଡ଼   ୬ଡ଼

"Peace be with you," Toribio pronounced as he made the sign of the cross.

"And also, with you," the congregation replied.

"I'd like everyone to now join us for the first night processional of the Fiesta de San Martín," the acting-bishop commanded.

The Reverend Father stood from his seat behind the acting-bishop. "And please, everyone pray for the safe return of Bishop Castillo."

"Amen!" Oralia said loud enough for her cousin to hear, causing him to turn and glare at her.

"So that's your cousin. He doesn't look anything like you," Francois joked.

"It's the robes. If I was wearing a mitra pretiosa you couldn't tell us apart," Oralia replied, causing Elisa to giggle.

"A what?" Francois asked.

"A mitre, you know, that fancy hat that the bishop wears," Oralia replied, disappointed that Francois didn't get the joke.

"I guess we're heading outside," Francois noted as he and the two women inched along, caught up in the throng of worshipers heading for the exit. "Any suggestions as to where we should view this spectacle?"

"It's not a spectacle," Oralia insisted, "Catholics take these processionals very seriously here in Madrid."

"Just exactly what is this processional for anyway?" Francois asked.

"It's to celebrate the Fiesta de San Martín," she replied.

"Your cousin said that, but what does the festival actually celebrate?" Francois persisted. "I know you're not honoring the San Martín who liberated Argentina from Spain."

"Of course not, he wasn't a saint," Elisa interjected. "Nor are we honoring San Martín de Porres. He was a saint, but he wasn't canonized until 1962. We're celebrating San Martín Caballero, the Patron Saint of those who hope strangers will aid them," Elisa continued to explain.

"How did he become a saint?" Francois asked.

"He was a Roman centurion who one day came upon a near-naked beggar on the road. He cut his cloak in half and gave it to the beggar. That night he had a dream in which the beggar appeared as Jesus, so he quit the army and became a monk. He was eventually appointed as the Bishop of Tours in France. I'm surprised you've never heard of him," Elisa said.

"I've never been much for religious cults," Francois replied, infuriating Elisa, who turned to try to walk away but was unable to navigate through the crowd.

"Christianity is not a cult," Oralia huffed.

"This cathedral is huge compared to the templo," Francois noted, realizing he had raised the ire of both Elisa and Oralia. "And everything looks so new."

"That's because it is new. Almudena was completed in 1993," Oralia replied.

"Yeah, but they probably started building it three hundred years ago," Francois replied, cynically.

"Actually, only one hundred and twenty-five years ago," Oralia replied, sheepishly, "But they only completed the crypts back then. They really didn't start building seriously until after World War Two."

"Wow!" Francois exclaimed as they walked out the door. "Look at all the people."

"Several hundred more will join in as the processional moves through the streets," Oralia said.

"I'll see you two later," Elisa remarked, "I see the inspector coming this way."

"Remember, don't mention anything about the librarian," Oralia warned.

"Don't worry, I won't," Elisa assured them as she headed to meet Inspector Romero.

"Why don't we go back to the templo and watch as it passes by there," Francois said.

"It doesn't go by there," Oralia replied. "They'd have to close down the Gran Via for a couple of hours for that to happen. It heads up Calle de Bailén to the monastery then meanders through the side streets headed back towards the Plaza Mayor. Once everyone is inside the plaza the different groups show off the shrines they carried and several bands entertain the participants. It usually takes a couple of hours."

"Why don't we beat the crowd and try to find a seat at the plaza, I could go for a glass of wine," Francois said.

"Don't you think we should try to find Kevin and Liz?" Oralia replied.

"I think there's a better chance of them finding us. We just need to be some place where that can happen and I think the Plaza Mayor is as good a place as any," he explained. "And if not, after the processional, we'll go back to the templo and wait."

Oralia didn't care much for Francois' plan, but lacking any ideas of her own, decided to go along with his suggestion.

൴   ൴   ൴

"Have you seen anyone who looks like the man you saw in the office today?" Inspector Romero asked Elisa.

"No, no one yet," she replied.

"Any idea where Francois might be?" Romero asked.

"I saw him and Oralia together leaving the cathedral after the Mass," she replied. "They headed down Calle de Alcala. I bet they wanted to get a good seat so they could watch the conclusion of the processional."

"You by chance didn't talk to Francois when he returned to the templo today did you?" Romero asked.

Elisa had a hard time hiding her guilt. "Oh look," she said, "here comes the bishop. That means the Reverend Father won't be far behind. That's strange."

"What's strange?" Romero asked turning to look at the processional.

"I gave the bishop a purple candle to carry. That's the color required for this processional. And why is that man carrying a green cross. That doesn't make any sense. Wait a minute... that looks like the other man in the photo Francois showed me."

Romero looked to see who Elisa was pointing to but only could see the green cross rising above the crowd. "Francois showed you a photograph?" Romero asked.

"I'm so bad at keeping a secret. God please forgive me," Elisa said crossing herself.

"Who was in the photo he showed you?" Romero asked.

"The man I saw in the office today, the one who killed Adela. You know that. Francois told me you found him dead in his apartment and said to keep it a secret," Elisa explained. "I'm not good at keeping secrets."

"And the other man?" Romero asked.

Liz took a careful look both directions. "I think you're…" she paused. "Isn't that Francois and Oralia sitting over there?"

"Let's join them," Kevin said moving ahead without hesitation.

༄ ༄ ༄

"Here comes the cross of jurisdiction," Oralia explained. "That means the acting bishop is coming and all these candle bearers are parishioners from the Cathedral Almudena. The Reverend Father and the group from the Templo Eucarístico will be coming along later."

"What's the cross of jurisdiction?" Francois asked.

"It's a cross specifically made for processionals. I guess it's like any other cross, but it's just on a long stick so you can hold it in the air. That one belongs to the bishop. It's always the first cross in any processional in the Bishop's metropolitan, that is, as long as he is in the processional."

"Him or his replacement, I would assume," Francois added, trying to get Oralia to talk more about her cousin.

"All the parishes have their own distinctive cross as do the cathedrals, temples, and even the monasteries. Some organizations within a cathedral even have their own crosses and sometimes emblems and banners," Oralia explained, ignoring Francois' taunt.

"Who does that green cross and emblem represent that's being carried behind the bishop?" Francois asked

"I don't recognize it," Oralia said. "I've never seen a cross with a sword and branch on it like that before. But look, coming through the passageway are several monks, it must belong to one of the monasteries here in the city."

"Those monks are wearing brown robes. Isn't that the color of the robes of the Templo Eucarístico de San Martín?" Francois asked.

"They are brown. Why in the world would templo monks be...," Oralia paused. "Look at the man carrying the cross and the one next to him. They're dressed just like the two men in the picture you showed me from the librarian's apartment. What's the other one carrying?"

"I'm not certain, but it looks like a book and you're right, they are dressed the same. They're even wearing white gloves."

"We should have a closer look," Oralia said, as they both stood up.

"Where are you going in such a hurry," a voice said behind them. They turned to see Romero and two other policemen standing there.

"No place in particular," Oralia said.

Romero looked over to where the two had been staring. "Curious about the green cross? Me too. As a matter-of-fact, that's why I came to the plaza. Your friend Elisa told me about the photo and how she thought the man carrying the cross was the other man in the photograph with Carlos Hernandez."

Suddenly, Oralia's eyes got big. Coming up behind Romero was Kevin and Liz dressed as monks and they hadn't yet realized Romero was right in front of them.

"Are you arresting me inspector," Oralia almost yelled, surprising both Francois and Romero. It also was enough to warn Kevin and Liz who turned a second before Romero turned around to see who else had heard Oralia and was now staring at them.

"Of course, I'm not arresting you, Ms. Toribio. Francois however..." Romero shrugged to let them know that his arrest was a real possibility depending on how they cooperated.

"We were on our way over to have a closer look at the same man Elisa described. The one carrying the book next to him is also dressed the same way," Francois explained.

"Why don't we all walk over and have a look," Romero suggested.

"Excellent idea," Oralia said, glancing back to make sure Kevin and Liz were safely away.

"That was close," Liz said.

"I can't believe we almost walked right up to Romero," Kevin exclaimed.

"Are they still there?" Liz asked.

"I'll look in a moment," Kevin said, "as soon as we're a little further away."

Liz couldn't wait and turned to have a look.

"It looks like they're all heading over to the processional." Liz said.

Kevin now turned to see.

"Looks like they're heading for that man carrying the green cross," Kevin replied. "Then again, maybe not."

"Neither of those two are the man I saw in the photo with the librarian," Francois said as they got closer.

Suddenly Romero grabbed Francois arm and turned sharply away and began walking quickly back towards the restaurant. Seeing this, one of the police officers did the same with Oralia.

"Heh, what's the meaning of this? Take your hands off of me," Oralia insisted.

"Are you arresting us after all?" Francois asked.

"Just be quiet and sit back down," Romero snapped.

"You two go wait over by the northeast passageway," Romero said to the two policemen.

"What is going on?" Francois asked.

"I'm not sure," Romero replied, looking nervously at the processional.

"You look like you've seen a ghost," Oralia said.

"Or maybe your boss," Francois quipped.

"Why do you say that?" Romero asked.

"You have the same expression on your face that I saw when we were shopping at the El Corte Inglés when you thought you saw your comisario there," Francois replied.

"You have a remarkable memory," Romero replied. "I did see my boss. He was the one carrying the green cross. See that man next to him? That's Gabriel Arciga, one of the members of the Council of Ministers. Arciga is one of the most powerful men in all of Spain."

"Did you know your boss was such a devout Catholic?" Oralia asked.

"I had no idea," Romero replied.

"Didn't you say in the El Corte Inglés that you thought you'd seen Arciga?" Francois asked.

"I didn't say his name, only that I was surprised to see one of the ministers without his bodyguards," Romero replied. "But yes, it was Arciga who I saw in the department store."

"Perhaps your comisario is the minister's bodyguard this evening," Oralia suggested.

The Plaza Mayor began to fill as the hundreds participating in the processional continued to pour in.

"Look," Oralia said, "There's the Reverend Father and the monks from the templo. The monks are carrying the oversized model of Jesus on the cross that sits in the sanctuary. That's got to hurt."

Both Romero and Francois looked to see what Oralia was talking about. More than a dozen of the brown clad monks were struggling to keep the icon above their heads, but as the three of them watched, the monks sat it in a stand that had been brought to the plaza earlier that day. When Francois and Romero looked back, the comisario and the minister had disappeared.

"Where'd your boss go?" Francois asked.

"I don't see the green cross anywhere," Oralia added.

"He must've left the plaza," Romero said. "At least I hope so."

"Do you know anything about the 'Seven of the Cross'?" Romero asked.

"Never heard of it," Francois replied.

"Me either," Oralia said, "Who are they?"

"That's why I asked, I've no idea. Liz told me, right before she and Kevin escaped, to see what I could find out about them. Liz said that this group is behind the evil that is taking over Madrid," Romero explained.

"Was the librarian part of this evil group?" Oralia asked.

"I'd guess that's why Liz was at the librarian's apartment and why she told me about the group," Romero replied.

"I knew it." Oralia said. "That librarian stole Bruno Mancini's journal just like my cousin stole the journal from my grandfather. I bet Bishop Toribio is part of this 'Seven of the Cross' just like the librarian was. There's something in those journals that they want no one to read and I intend to find out just what that is."

"We found no journal at the librarian's apartment," Romero replied.

Oralia looked down at the ground refusing to meet the inspector's stare.

"Francois, you didn't..." but before he could finish his question, several people screamed as pandemonium seemed to break out in the Plaza Mayor.

୨୦   ୨୦   ୨୦

"What's going on?" Liz asked.

"I don't know. First, they were headed towards that man with the green cross and the next thing I know, they make a quick about-face and go sit back down. I'm not sure what to make of it," Kevin replied

The plaza was becoming crowded as parish after parish entered through the passageway and set their icons in prearranged areas, vying for recognition as parish bands played loudly trying to encourage people to come and view the displays.

"He must've recognized the man with the cross," Liz suggested.

"And didn't want the man with the cross to recognize him," Kevin added. "Do you see where he went? I lost him in the crowd."

"Too many people, I can't even see where Romero went," Liz replied.

"Me neither, but I'm sure he's still sitting over at the restaurant. Let's head to the north porticoe, maybe we'll have a better view from there."

"You know that man carrying the green cross was dressed just like the librarian," Liz said.

"So was the man next to him," Kevin replied. "You'd think we'd be able to find that green cross somewhere in this crowd."

"Not if they don't want it to be found," Liz replied.

Liz spun quickly around. "I got a feeling something really evil is about to happen."

"Is that a power Nephilim possess or is it just a woman's intuition?" Kevin asked.

Liz didn't reply, she was watching as two monks dressed in brown tunics identical to theirs removed a third monk's tunic to reveal a dazed woman.

"What's wrong?" Kevin asked.

"Those two monks just handcuffed a woman to that display," she replied "I think the woman was drugged. We need to..." but before she could finish, about twenty-five feet past the first display, a second identical display with another woman handcuffed to it, suddenly burst into flame.

"Oh my God," Kevin exclaimed, fighting through the fleeing crowd, as he rushed towards the screaming woman.

"It's too late to save her," Liz yelled, "try to free the other woman."

Kevin had just reached the closer display when it too burst into flames. Without giving any thought to his own well-being he reached into the fire to try to pull her free, but she was handcuffed to the frame. The sleeves of his monk's tunic burst into flames and then suddenly, they turned into frozen icicles that shattered and fell to the ground.

"What the hell?" Kevin said.

"Free her quickly," Liz said, removing her hands from the now frigid display. "We've got to get out of here."

"You stopped the fire by freezing it," Kevin exclaimed, "just like Lucienne froze the hearts of her victims."

273

"Kevin, are you alright?" Francois yelled running towards them with Romero close behind.

"Ronda," Liz whispered.

"What?" Kevin said, turning back to Liz.

"Ronda, in the morning, the Parador," Liz said, then bolted into the crowd.

"Bridges, don't move," Romero shouted. "You're under arrest."

"Hurry," Kevin shouted, "She's cuffed to this thing, hurry before the flames restart."

Romero had witnessed the first woman burn at the stake and wasn't willing to see it happen again. He ignored Kevin while he struggled to un-cuff the woman.

"Liz turned the flames to ice," Oralia said in awe. "It was a miracle. She actually turned flames into ice."

Several others who had witnessed Liz's act dropped to their knees and began praying, thanking God for His divine intervention.

Two of the waiters from one of the restaurants inside the Plaza Mayor had used extinguishers to stop the fire which had burned the first victim, but gas from a tank that fed the fire continued to hiss ominously.

"Somebody call the fire department," one of the waiters shouted, while another tried to cover the blackened incinerated body still cuffed to the pyre.

A crowd pushed in with several people trying to help Romero, but also allowing Kevin to fade into the gathering throng.

"Bridges. Kevin Bridges." Romero shouted when he realized Kevin had snuck away, "Get back here."

A roar of screams again erupted in the plaza as the first pyre covered in the tablecloths burst into flames once more. There was nothing left in the two fire extinguishers to quench the flames this time.

"We've got to get her off of here," Francois yelled at Romero, as he frantically ripped apart the display trying to pull the woman's legs free while Romero continued to struggle with the handcuffs.

"The gas valve, turn off the gas valve," Romero shouted.

"My hand is too big, I can't get it in the opening," Francois shouted back.

"Move over," someone screamed, shoving the much larger man out of the way.

It was Kevin. He reached inside the small housing opening just as the display ignited once again.

"Get back," Romero shouted, but Kevin had grabbed the valve and turned it off, stopping extra gas from flowing but doing nothing to extinguish the flames already consuming the display and Kevin's brown tunic.

Francois yanked him away from the burning pyre and started rolling him on the ground just as the first fire fighters arrived and covered Francois, Kevin, Romero and the woman on the display in thick foam.

"Why'd you come back?" Romero asked Kevin.

"You needed help. Besides I wanted to see if Lucienne would show up," Kevin explained.

"Why do you think Lucienne would come here?" Francois asked.

"It's hard to explain let alone understand," Kevin said.

"What about this case hasn't been hard to understand," Romero replied. "Let's hear it."

"I thought Lucienne might appear because of the death of that woman on the other stake," Kevin said. "You see, a Nephilim can be called forth from Tartarus by a murderer of another human. I thought that if for some reason Lucienne had gone back to Tartarus, this might be the way one of the 'Seven' would call her back."

"You're right, I've absolutely no idea what you are talking about," Francois said.

"Are you saying that one of the 'Seven of the Cross' Liz told me about is behind this?" Romero asked.

"I'm not sure. I only know that when Adela was murdered at the templo by the librarian, he summoned forth Lucienne. That was why she appeared suddenly in the mausoleum. That's also why we discovered Liz at the librarian's apartment. Lucienne killed the librarian and then summoned forth Liz to take the blame for the murder," Kevin explained.

"Are you telling us that this Lucienne and Liz are both Nephilim?" Oralia asked.

"That's what Liz told me," Kevin asked.

"And you believe that?" Romero asked.

"I'm not sure what to believe anymore," Kevin replied. "Liz did say that the 'Seven of the Cross' were prominent men who believed in the ways of the Inquisition and burning at the stake was a common practice during the Inquisition."

The fireman had finally cut the woman free from the display and medics were working on her. Medics were also checking out the burns on Kevin's arms and Francois and Romero's hands.

"You men are extremely lucky you weren't hurt any worse than this," one of the medics said.

"Luck had nothing to do with it," Kevin replied.

"You think God intervened to save this woman's life?" Romero asked.

"Absolutely." Kevin replied without hesitation.

"I wish I had your faith," Francois said.

"Hang around long enough and a little faith might rub off on you too," Kevin replied.

"Whoa," the other medic gasped, "Look at this lady's back. It looks like someone skinned her."

Everyone went over to look.

"I've seen this before," Oralia said. "It's just like the drawings I saw in my ancestor's journal. They used the skin to make a cross."

"Like the cross found embedded in Adela's head," Kevin noted.

Everyone stood quietly.

"What now, Romero, am I under arrest?"

Romero hesitated, obviously troubled by what he had seen and heard and what his boss had ordered him to do. "You know as well as I do that your diplomatic immunity won't allow me to arrest you, but it does allow me to escort you to the airport and see that you leave my country."

"If you did that, you wouldn't know where to find Liz and Lucienne," Kevin replied.

"I'll have two of my men take the two of you back to your hotel so you can change clothes. Then I want us all to meet back at the Templo Eucarístico. There are several questions I need answered before anybody does or goes anywhere."

"They could ride back with me," Oralia offered as she stood close to Francois "I'm heading back to the templo."

"I think it best if two of my officers keep them company," Romero replied. "However, I'd like you to find the Reverend Father and meet us at the templo. I've a few questions for the two of you as well."

"Great," she replied. "I've a few questions I need answered too, and what better place to find those answers than in the Lord's house."

"Amen," Francois replied, tongue-in-cheek, causing both Romero and Kevin to glare at him and Oralia to sock him in the arm.

CHAPTER TWENTY-SIX

"Conspiracy"

"You assured me that this Vatican investigator wouldn't interfere in our plans," Toribio complained to Comisario Diaz. "It was Mr. Bridges who helped free the harlot who was sentenced to die."

"It's not Kevin Bridges we need to worry about," Diaz snapped back. "Didn't you see that woman dressed as a Templo Eucarístico de San Martín monk? She turned the fire into ice, she must be an angel of God," Diaz declared.

"She is no angel, the 'Light' has assured me of this," Toribio replied.

"You knew of this woman and didn't tell us?" Diaz roared.

"I didn't know the extent of her powers until I saw what she did in the plaza," Toribio explained. "You knew of her as well. She is the Interpol agent who allegedly has been tracking Lucienne for some time. She and the French prefect arrived with the Vatican investigator. Had your people arrested Bridges the other two wouldn't have been a problem."

"That was the Interpol agent? Perhaps we should consider postponing our…" Diaz was interrupted.

"We'll not postpone anything," Toribio asserted. "I'll contact the 'Light' to see what can be done about this woman. Meanwhile, we will continue to prepare just as planned."

"I saw Inspector Romero help rescue the accused at the Plaza Mayor. I'll contact him to make sure Kevin Bridges was arrested and is sent back to Rome," Diaz explained.

"I think you should tighten the reigns on Inspector Romero as well. What was he doing at the processional?" Toribio asked.

"Trying to capture Bridges as he was ordered to do," Diaz replied.

"Let's hope that's the only reason he was there," Toribio said.

༄ ༄ ༄

"I thought we were going to get me a sports coat," Kevin said.

"I wanted to talk to you in private," Romero replied.

"We didn't need to go up to the hotel roof just to talk. You must have a reason for coming here."

"I do. This is the tallest building on the block next to El Corte Inglés," Romero replied, taking out a camera with a telephoto lens.

"So?"

"So, have a look at that private dining room on top of El Corte Inglés," He said handing Kevin the camera. "Any of those men look familiar?"

"Should they?"

"How many men do you see?"

"Five, no, wait. Two more just got off an elevator. That makes seven. Are you suggesting these men are the 'Seven of the Cross'?" Kevin asked.

Romero took back the camera and started snapping pictures. "One of those men is my boss, Comisario Diaz. He was the one carrying the cross on that green background in the processional."

Kevin grabbed the camera back and looked again. "You're right, he is the one who was carrying the cross."

"Of course I'm right, you think I wouldn't recognize my own boss? The one standing next to him is Gabriel Arciga, from the Council of Ministers. He was also in the processional."

"What are you suggesting?"

"After you and Francois left me at the El Corte, I did a little investigating."

"That's right, you said you thought you saw your commander and one of the ministers when we were there shopping."

"When Liz asked me to see what I could find out about the 'Seven of the Cross' I gave it no thought. But then when I saw Diaz marching in the processional and with what you told me and what happened in the Plaza, it all made perfect sense."

"What made perfect sense?" Kevin asked.

"When I went snooping around the store, I made my way into that dining room. Whoever was there must have just left because there were still place settings where seven people had just eaten. I'm guessing it was those seven men we're now looking at."

"You think those men are the 'Seven of the Cross' Liz was talking about?"

"She did say they were powerful men. One of the others is, Señor Guidino, the executive Vice-president of the El Corte Inglés Conglomerate. I saw his picture on the wall when I was looking around."

"Know anything about any of the rest of them?" Kevin asked.

"That's the scary part. Look at the one at the head of the table. Recognize him?" Romero asked.

"No, should I?"

"I would think you should. That's Father Toribio, the acting-bishop of Madrid. Oralia's cousin."

"What do you intend to do about it?" Kevin asked.

"Nothing, absolutely nothing, at least for right now. Diaz called me on my way here. He wasn't very happy about what happened in the Plaza Mayor."

"Not happy that it occurred or not happy that you interfered?" Kevin replied.

Romero gave Kevin a stern look. "When I told him that you somehow got away in the midst of the chaos, he was irate, threatening to fire me if I don't take you and Liz into custody this weekend. The trouble is, I'm starting to believe this whole supernatural spiritual warfare story about Lucienne," Romero said.

"So am I, and it scares me," Kevin replied.

෨ ෨ ෨

"Where's Kevin?" Oralia asked when Francois walked in

"He and Romero went over to El Corte Inglés before they closed. Kevin needed a sports jacket. I told him to buy one when we went there the first time, but he wouldn't listen."

"Look at this entry in Bruno's journal," Oralia cried. "Someone added it after his death. It describes how and where his body was found. He was found in the crypt room and had a handprint burned onto his chest, just like Lucienne did to the librarian."

"And to the hotel security guard, and tried to do to the radiologist in New York and who knows how many others," Francois added.

"This proves that my ancestor Raul Toribio didn't kill Bruno as he's accused of doing," Oralia exclaimed.

"Praise the Lord," the Reverend Father replied.

Oralia's smile turned to a frown. "But it doesn't prove he didn't kill the other monk and then take his own life as he's also accused of doing."

"God will lead us to the truth," the Reverend Father assured her. "Just have faith."

"I do have faith," Oralia replied.

"I wish I did," Francois admitted.

"We all are given a measure of faith by the Lord," the Reverend Father chastened, "what we do with that measure of faith is up to us."

"You know Romero will probably take the journal when he arrives," Francois warned Oralia.

"I know, but now that it has been found I'm sure I'll get the chance to study it," she replied. "What about the cross?"

"I don't think we need to mention that quite yet," Francois replied, looking at the Reverend Father.

"Mention what?" the Reverend Father said smiling.

"Yes, mention what?" Romero said, as he and Kevin entered the room.

"Oralia was just reading from Bruno Mancini's journal. It seems that Mancini was found on the crypt room floor with a hand print burned through his clothes and onto his chest," Francois said. "Does that sound familiar?"

"Here's her name," Oralia exclaimed. "The name of the murdered witch was…"

"Lucia de la Cruz," Kevin interrupted.

"That's right, how did you know that? I hadn't told anyone," Oralia said.

"Liz told me," Kevin said.

"Well, did she tell you the witch had the cross stuck in her head just like Adela when they found her?" Oralia asked.

"It says here Bruno had to turn it like a key in a keyhole to remove it and when he did her brains came out. That's disgusting."

"What happened to Liz?" Francois asked.

"Which time are you asking about?" he replied.

"I want to know what happened to her now, and where we can find her," Romero insisted.

"She said that Lucienne or Lucia, whatever name you call her, is on her way to a place called Ronda. That's where the doctor is staying, at the Parador," Kevin explained. "She told me to meet her in the morning."

"Ronda. That's more than a six-hour drive," Oralia said.

"Not the way I drive," Romero replied.

"Don't you want to look at the photo I took from the librarian's apartment?" Francois asked.

"Oh yes," Romero replied, but Francois knew that Romero's sense of urgency to do so seemed to have waned.

Romero took the photo from Francois then passed it along to Kevin who feigned interest in it as well.

"We need to be going if we're going to make it to Ronda before sun up," Romero said looking at Kevin.

"Don't think for a minute that you're leaving me here," Francois said to Romero. "I've been half-way around the world following Lucienne and don't intend to be left behind now."

"Nobody's leaving you behind," Kevin assured him.

"What can we do to help?" the Reverend Father asked.

"Oralia can try to find out what that green cross we saw in the processional stands for," Romero suggested.

"And see what else she can learn from Bruno Mancini's journal," Francois said.

"I don't want to know anything about that. At least not yet," Romero interjected.

"Then forget what I just said, Oralia," Francois said, smiling.

"What can I do?" the Reverend Father asked.

"Continue to pray for the bishop's safe return," Kevin replied.

"Amen," Oralia added, as Kevin and Romero glanced at each other.

"Are you sure this is how you want to handle this?"

"I know of no other way," Liz replied.

"What about the Inspector from Cuerpo Nacional? Maybe you should let him arrest her."

"That will never happen. You know as well as I that the deceiver has a strong influence over the Cuerpo. Besides, Lucienne would never allow herself to be caught by a mortal," Liz replied.

"Was it wise to tell Mr. Bridges to meet you in Ronda?"

"It's something I must do. I've jeopardized his reputation and made him a wanted man. I only hope he wasn't captured in the plaza and that he's able to get here in time. He's the one human who will understand what I do."

"How can you be sure Lucia won't again be summoned forth by this 'Seven of the Cross'?"

"I can't be, but I pray that Kevin, Francois and Inspector Romero will stop this group before they can murder anyone else or spread further evil in Madrid," she said.

"And I pray your prayers will be heard and answered."

CHAPTER TWENTY-SEVEN

"Rebellion"

"**The desk clerk says** nobody closely resembling Lucienne has checked in nor did he see anyone who looks like her in the bar or restaurant last night," Romero said.

"I'm not sure if I'd trust the memory of a hotel desk clerk," Francois replied. "Besides, how long has he been on duty? Lucienne might have checked in before his shift began."

"Maybe one of you should have a look at the security tapes and see if this Lucienne or Liz appears on them," Romero suggested.

"There's no way Liz could have arrived here last night. At most she had a three-hour head start on us," Kevin replied. "Still, the tapes might tell us if Lucienne is here."

"I'll take a look at them," Francois offered, "but don't even think about taking on Lucienne without me."

"I promise you that won't happen," Romero replied.

"What about the doctor?" Kevin asked.

"He and his friend should be coming down to breakfast in about ten minutes. They are checking out this morning and headed for Marbella," Romeo replied.

What's Marbella?" Kevin asked.

"It's a city along the coast; mostly high-end resorts and golf courses."

"What'd this place use to be? It couldn't have been built as a hotel," Kevin said.

"No, this was the old town hall. Most of Spain's Paradors were at one-time castles, palaces, or monasteries. They are the guardians of our cultural heritage," Romero explained.

"It's an incredible view," Kevin said. "That bridge is a work of art."

"That's the Puente Nuevo," Romero replied.

"You're joking, right?" Kevin replied.

"No, that's its name, Puente Nuevo, the new bridge. It's the newest of the three bridges that cross over el Tajo gorge into the old city. Of course, it was named that when it was built in 1793."

"It certainly is a spectacular sight. How far…" Kevin suddenly stopped in mid-sentence.

"What's the matter?" Romero asked.

"The woman on the bridge, that's Liz."

"Are you sure?" Romero asked.

"I'm almost positive. I'm going out there," Kevin said heading for the door.

"The doctor is due at any moment, what if Lucienne shows up here? Who will protect the doctor?" Romero asked.

"Francois," Kevin yelled.

Hearing the urgency in Kevin's voice Francois bolted from the security office. The few guests making their way down for breakfast also turned sensing trouble.

"Liz is on the bridge outside. I'm going to talk to her but someone must stay here to protect the doctor in case Lucienne shows up."

"Romero can stay here, he's got the gun," Francois replied.

"No, I'm going with Kevin," Romero replied, handing his gun to Francois. "Go find the doctor and don't let him out of your sight. Have the hotel security go with you."

Romero turned to the desk clerk. "You call the local police and tell them Cuerpo Nacional needs two squads here now."

A slight nod from Kevin assured Francois that he agreed with Romero's plan. Five seconds later Kevin and Romero were out the door.

૭ ૭ ૭

"Good morning, Reverend Father," Oralia said as she arrived at the templo office.

"I trust you slept well," Reverend Father replied.

"Of course not. I was up half the night reading Bruno Mancini's journal and the other half was spent worrying about Francois, Kevin, and the inspector. Have you heard from them?"

"No, but I'm sure they are safely in Ronda. Perhaps you should've spent your time praying for them rather than worrying about them. God will watch over them."

I've been bothered about something," Oralia said. "There's something odd about that cross the librarian used to murder Adela," she said, as she pulled the cross from the desk drawer.

"You know you really should've told Inspector Romero that you borrowed an important piece of evidence."

"Had I done that I'd be in jail. Then what help would I be?" She turned the bag holding the cross in her hands trying not to smudge any possible fingerprints or knock off any of the dried blood. "I knew there was something different about this cross," Oralia exclaimed to the Reverend Father. "Look at this symbol on the top. That's different from the cross drawn in Bruno Mancini's journal."

"Perhaps, your ancestor failed to include all the details when he originally drew it," Reverend Father replied.

"Maybe, but I've seen that symbol before. I just can't remember where," Oralia replied.

"I must say it looks somewhat familiar to me as well," Reverend Father said as he prepared to leave.

"Are you going to check on the miracle of the Madonna?" Oralia asked.

"No, I'm afraid that the acting-bishop has called another meeting to discuss tonight's processional. Several people have demanded the church cancel it after what happened last night in the Plaza Mayor. I for one would tend to agree with them. However, I'm sure Father Toribio has a different view."

"I can't stand to even hear his name," Oralia replied. "Has there been any news regarding Bishop Castillo? The Cuerpo seem to be dragging their feet in searching for him."

"So it would seem. I've directed the monks to continue to pray for his safe return. I'm sure it's all part of God's plan. Don't forget to research that green cross and emblem as Inspector Romero requested."

"That's right, I was so caught up in reading Bruno Mancini's journal I'd forgotten all about it."

"I'm sure with your computer skills it won't take long for you to find out its meaning. I know this is your day off, so if you are gone when I return be sure to leave me information about what you discovered."

"I will, but I doubt I'll be going anywhere until I hear from Kevin and Francois."

"God be with you."

"And with you," Oralia replied, as she sat down at the computer.

"And especially with Kevin and Francois," she prayed silently as the Reverend Father headed out the door.

"You didn't give him your only gun, did you?" Kevin asked, as they headed towards the Puente Nuevo.

"Of course not," Romero replied. "Although, I'm not sure what good a gun will be if what you've told me is true."

Liz stood in the middle of the bridge watching as the two men approached.

"You don't look very pleased to see me," Kevin said as he hugged Liz.

"Or is it my presence that makes you sad?" Romero asked.

"No, I'm saddened by what must be done," Liz replied, making both the men a little nervous.

"What do you mean?" Kevin asked.

"Lucienne is here in Ronda, but she's not here to kill the doctor. If she wanted him dead, he'd already be dead. This was never about throwing doubt into the miracles attributed to Pope John Paul II. Perhaps it started that way, but it's turned into something else, something much more sinister. Satan wants to disgrace you, Kevin, and put everything you've accomplished for the Church in doubt."

"That's absurd. I've not done that much." Kevin exclaimed.

"Then possibly Satan wants to stop what you may someday accomplish," Liz suggested.

"That's nonsense," Kevin replied.

"She wanted you here. She wanted all of you here," Liz said.

"Why, would she want that?" Romero asked.

"She wanted you out of Madrid. You're interfering with her plans there."

"What plans?"

"That I can't tell you," Liz replied.

"Can't or won't," Kevin asked.

"Can't. I don't know what evil Satan has planned for Madrid. I only know that Lucienne is merely a servant sent to spread evil. One of your problems as human beings is that you are so used to living in the blessings of the Lord that when you see the work of Satan you are so shaken."

"All this talk of Satan gives me a chill," Romero said.

"The chill is real, I feel it too," Kevin said.

"Lucienne approaches," Liz said. "The time is near."

Romero pulled his other gun but dropped it immediately and screamed. "It felt like it was on fire." Suddenly, he began to shudder uncontrollably.

"Liz, stop this!" Kevin demanded.

"There is nothing Liz can do," Lucienne said, crossing the street and onto the bridge. Lucienne had been watching from her hiding place on a covered stairway leading down to an outdoor restaurant on the cliff face of the gorge.

"Lucienne you don't need to do this," Liz ordered.

"Of course I do. It is what Satan commands of me, just as he commanded you to lure the miracle investigator here. It's your duty as a Nephilim."

"I warned you of this," Romero said through chattering teeth. "She's always been a servant of Satan."

"It has always been and will always be a battle between the Kingdom of God and the Kingdom of Satan," Liz replied. "Just remember, the only victory Satan has is the one you give him."

"Enough of this," Lucienne demanded. "It is time for the inspector to die and Kevin to take the blame."

Now Kevin began to shake as his body temperature fell. Lucienne picked up the inspector's gun and placed it in Kevin's hand. He was unable to resist, but before Lucienne could pull the trigger, two police cars skidded to a stop at either end of the Puente Nuevo and Francois had come running and was almost upon them.

"Oh well, I guess it's Kevin who must die," Lucienne said.

Warmth had started pulsating through Kevin's body and the chill was almost gone.

"Not this time," Liz said as she grabbed and pushed Lucienne over the railing of the bridge.

"No," Kevin yelled and grabbed for Liz, expecting to pull her back. However, his arms passed right through what should have been solid body and he too toppled over the bridge railing.

Kevin watched as Lucienne and Liz both disappeared, but not into the el Tajo gorge below as one would expect. They had just faded into nothingness. Even more puzzling to Kevin was why he wasn't plummeting to his death.

"There's no way I'm going to let you get off that easy," Francois' voice said from above him.

It was at that moment Kevin realized Francois had grabbed his leg just as he was about to plunge to his death.

"You can pull me up anytime now," Kevin said.

"I would if you weren't so damn heavy and cold to the touch," Francois replied. "A little help here," he called out to the police who finally found the courage to approach.

"How's Romero?" Kevin asked as Francois and two policemen pulled him back to safety.

"Frozen but alive," Romero called out from the curb.

"What happened?" Francois asked.

"Liz saved our lives," Kevin replied. "Lucienne was about to kill us both when Liz knocked her off the bridge."

"That's over a hundred and twenty-meter fall. No one could survive that. I'm sorry," Romero said.

"Thanks, for saving my life," Kevin said.

"You're welcome, but now what do we do?" Francois replied.

"I'll have the local authorities retrieve the bodies," Romero said.

"There will be no bodies to find," Kevin affirmed.

"Yesterday I would have said that was ridiculous," Romero replied, "but today, I know better."

"What happened to them?" Francois asked.

"Remember when Liz told us about a place called Tartarus?" Kevin asked.

"I remember you saying that name at the Plaza Mayor, but I didn't know what it meant," Romero said.

"I think Liz came here to force Lucienne back to Tartarus," Kevin explained.

"Is Tartarus another name for 'Hell'?" Romero asked.

"Something like that. I'll explain it to you later," Francois said, not completely satisfying Romero.

The police collected Francois' and Kevin's passports.

"Like Liz told us, Lucienne wanted us to come to Ronda. She wanted us out of Madrid. That's where we need to be, and the sooner the better," Kevin said.

"I'm afraid the local police will insist we stay around for a while," Romero replied, after having handed his identification to one of the local authorities.

"You're with the Cuerpo Nacional, pull rank on them," Francois insisted.

"If I did that, they would call my comisario and I don't think that would be a good idea," Romero replied, looking at Kevin.

"When they don't find any bodies, they'll probably call him anyway," Francois suggested.

"Let's hope not," Romero replied.

"At least call the templo and let Oralia and the Reverend Father know what happened," Kevin said.

"It's still too early. No one will be there yet. I'll give Oralia a call a little later when we have a better idea about how long we're going to be stuck here," Francois replied.

"You couldn't ask for a more beautiful place to be stuck," Kevin replied.

All three men looked out across the gorge each wondering what was next.

"Mr. Bridges, you are under arrest," one of the local police announced after studying the identification supplied by the three men.

"I was afraid of this," Romero replied.

"Then do something about it," Francois ordered.

"Don't worry, I'll take care of things," Kevin said, as he was led away.

೪ ೪ ೪

"Well it's about time." Oralia said to herself.

Oralia had been searching the web for almost an hour trying to find the meaning of the green cross and emblem.

"Oh my!" she said as she continued to read. "I better print this."

She had discovered that the emblem was actually the seal of the Spanish Inquisition and the green cross was used in the processional for the auto de fe.

"That woman burned at the stake must have been part of the auto de fe." Oralia gasped at her realization. "I've got to call Kevin."

Oralia tried calling but there was no answer. Kevin had lost his Blackberry sometime after leaving the librarian's apartment. She decided the best way to contact him was to call the Cuerpo Nacional and try to get someone there to contact Inspector Romero in Ronda. After being transferred to three different people at the Cuerpo, none of whom even knew Romero was in Ronda, Oralia was about to give up when a voice answered, "Comisario Diaz, may I help you?"

Oralia panicked. "I'm sorry, I must have the wrong number," she said, quickly hanging up.

"What a bonehead I am. That was the Inspector's boss, the one who was carrying the green cross and seal of the Inquisition. I sure hope I didn't screw up."

"I guess I'll just have to wait and talk to Kevin and Romero when they return," she said stacking the information she had printed on the desk.

Oralia picked up the clear bag containing the cross and looked at the top of it once again.

"I know I've seen that design somewhere before," she said, trying to jar her memory.

She picked up Bruno's journal and began thumbing through the pages furiously.

"I knew it." Oralia dropped the journal leaving it open on her desk, grabbed the cross, and then ran out of the room and down the steps to the mausoleum. It took her a few minutes but she finally found what she was looking for.

"Just like the journal said. *'Ask and it will be given to you; seek and you will find; knock and the door will be opened to you.'*"

Oralia had found the crypt with the verse from Matthew 7:7, but just as the journal said the 7:7 was missing and in its place was the strange symbol. She held up the end of the cross.

"A perfect match," she exclaimed.

She touched the symbol and could feel the smooth worn edges.

"They must go together," she deduced, but how would she know for sure unless she removed the cross from the evidence bag.

"I could go to jail for tampering with evidence. Then again, we already know it was the librarian who killed Adela and he's dead." Oralia debated with herself for almost a minute.

"I've got to try it," she finally blurted out and removed the cross from the bag.

The symbol fit perfectly and as she pressed it against the stone, she heard the sharp click of a bolt releasing, but nothing happened.

"That's strange," she said as she started pulling on the edges of the crypt. "Something has to open."

For five minutes she yanked, pulled, and pried with no luck. Exhausted, she sat down on the bench across from the wall of crypts to think and rest.

"It doesn't make any sense. I know I heard it unlock," she said as she stared at the crypt and reread the passage from Matthew.

Her face lit up as the puzzle finally became clear. She rose and stood before the crypt and began to recite.

"*Ask and it will be given to you; seek and you will find; knock and the door will be opened to you.*" As she said the last line she pounded on the top right corner of the crypt. The door gently swung open. At the same time a buzzer sounded and a light began to flash in a room just a few blocks away.

CHAPTER TWENTY-EIGHT

"Determination"

Lucienne's screams echoed off the canyon walls, then suddenly stopped as the transition back to Tartarus seemed to explode every cell in her body.

Lucienne raged. "What have you done?"

"I've brought you back where you belong. Where we both belong," Liz replied.

Lucienne burst into laughter. "Maybe this is where you belong, but I assure you I don't intend to be here long."

"No one knows you're here. There's no one to summon you forth," Liz insisted.

"It's the duty of the 'Seven of the Cross' to summon me every time they sacrifice one who is not worthy," Lucienne replied. "And with the second and third processional still to come, I'm sure there will be several found to be unworthy. I expect to be summoned within a few hours."

Liz was devastated. That wasn't how things were supposed to work out. She had sacrificed her own freedom to stop Satan's servant from executing further evil in the hope that God would then show mercy on her.

"You thought God would see your sacrifice and take you out of this place, didn't you?" Lucienne realized and laughed. "You fool. The great deceiver has worked his spell on you once again. You don't bargain with God. God won't release you from this place. Satan showed you the way out of here once before and again you have forsaken him. This time I shall not summon you forth. It's here where you'll spend eternity."

Liz realized that what Lucienne had said was true. There's no bargaining with God. Christ had said there is only one way to the Father and that was through him. But, didn't God realize that as a Nephilim she was never afforded the opportunity of the Way. The demons of doubt swirled around her head and she brushed them away as one would a fly.

"Demons of doubt, I rebuke you," Liz shouted.

"How ironic that a demon such as you think yourself capable of rebuking your own kind. Do you forget that this is where demons roam, that God created this place for disembodied spirits? In a few days the shell you now wear will be worn away by the hellish grit of Tartarus and then you too will be nothing more than one of these devilish apparitions of evil," Lucienne said.

"That will never happen," Liz snapped.

"Oh, it will."

"Somehow, I'll stop you," Liz threatened.

"Maybe I'll drop by again to see how you're getting along. Or if you ever return to demonize mankind as God ordained, make sure you stop by and say hello." Lucienne laughed so hard that she choked on the chalky dust pervading the darkness and began to cough.

"This isn't over," Liz warned.

"It is for you," Lucienne replied and disappeared into the darkness.

૭ ૭ ૭

Oralia peered inside the crypt.

"It's empty. What's so important about an empty crypt that it needs a secret lock?" she said to herself.

She sat back down on the bench and stared at the open crypt.

"That's an awfully big crypt. What would they have stored in such a big crypt?" she pondered.

"Wait a minute, maybe it's not a crypt at all. Maybe this is how the librarian escaped without showing up on the security cameras."

Oralia stuck her head inside.

"Those are scuff marks. Somebody wearing black shoes scuffed them climbing in here. It has to be a secret passage just like Bruno surmised in his journal."

Oralia was getting excited and was about to climb in when her better judgment kicked in.

"No, I better call Kevin and the Reverend Father first," she decided and climbed back out.

She stood in front of the crypt debating herself.

"But I already tried to reach Kevin through the inspector and couldn't do it. And the Reverend Father will be meeting most of the day with the bish… acting-bishop," she said correcting herself, anxiously tapping her foot.

"Still, if I were to get stuck in the crypt or wherever it leads, no one would know where to find me or even look for me. That would be bad."

"I know, I'll leave a note on the Reverend Father's desk telling him what I've discovered and what I intend to do," she decided.

"Just what is it I intend to do and what do I expect to find?" she thought.

"I better try and reach Kevin again before I get myself into worse trouble than I'm already in," she concluded.

She closed the door to the crypt and heard the bolt click back into place. Just to be sure, she inserted the symbol on the cross into the stone, heard the click, and then knocked. Again, the crypt door gently swung open.

"Good, I don't want to look silly if it doesn't work when Kevin tries it," she assured herself.

Once more she closed the door hearing the click and headed up the stairs out of the mausoleum.

She saw the man standing at the top of the steps before she was halfway up. She recognized him at once.

"You must be Oralia Toribio," Comisario Diaz said.

"Yes, and you are?"

"Oralia, you know who I am. You called me less than an hour ago trying to contact Romero, but you hung up before we had a chance to talk. I was rather surprised to hear that he was in Ronda. He usually keeps me better informed about his investigations. You wouldn't know what he is doing in Ronda or who he might be with would you?" Diaz said as he started down the steps.

Oralia was holding the cross behind her back not wanting the comisario to see what she was hiding. She began to back down the steps at the same pace Diaz came down.

"Don't be afraid, I just want to talk to you," Diaz assured her.

"Yeah, I bet," Oralia said, turning quickly and running for the crypt that held the secret passage, making sure she smashed the fire alarm along the way.

"Now why did you have to go and do that?" Diaz said, chasing after her.

Oralia had reached and opened the crypt when she felt a sharp pain on her shoulder. The fire alarm echoed through her head and the chamber. Her body began to spasm as she turned and collapsed into Diaz' arms.

"I can see why your cousin doesn't care much for you. You are a real pain in the ass," Diaz said as he stuffed her body into the open crypt then climbed in behind her pulling the secret door closed.

※ ※ ※

"I told you that you should have called your boss when all this first went down," Francois reminded Romero. "I'm sure hearing about it from the local police didn't make him happy."

"He didn't hear about it from them. He was completely surprised when I told him Kevin was in jail. Somebody else told him I was in Ronda," Romero explained.

"Somebody else? Who else did you tell we were coming?" Francois asked.

"Nobody. I didn't see anyone nor did I call anyone before we left last night," Romero replied.

"Your phone must have a GPS tracker on it or something," Francois suggested.

"I don't believe so."

"Maybe the car is bugged," Francois said.

"No, somebody had to tell him and since the three of us were together it had to be either the Reverend Father or Oralia," Romero said.

"That's not likely," Francois replied.

"You got any better suggestions?"

"Maybe your comisario had men staking out the hotel, watching for the doctor or Kevin and Liz. Or maybe Lucienne told him." Francois got quiet reflecting on what he had just suggested. "Ooh, that would be bad. That would mean…"

"I know," Romero interrupted," I've already shared my concern with Kevin. We think the comisario may be part of this 'Seven of the Cross' Liz warned us about. The problem is, Lucienne knew nothing about our plans to come here and had she called the comisario this morning, he would have known about you and Kevin also. He didn't know Kevin was in jail until I mentioned it. That's why I don't think it could've been her who contacted him. That brings us back to Oralia and the Reverend Father. Were you ever able to get a hold of them today?"

"No. I tried several times and left a couple of messages, but no one from the templo has returned my calls," Francois said. "Why did you tell your boss you came to Ronda?"

"To catch Kevin and Liz, of course. Once he found out Kevin was in jail he seemed to calm down. I never mentioned Liz or Lucienne. Now he wants me to stay here until Monday when he'll send a car to come transport Kevin back to Madrid."

"Sounds to me like your boss wants you out of Madrid and out of the way until the processionals are over just like Liz said," Francois surmised.

"I'm starting to get that feeling as well."

"What else do you know about this 'Seven of the Cross'?" Francois asked.

"I'll tell you what I know on the drive back to Madrid," Romero said. "Right now, we need to figure out a way to get Kevin out of jail so we can get back there before something else happens."

"Unless it already has," Francois said looking at his watch. "There's no way we'll make it back in time for the processional."

"I know, but I'm sure the Madrid police will have a lot more men patrolling the plaza and the streets after what happened last night. I really don't think the 'Seven' would try anything so blatant again so soon."

"I don't know. Why else would your boss and Lucienne want us out of Madrid if nothing else was planned?"

"Like you said, there's no way we could get there in time, so let's just concentrate on the task at hand and pray that God will suppress the evil that grows in Madrid," Romero replied. "Tonight, we put it all in His hands."

"Maybe He could give us a hand getting Kevin out of jail," Francois suggested.

"Maybe, who could give you a hand?" Kevin said cheerfully, as he was escorted into the lobby of the police station.

"I've been ordered to transfer the prisoner into the custody of the Cuerpo Nacional as quickly as possible," one of the civil guard officers explained. "And since you are here, the prisoner is now your responsibility."

"Who authorized this?" Romero demanded, trying to sound put out by such an inconvenience.

"Our sergeant received a call from él Presidente Zapatero himself," the officer said with concern in his voice.

"How did you pull that off?" Francois asked.

"I insisted that they allow me to make my one phone call" Kevin responded.

"Are you telling us you called Zapatero?" Romero said.

"Of course not," Kevin replied. "I called the Pope. He called Zapatero."

"Ask and it will be given to you," Francois said.

Both Kevin and Romero looked at him curiously.

"What? Just because I don't believe in all this religious mumbo-jumbo doesn't mean I can't occasionally quote it."

Romero smiled and shook his head. "I think it's time we get back to Madrid."

"Then what are we waiting for," Kevin said, as the three headed out the door.

"Surely you don't plan to continue with the fiesta and processionals after what occurred in the Plaza Mayor," the Reverend Father insisted.

"A tragedy beyond imagination," Bishop Toribio exhorted, "but one through which we must abide and endure."

The Reverend Father knew that further argument would be useless. "Has there been any news from the Cuerpo Nacional regarding the bishop?" he asked.

"Comisario Diaz of the Cuerpo Nacional has informed me that they have reason to believe that an ETA operative who goes by the name Txeroki may be responsible for his kidnapping," Toribio explained.

"Txeroki, that sounds like an American Indian name," one of the other pastors in the room said.

"So, it does," Toribio mocked coldly, leaving little doubt such interruptions wouldn't be tolerated.

"Have these terrorists made any demands?" the Reverend Father asked.

"We don't know for certain these ETA terrorists are even involved. None of the tips the Cuerpo has received have been substantiated. What we need to do is continue to pray for his safety. Would you please lead us in prayer Reverend Father? But first I must excuse myself for an important call from the Vatican. My assistants will explain your duties for today's fiesta and processional. God be with," Bishop Toribio said.

"And with you," the pastor's responded.

Toribio came to where the Reverend Father had kneeled down and held out his hand for the Reverend Father to kiss his ring.

As distasteful as doing so was, the Reverend Father knew it was his duty to kiss the ring, even if Toribio wasn't yet officially the bishop of the Madrid Metropolitan. It was a purposeful action on Toribio's part intended to humiliate the Reverend Father in front of the others who supported him over Toribio.

"Why do you let him treat you that way?" one of the other pastors said softly after Toribio left.

"We should all humble ourselves before God and God's chosen servants," the Reverend Father replied, but then whispered, "And you'd be wise to keep such opinions reserved, for there are many here whose devotion to the acting-bishop surpasses their devotion to our God."

The other pastor bowed his head knowingly.

As instructed, the Reverend Father led the prayer for the real bishop's safe return, although in his heart he knew that somehow Toribio was behind the disappearance.

For the rest of the morning the participants discussed and argued about the processional order, who would participate in saying Mass, and how many local bands would be allowed to join in the processional.

The Reverend Father sat with his head bowed. Many thought he was dozing but those near him could hear his continuing prayer in English, Italian and Latin for the safety of those who now struggle with Satan's demons for the very soul of Madrid.

CHAPTER TWENTY-NINE

"Persecution"

Oralia blinked, trying to focus. She lifted her right hand to rub her eyes, or at least the brain sent the message to lift the right hand, but nothing happened.

"What's going on?" Oralia said, still trying to clear her foggy head, but with little success. The drugs she'd been given after Diaz had zapped her with a taser clouded her mind.

"What's that awful smell?" she said, and tried to straighten up, but again found her constraints keeping her from doing so.

Finally, her eyes began to clear and in the dim candlelight she could see the wooden device that restrained her.

"How in the world did I..." she paused, "Diaz!"

Suddenly her brain began to register the signals of pain from the various areas of her body. Her back ached from being hunched over, her shoulder ached where he had tasered her, her arm ached where they had administered the drugs, and worst of all she felt as if she had been violated.

"Thank God you're alive," a hoarse voice said from across the room.

"Who's there?" Oralia demanded, not yet able to see clearly in the dimly lit room.

"I'm Bishop Castillo," the man whispered.

"You're alive," Oralia replied. "Our prayers have been answered. I'm Oralia, the Reverend Father's secretary at the Templo Eucarístico de San Martín"

"Bless you Oralia. Tell me, does the Virgin still cry the tears of blood?"

"She does, and the Vatican has sent an investigator to find out why. In fact, a French Prefect and an Interpol agent have come too."

"All because the Virgin cries?" the Bishop asked.

"No, it has become much more complicated. A group called the 'Seven of the Cross' is believed to…" Oralia suddenly stopped.

"What is it?" the Bishop asked.

"I've just realized we're captives of this group and they intend to kill us," Oralia began to cry.

"Ohhh," a third voice moaned somewhere behind Oralia.

"Who's there?" Oralia called out.

"She cannot reply," Bishop Castillo said. "They keep her chained to the bed and heavily drugged. There used to be three of them but they removed two of the girls several hours ago."

"They took two of them out last night?" Oralia asked.

"I'm afraid I have no sense of day or night down here. All I can tell you is that it seemed like several hours ago," the bishop explained.

"I wish I could turn to see you, but I can't seem to move," Oralia said.

"They've placed you in the stocks," he said.

"Are you in stocks also?" Oralia asked.

"No, I'm tied to a garotte," the bishop replied.

"I don't know what that is," Oralia replied.

"Let's just say it is a device designed to execute people either very slowly or very quickly. Fortunately, our captors have chosen not to make my death too quick."

"Is it painful?" Oralia asked.

"Not as much as it could be," the bishop replied, trying to give Oralia some hope.

"What are we going to do?" Oralia asked. "And what's that awful smell?"

"I'm afraid part of that smell is coming from me. I've been tied here for several days, but mostly what you smell is death," Bishop Castillo replied. "As for what to do, we'll pray for God's intervention. Now that I know that there are those who have come to help, my strength and my faith grow stronger. Always remember, we will be healed by the stripes on His back. Now pray with me."

Oralia recited the Lord's Prayer along with the bishop, but her thoughts were with Kevin and Francois. Her prayer was that they would figure out where she was by the journal she had left on her desk. That is, if they had survived Ronda.

୨ ୨ ୨

"Wow! Francois explained. "That's an incredible theory. How do you plan to prove it?"

"With your help I hope," Romero answered. "I'm afraid Kevin will be unable to move around Madrid quite as freely as may be necessary, so I'm counting on you."

"There's no way your keeping me out of this," Kevin swore.

"If the comisario has heard that you were released to me, he'll have the entire civil guard searching for both of us," Romero said.

"If he does find out, tell him you have me under house arrest at the templo. Tell him the Vatican couldn't arrange for my flight until Monday evening." Kevin suggested.

"That just might work," Romero replied.

"Works for me," Francois snipped.

"I have to stop by my office to see what my men have learned about what happened at the Plaza Mayor," Kevin said.

"I think it would be wiser to take the two of you to the templo rather than the hotel," Romero said.

"I agree. What I don't understand is why no one from the templo has tried to reach us. I've left several messages," Francois noted.

"The second processional should have ended a couple of hours ago. Nothing came over the radio about trouble or anything unusual happening. The Civil Guard had a huge presence this evening, I'm sure."

"Oralia and the Reverend Father should have been back to the templo by now. I'm getting a bit concerned," Francois said.

"I'm more than a bit concerned. I'm guessing Oralia called the Cuerpo trying to get a hold of us. That's how Diaz found out you were in Ronda. If your comisario and the acting-bishop are in this as deep as we all seem to believe, then Oralia and Reverend Father could be in big trouble."

"There's nothing we can do until we get back to Madrid and that won't be for several more hours, so I suggest you both try to get some sleep," Romero said.

"What about you? You've been awake just as long as us," Francois said.

"When I stop for gas, I'll let one of you drive. Just promise you won't get us lost," Romero replied.

"God will show us the way," Kevin replied.

"*For this God is our God for ever and ever; he will be our guide even to the end*," Romero recited. "That's from Psalm 48."

"Very impressive. How do you remember that?" Francois asked.

"It's amazing what you can remember when a nun is whacking your hand with a ruler every five minutes in school," Romero replied.

"The joy of growing up Catholic," Kevin added, then lay back to try to sleep.

֍   ֍   ֍

"I'm pleased all went well with the processional," Bishop Toribio said, congratulating the other six men sitting around the table in the private dining room atop El Corte Inglés.

The processional had ended shortly after midnight and the 'Seven of the Cross' had gathered to discuss their plans for the final night of the Fiesta de San Martín.

"The crowd was almost twice what is was the previous night," one of the men replied.

"And Sunday's processional should be larger yet with él Presidente and possibly the King himself participating in the processional," Toribio beamed.

"There's still no assurance the King will participate," Minister Arciga interjected. "There's a fund raiser at the Prado that he and the Canadian Prime Minister will attend. I too must attend, but it is scheduled to end before the processional."

"The head of his personal security team is hesitant to allow his participation after what happened in Plaza Mayor Friday night. I've assured him that the Cuerpo Nacional will have a full contingent of officers to assist in providing protection but he is still leery. I'm afraid if I push the issue he may become suspicious," Diaz explained.

"Just make sure Zapatero is there," Toribio insisted. "If he fails to come, all our preparation will be for naught."

"What about the 'Light'? Won't she be upset if the King fails to join the processional?" someone asked.

"The 'Light' has spread evil for generations and will continue to do so for generations to come. Of course, she'll be disappointed, as will our master, just as we shall be, but our lord's kingdom cannot be stopped," Toribio replied.

"Where is the 'Light'?" someone asked. "I thought she was to join us tonight."

"As did I. After the meeting I want you two to summon her forth in case she has returned to Tartarus," Toribio ordered pointing to two of the men at the end of the table. "Another of the street whores awaits you in the torture chamber."

"What about the bishop? How long must we keep him alive," one of the others asked.

"The 'Light' will let us know when and how he is to die," Toribio assured them. "Perhaps even tonight when so many others will die, will the bishop finally meet his God."

"Has the fugitive who interfered with our ceremony on Friday been apprehended?" one of the 'Seven' asked.

"If you are speaking of Kevin Bridges, the investigator from the Vatican, then the answer is yes," Diaz replied. "He was arrested in Ronda by one of my men, Inspector Romero."

"But wasn't it Romero who also interfered in the executions?" another asked.

"Yes, but I have ordered him to remain in Ronda with the prisoner until Monday when arrangements can be made to bring Bridges back to Madrid. They won't interfere this time, I assure you," Diaz replied.

"I want nothing to go wrong tonight in the plaza. Zapatero mustn't be allowed to escape," Minister Arciga demanded.

"Rest assured that all will go as planned," Toribio replied. "By this time next week, you'll be the one known as, él Presidente."

"Several of the gates into Plaza Mayor will be closed and locked as a security precaution for Zapatero's appearance in the plaza. I will know which ones when I meet with his chief of security at 8:00 a.m. this morning. Have you prepared the trucks we'll use to block the other gates?" Diaz asked one of the men.

"Four trucks were rented yesterday and are parked in the loading docks below. No deliveries are scheduled on Sundays so we won't be disturbed when we load the explosives onto the trucks," Guidino explained.

"What about the gas canisters? Have they all been hidden in the service tunnels below the plaza?" Toribio asked.

"They are in place but the explosives still need to be set," Diaz replied.

"Just make sure you set them correctly," Toribio said to Diaz, with a knowing look.

"Now I suggest we all go home and get a few hours rest. We will meet back here at 1:00 p.m. for lunch and to go over our plans one final time. By then we should have the information from Zapatero's security chief," Toribio instructed.

Arciga and two of the other 'Seven' left to get some rest. Toribio and Diaz remained behind to instruct the two charged with summoning forth the "Light".

"There is another issue that concerns me," Diaz began. "The secretary from the Templo Eucarístico discovered the crypt entrance into the catacombs."

"Oralia! Are you sure?" Toribio asked.

"I was in my office when the alarm was tripped. I went there immediately and discovered her coming out of the crypt room. She knew who I was and tried to escape through the secret passage."

"Did you kill her?" Toribio asked.

"No. She set off the fire alarm as she ran. I used my taser on her and took her to the torture chamber where I drugged her and placed her in the stocks," Diaz explained.

"And that's all you did?" Toribio asked.

Diaz smiled deviously, "Not quite. She got what she deserved."

"You two take the elevator to the catacombs and deal with the whore, then summon forth the 'Light'. We must make sure she's here in case we run into any other unexpected roadblocks," Toribio insisted.

"What about the secretary?" one of them asked.

"Leave her alone, at least for now, but do with the whore as you wish. Just be sure she dies and you summon the 'Light'," Toribio demanded.

One of the men inserted his ring into the matching inverted design on the elevator panel. The door opened immediately and the men left, anxiously anticipating the task ahead.

"Tell me about the woman from Interpol," Toribio said as soon as the elevator door shut. "Was she in Ronda as well?"

"Inspector Romero made no mention of any woman," Diaz replied.

"I questioned the 'Light' about this woman. Lucienne wouldn't admit it, but I believe Liz Purdue is a Nephilim, the same as the 'Light'," Toribio said.

"That would make sense. Several people at the Plaza Mayor said that a woman seemed to stop the fire meant to consume our intended victim by freezing the flames. But if she's a Nephilim, why would she interfere? She's a servant of Satan just like us." Diaz exclaimed.

"I don't know. And what I don't know worries me," Bishop Toribio replied.

CHAPTER THIRTY

"Isolation"

"**Morning already?**" Francois yawned. "Where are we?"

"Almost home," Romero replied.

"Paris?" Francois replied.

"Forgive me, your home away from home. We're almost to the templo," Romero explained.

"You are kind of quiet this morning," Francois said to Kevin.

"I'm just thinking," Kevin replied

"About what?" Romero asked.

"I'm thinking there must be a reason why the Madonna continues to cry the blood of Christ," Kevin said.

"The blood of Christ? That's a rather large leap of faith wouldn't you say?" Francois replied.

"Sometimes you need faith over reason," Kevin said.

"So, what's the plan?" Francois asked.

"First, we're checking in at the templo to see what information Oralia has for us and to ask the Reverend Father how the processional went last night," Romero said.

"And to see why we haven't heard from them in over twenty-four hours," Kevin added.

"You and I are going to drop by my office to see what my crime scene specialists have found out about that cross used to kill Adela and about the two women in the Plaza Mayor Friday night," Romero said.

"Uhmm, about that cross," Francois hesitated.

"Don't tell me you also stole it from the crime scene," Romero exclaimed.

"Oh no, I didn't steal it," Francois quipped. "Oralia did."

"That's just great!" Romero huffed.

"Don't worry it's in the drawer at the templo. You can pick it up when you drop me off," Kevin said. "Oralia thought she was doing the right thing."

"Two days ago, I would have locked her up and thrown away the key," Romero said. "But today, I'm not even sure I'd scold her."

"Look up there," Kevin said as they headed up the Grand Via, "the lights are on in the dining room on top of El Corte Inglés."

"You wouldn't mind if I just dropped you off at the templo, would you? I think Francois and I need to take a closer look at that dining room."

"I thought you wanted to check in with your office?" Kevin replied.

"Just as soon as we have a look from the roof of the Atlantico," Romero replied.

"Don't leave me alone for too long. I don't want to have to go looking for you two," Kevin threatened.

"Don't even think about leaving the templo until we get back," Romero warned.

"Just be careful. I'm not sure who we can trust anymore," Kevin said, as he climbed out of the car.

"You remember that too," Francois reiterated, "and say hello to Oralia for me."

"Who's there?" Oralia called out when she heard the crack of the locks to the door of the torture chamber release.

"Quiet," the bishop whispered, "pretend you have passed out and they may leave you alone."

"Water, I need water," the woman chained to the bed begged when she heard the noise.

A torch was lit at the top of the staircase and shadows cascaded along the walls as the two men descended the stairs.

"Water, please, I need water," the woman cried out softly as the men approached.

"Shut up, whore," one of the men bellowed.

"For the love of God, give the poor girl some water," the bishop rasped.

"This isn't about the love of God," one of the men laughed. "This is about the love of death and if you don't shut up, it just might be your death."

The man slightly turned the bar on the back of the garrote tightening the rope ever so slightly around the bishop's neck.

"Aahhh," a gargled moan wheezed from the bishop's constricted throat.

"Easy, we don't want to snap his spine. At least not yet," his partner warned.

"Leave him alone," Oralia shrieked.

The man turned and slapped Oralia with the back of his hand.

"No woman talks to me that way," he growled, grabbing her hair and jerking her head back to face him.

"Her time will come," his partner said, pulling his friend away. "The whore will be more than enough entertainment for tonight."

"Where is the absinthe? The smell down here seems stronger than usual," one of the men said.

"Here," his partner replied, pulling a flask from his jacket pocket. "Maybe the whore would like some, too."

"Why waste it? She won't be alive long enough to enjoy it."

"No, no," the woman moaned, as the two men began their violent torment.

Oralia cried as she listened to the sound of the men beating the woman to death. The woman's screams turned to moans and were soon drowned out by the rhythmic creaking of the rusted bed.

"Oralia," the bishop whispered. "Oralia, he called again.

"Yes, your Eminence?" Oralia replied weakly.

"Do you know the psalm of David?" he asked.

"The twenty-third psalm? Yes, I know it," she replied.

"Then say it with me," the bishop ordered.

"*The LORD is my shepherd, I shall not be in want.*
    He makes me lie down in green pastures,
he leads me beside quiet waters,
    he restores my soul."

Even as they prayed Oralia winced at each creak of the rusty springs as the men continued the brutal attack on the lifeless woman.

"*He guides me in paths of righteousness*
    for his name's sake.
Even though I walk
    through the valley of the shadow of death
I will fear no evil
    for you are with me;"

The moans had stopped and Oralia could hear the rattling of chains.

"She's passed out again," one of the men complained. "Let's put her on the rack and hear some real screams."

Oralia could hear the men dragging the body from the bed to another area somewhere further behind her.

"*your rod and your staff,*
they comfort me." the bishop continued.

"Oralia, you must continue to pray with me," he insisted. "We must pray for her salvation."

"*You prepare a table before me*
in the presence of my enemies."

Oralia could hear the noise as the ropes were ratcheted tighter.

"*You anoint my head with oil;*
my cup overflows."

Tendons and muscles ripped as the woman's limbs were torn from their sockets. Yet she did not cry out as the men had hoped.

"*Surely goodness and loving kindness will follow me*
All the days of my life,"

"Damn, the whore up and died on us before we could finish," one of the men complained.

"*and I will dwell in the house of the LORD*
forever."

God had been merciful, allowing the woman to die long before the men had finished their sadistic ritual.

"Let's have some fun with that one," one of the men said pointing towards Oralia.

"No, you heard what the bishop said. We can't touch her until after tonight. Besides, I need some rest. We've got a busy day and I need some sleep before all the work begins," his partner explained.

"What about the whore?"

"Leave her on the rack. We can throw her in the pit later."

"I'll be seeing you later," one of the men said as he patted Oralia on the behind.

Oralia gritted her teeth in anger, knowing a smart remark could cost her dearly.

The men were half way up the stairs when one of them grabbed the others coat sleeve.

"Hell, we almost forgot to do what we were sent here for," he said.

"I'm glad you remembered," his partner replied, as they walked back down the steps.

"As Satan commands I have sacrificed a body so his servant, Lucia can return and his will be done," the man recited.

"It's Lucienne," the other man corrected. "She goes by the name of Lucienne now."

"Lucia, Lucienne, it doesn't matter. They both mean the 'Light'," his partner corrected. "Satan knows who the hell I'm talking about."

"Have another drink of absinthe," his partner offered. The other man gladly took the flask and took a large gulp. The men waited expecting Lucienne to appear at any moment.

"Looks like she's not coming," one of them said after a couple of minutes. "She must already be here."

"We should give it a few more minutes," the other said looking at his watch. "We don't know how long the whore had been dead before we noticed.

"Then you wait for her, I'm going home to get some sleep. This place stinks and I've had more than enough absinthe to drink."

The man started back up the stairs.

"Wait for me," his partner called. "If she does show up, I don't want to have to face her alone."

"Leave the torch just in case she does show," his partner suggested.

"Remember me in your prayers Father," the other man called out to Bishop Castillo and then laughed.

"And don't forget about our date tonight, sweetie," the other man said to Oralia.

"Lord have mercy on their souls," the bishop whispered hoarsely.

Tears began to flow down Oralia's cheeks as the chamber's door locks snapped back into place and the men's final words echoed in her head.

CHAPTER THIRTY-ONE

"Darkness"

Even at this early hour the sanctuary was crowded with worshipers praying before the weeping Madonna. Among them was the Reverend Father who Kevin recognized upon entering the church.

"Father please forgive my interrupting your prayers, but we have been trying to reach you or Oralia since yesterday morning. Is everything okay?" Kevin asked.

"Thank you, Lord," the Reverend Father said as he crossed himself. "God has answered one of my prayers and returned you safely to the templo. I didn't know how to reach you. Oralia had that information and I've been unable to contact her since I left for the meeting with the bishop yesterday morning."

"She wasn't at the processional?" Kevin said.

"She wasn't anywhere that I would've expected to see her and she never returned to the templo last night. I'm very concerned. That's why I'm here now, praying for her safety and for guidance as what to do next."

"Did you check her desk? Maybe she left us a note," Kevin suggested.

"I did look. The only thing I found out of the ordinary was Bruno Mancini's journal. It was lying open on her desk."

"She wouldn't leave the journal just lying there for no reason. It must be a clue," Kevin said, as he and the Reverend Father rushed to the office.

"Maybe she dropped it and ran out when the fire alarm went off," Reverend Father suggested.

"There was a fire?"

"No, it seems someone pulled the alarm at the entrance to the mausoleum."

"Did the fire brigade search the mausoleum?"

"I know what you're getting at. They searched everywhere but found no fire. Nor did they find Oralia," Reverend Father answered.

Kevin didn't like the sound of that. He picked up the journal and began to read. "It's talking about a specific crypt in the mausoleum. There's a crude map of the room and note about a mislabeled scripture from Matthew. Wait a minute. I know that symbol." Kevin said excitedly, as he reached into his pocket. "It's the symbol on the librarian's ring."

Kevin held the ring next to the journal so the Reverend Father could see the resemblance.

"God help us! I knew I'd seen that symbol. Bishop Toribio wears an identical ring," Reverend Father exclaimed. "What does it mean?"

Kevin didn't want to worry the Reverend Father anymore than he already was so decided not to tell him what he and Romero had seen at the El Corte Inglés.

"I'm not sure, but I do intend to find out," Kevin replied.

"Are these of any importance?" Reverend Father said picking up two pieces of paper from the printer tray.

Kevin scanned the papers. "Very important. It seems that the emblem we saw that was carried in Friday's processional was the emblem of the Spanish Inquisition."

"What about the green cross?" Reverend Father asked.

"It was the cross of the auto de fe." Kevin replied.

"Why would that be significant?" Reverend Father asked.

"Because the auto de fe was the processional of the guilty, right before they were to be put to death," Kevin explained.

"Just like what happened on Friday," Reverend Father replied. "God help us."

"I need to let Romero know what Oralia discovered," Kevin said.

"And I shall call for a meeting of all pastors in the Metropolitan after this morning's Mass. I'll explain what we've discovered and we shall confront Bishop Toribio with the evidence."

"I don't think that's such a good idea right now," Kevin replied. "There's more to this story that we need to find out before we go accusing or confronting anybody. My recommendation is to go on like nothing is out of the ordinary. Romero and Francois will be back in a couple of hours. I'll let Romero know about the bishop's ring and we'll decide what our next move will be. Until then, I'm going to see what else I can learn from this journal and you should get ready for Mass."

"I'll do as you wish if you promise you'll find out what happened to Oralia," Reverend Father insisted.

"I've got a feeling Bruno Mancini's journal may just hold that answer too," Kevin replied.

"Exactly what was it you were expecting to see in the dining room?" Francois asked.

"I was hoping the 'Seven of the Cross' would be meeting," Romero answered.

"So, none of those workers setting up the table are part of the 'Seven'?" Francois joked.

"No, but you can bet they're setting up for a lunch meeting and my money says it will be for the 'Seven'," Romero replied. "Now try not to attract attention. I don't want any of my officers calling my comisario because some crazed French Prefect was asking too many questions," Romero warned.

"My lips are sealed. No, forget I said that, especially after what Lucienne did to that hotel security guard back in Paris," Francois cringed as he remembered the guard's mouth seared shut.

"Romero, what the hell are you doing here? You're supposed to be in Ronda with that serial killer from the Vatican," one of the Cuerpo officers asked.

"He's no serial killer," Francois interrupted.

The officer stared at Francois with obvious disdain. "The comisario must have called twenty times looking for you Friday night and Saturday morning. If it hadn't been for some crazy lady who kept calling and telling us you were in Ronda and that it was urgent she get a hold of you, we never would've known where the hell you were."

"Did you bring back the killer?" the officer asked.

"Somebody from the Council of Ministers came and picked him up. It seems that this Kevin Bridges had diplomatic immunity. I'm sure he's already back in Rome by now," Romero lied.

"The comisario won't be too happy to hear that."

"I plan on calling him myself later today with the news," Romero replied.

"I've some information about that woman you saved in the Plaza Mayor the other night. She was a prostitute that worked the Gran Via. She'd been reported missing by another prostitute, one called Misty, but you know the local police hear that all the time, so they didn't take it serious."

"How is she?" Francois asked, interrupting again.

"How is she?" Romero asked when the officer didn't reply to Francois query.

"Dead!"

"Dead? What happened?" Romero asked.

"Preliminary guess is a drug overdose. When we took her to the hospital she was pretty beat up and groggy, like she'd been drugged. She had abrasions on her hands and ankles where she'd been shackled. Someone had been torturing her for some time. She had a large piece of skin cut out of her back."

"I know, I saw it Friday night, but did she say anything that might help find who did this to her?" Romero asked.

"At first just a lot of bizarre mutterings about, brown monks, dark tunnels, torture chambers, and elevators. Complete nonsense." the officer replied.

Romero's interest piqued at the mention of elevators, but tried not to show it.

"She seemed to be getting better and told us that they were still holding this girl called Misty. I've got some local police walking the streets asking around to see what they can come up with."

"So, what happened?" Romero said.

"I don't know. The doctor gave her something to rest so I came back here. When I got back, Diaz was here looking for you. Just about that time the lady who'd been calling for you called again saying you were in Ronda and it was imperative she speak with you. Diaz took the call. When he hung up, I told him about what the prostitute had said. He seemed pretty upset. He went into his office and got on the phone. I got back to work and about an hour later the hospital called saying the woman had died. When I went to tell Diaz, he was gone."

"They gave no reason?" Romero asked.

"No, the doctor said he'd let us know what they find from the autopsy."

Romero and Francois exchanged glances. The news was worse than they both expected.

"Was there any trouble at last night's processional?" Romero asked.

"No, nothing out of the ordinary. We had an extra two dozen officers patrolling the Plaza Mayor and the processional route. It was a good thing too, for almost twice the crowd showed up after hearing about all the hysterics on Friday night."

"What about for tonight?" Romero asked.

"The comisario wants as many men out there as possible. Él Presidente Zapatero will be marching in tonight's processional. We plan on putting another hundred uniformed officers on the streets."

"Zapatero! Maybe that's why Lucienne wanted you out of Madrid," Francois suggested.

"Who is Lucienne?" the officer asked.

Romero's glare reminded Francois that he was to keep his mouth shut.

"Lucienne is an acquaintance in Ronda," Romero said trying to cover Francois' gaff.

"What does she have to do with Zapatero?" the officer pressed.

"Any idea where I can reach the comisario?" Romero asked trying to change the subject.

"I was surprised when he dropped by the office yesterday asking about you. I guess you could try his cell phone but, you know as well as I, he never answers. Leave him a message and hope he calls you back."

"Then I guess that's what I'll have to do," Romero said, hoping to satisfy the officer's concerns.

"Are you planning on being at the Plaza Mayor tonight? Diaz said get as many officers there as possible," the officer said.

"I wouldn't miss it for the world," Romero replied.

"Should be quite a religious spectacle," Francois added, causing both the other men to look at him with furled brows.

ঌ ঌ ঌ

"Oralia, Oralia," Bishop Castillo wheezed. "God has sent us an angel of mercy."

Oralia was able to turn her head just enough to glimpse the amorphous shape as it began to take human form.

"That's no angel," Oralia said. "That's one of Satan's demons. She was the one those two men summoned forth."

"And it was about time they did," Lucienne responded. "Tartarus can be so foul at times. Speaking of foul, doesn't anyone bother to take out the trash here? There are putrefying bodies laying everywhere. I'll have to speak to the 'Seven' about this. Why can't they summons me from some expensive spa or luxury hotel? This just won't do at all."

"The Lord rebuke you." Oralia began to chant.

"Oralia, it's so good to see you again. I see you've become acquainted with the 'Seven of the Cross'. Gabriel will certainly enjoy your company. He likes mouthy women, or at least he likes to whip them if I recall his sexual preferences. And Bishop Castillo, I'm surprised to see that Bishop Toribio has allowed you to live for so long. Perhaps he's saving you for the *coup de grâce* later this evening."

"Whatever it is you've planned, will not succeed," Bishop Castillo warned. "The Kingdom of God is here to invade our world and give hope to this dark place."

"There is no hope for God's Kingdom. There is no hope for mankind and, believe me for what I say is true, there is no hope for either of you," Lucienne began to laugh hysterically at her mocking of Jesus' word as she dashed up the steps.

"What was that evil creature?" Bishop Castillo asked, his voice growing weaker.

"Lucia de la Cruz, the one they now call Lucienne. Kevin says she's a Nephilim," Oralia explained.

"Lucia de la Cruz. Light of the Cross," the Bishop barely whispered. "A Nephilim…"

"Bishop Castillo, are you, all right?" Oralia called when his whisper turned to a gasp.

"Bishop Castillo," she called again, but still there was no response.

"God please help us," Oralia began to pray when suddenly she remembered something she had read in Bruno Mancini's journal.

"Pray in Latin. Satan hates it when you pray in Latin."

"If Satan hates it, maybe God is more likely to hear it," Oralia thought and began the only prayer she knew in Latin. The Lord's Prayer.

PATER noster, qui es in caelis, sanctificetur nomen tuum.
Adveniat regnum tuum. Fiat voluntas tua, sicut in caelo et in terra.
Panem nostrum quotidianum da nobis hodie,
et dimitte nobis debita nostra sicut et nos dimittimus debitoribus nostris.

Et ne nos inducas in tentationem,
sed libera nos a malo. Amen.

It was all Kevin could do to keep from rushing down to the mausoleum and seeing if the ring was the key to some secret passage. He had promised he wouldn't go anywhere until Romero and Francois returned, but he also promised the Reverend Father he would do everything in his power to find Oralia. She was undoubtedly in serious trouble and Kevin knew that the mausoleum was most likely the clue to finding her. Still, with exploring the mausoleum the obvious and immediate thing he should do, Kevin felt it placed upon his heart to further explore the journal. It was one of those God things that are so very hard to explain, yet so easy to understand when you've come to know Jesus. There was something more God wanted him to learn from the journal before he took any action.

"The cross must be the key," Kevin said talking to himself as he often did when trying to figure something out. He opened the drawer where Oralia had placed the cross earlier.

"Where's the damn…" Kevin started to say but stopped, as he rifled through the desk drawers.

"Oralia must have taken it," Kevin said to himself. "But why? What was it she said about the cross?" he said trying to remember, "something about Bruno having to turn it like a key to get it out of the witch's skull. Maybe it really is a key."

He continued to read the journal hoping something else helpful could be found. He was nearing the end of the journal when he read Bruno's request for two containers of the Madonna's bloody tears.

"*But now in Christ Jesus you who once were far away have been brought near through the blood of Christ.*" Kevin read and he understood.

"But Liz already took Lucienne back to Tartarus," he thought. "At least that is what Liz said she was going to do."

Kevin grew agitated. He found a jar full of instant coffee sitting on a shelf. He poured out the coffee crystals into an empty cup too small to hold the jar's contents. The crystals spilled all over the desk. He knew he should write the Reverend Father a note, but something told him time was now of the essence. He ran out into the packed sanctuary and slowly worked his way to where the Madonna stood crying.

"I need you to fill the jar with the bloody tears," he ordered one of the monks assigned to keep the crowd from touching the statue.

"Bishop Toribio has ordered that no..." the monk began.

"Father Toribio is not yet the bishop and if you don't do as I say, I can assure you that it won't be Father Toribio who you must answer to, but God himself," Kevin warned sternly.

Something in Kevin's voice told the monk that no truer words could be spoken. He took the jar and did as Kevin requested. The Mass was nearing completion but Kevin knew he could wait no longer to inform Reverend Father of his plans, but as he hurried towards the steps leading to the mausoleum the Reverend Father's words to the congregation confirmed what he knew God had called him to do.

"*How much more, then, will the blood of Christ, who through the eternal Spirit offered himself unblemished to God, cleanse our consciences from acts that lead to death, so that we may serve the living God!*"

"It is a God thing. No sin can stifle his forgiveness." Kevin said, as he took the steps two at a time.

CHAPTER THIRTY-TWO

"Obsession"

"**Él Presidente Gabriel Arciga!** I do like the sound of that," Arciga said proudly.

"And by this time tomorrow it will be so," one of the 'Seven' replied.

"It will be so if Lord Satan desires such," Diaz warned. "Don't ever forget who it is we serve."

"You serve the 'Light', of course," Lucienne said as the elevator door opened revealing her and Bishop Toribio.

All conversations ceased as the remaining members of the "Seven of the Cross" all respectfully and a bit fearfully found their ways to their assigned seats.

"Now what was it you were saying?" Toribio asked Diaz.

"I was only warning my brothers that Brother Arciga will be the next él Presidente if and only if that is what Satan desires," Diaz replied.

"And what about what I desire?" Lucienne asked. "Don't you wish to please me?"

"We worship the 'Light'," Diaz assured her. "And as our Lord Satan's emissary, we will do all you ask, for we know it will please him."

"And pleasing him, pleases me," Lucienne responded, sitting down next to the bishop.

"Now let's eat before it gets cold," Bishop Toribio announced.

A buffet of breakfast and lunch foods had been delivered just moments before the men arrived. It was the duty of Señor Guidino, the vice-president of El Corte Inglés, to ensure that the identities of the other members of the "Seven of the Cross' were protected and their favorite foods always prepared. It was his building that supplied the access to the catacombs and torture chamber through the private elevators he had installed. His facility was also the staging ground for the attack on tonight's processional. Still, Señor Guidino felt his membership in the 'Seven of the Cross' was tenuous at best. A feeling shared by several other members but not discussed out of fear of the 'Light'. The librarian's violent dispatching by Lucienne, though discussed, left a seed of uncertainty in many of their minds. Who would be the next member whose usefulness to the 'Seven' would be trumped by the 'Light's' desire to admit a worthier member? The librarian had been essential in researching and writing the Libro de Reglas that documented the history of the 'Light' and of the "Seven of the Cross", yet his value to the society had waned. How soon would the 'Light' decide another of the 'Seven' had outstayed his welcome?

"Minister Arciga, what have you heard about the King? Will he be joining Zapatero at the processional?" Toribio asked.

"The King will be hosting the Canadian Prime Minister at the Prado this evening. I too must attend," Arciga replied.

"What about Zapatero?" Toribio now asked of Diaz.

"Zapatero will also be in attendance at the Prado, but his security chief assures me that he'll leave in plenty of time to participate in the processional. It seems his popularity among Catholics needs a boost," Diaz replied, trying to ignore Lucienne's glare of displeasure.

"The bishop informed me that you have Kevin Bridges in custody. Is this true?" Lucienne demanded.

"He was arrested in Ronda early yesterday morning. I've ordered one of my men to stay with him until Monday and then bring him back to Madrid," Diaz replied.

"Would that be your Inspector Romero?" Lucienne said. "If so, I think you'd better verify that he and Bridges are still in Ronda. I hear he interfered in Friday's celebration in the Plaza Mayor."

"Romero would never dare to defy a direct order from me," Diaz insisted. "But I'll do as you suggest and call the Ronda civil guard."

"It wasn't a suggestion." Lucienne sneered.

"I'd like to hear what you know about this woman investigator from Interpol. There are rumors that she possesses some extraordinary powers. Powers remarkably similar to your own," Diaz challenged.

"No one but Satan has powers equal to mine," Lucienne snapped back. "This woman you speak of will cause us no more trouble. I've seen to that."

A noticeable chill came over the dining room.

"Why don't we all relax and enjoy our lunch," Toribio suggested.

"Excellent idea," Arciga added. "Has anyone else tried the salmon? It's to die for." But no one was in the mood to respond.

୨ଚ   ୨ଚ   ୨ଚ

Although the map had been drawn almost three centuries ago, the mausoleum had changed very little and Kevin was able to immediately find the crypt with the verse from Matthew labeled with the strange symbol.

"A secret passage, who would've believed it?" Kevin said as he stuck the ring into its identical inverse.

The crack of the bolt releasing echoed through the mausoleum.

"Well that was easy," Kevin said, trying to pull the front of the crypt open with no success.

"I've no time for this," Kevin said in frustration. "I need to get in there now."

Just like Oralia had done, Kevin struggled trying to open the crypt every way imaginable until in frustration he pounded his fist on the scripture passage and the door gently swung open.

"What do you know? Just like Matthew said, '*Knock and the door will be opened to you.*"

Kevin's faith was growing greater by the minute.

"You all know your assignments. We'll meet back here at 10:00 p.m. to enjoy the spectacle, when Satan digs his claws not only into Madrid, but into all of Spain. The coming of the 'Light' supported by the 'Seven of the Cross' is now upon us. The time has come to expand Satan's realm and ascend to power." Toribio declared.

He held up a glass of the emerald colored absinthe. The other six men did likewise.

"All hail the 'Light', all hail Satan," Toribio toasted as soothing warmth now seemed to envelope each man in the room.

A second glass of absinthe was poured for each of the men.

"Now I propose a toast," Lucienne said, lifting her glass and beginning to slowly walk behind all the men standing at the table. A shared nervousness was felt by all but Toribio.

"You all have served me well. Your deeds have been documented in the Libro de Reglas and Satan shall hold a special place for each of you in his kingdom. Tonight, is our time to show the world just how powerful his kingdom is. We cannot fail. Zapatero must die as must thousands more. I expect no less. It's been almost three hundred years since Satan deceived God into allowing the seven accused in the Templo Eucarístico de San Martín auto de fe to be freed. It was Satan who arranged for my freedom from Tartarus through the body of the accused heretical witch Lucia de la Cruz. And it was Bishop Toribio's ancestor, Jayro Toribio, who acted on Satan's commands. That's why I'm the 'Light of the Cross' and you're the 'Seven of the Cross', symbolic of the seven heretics Satan freed from the Inquisitor's torture, now, forever compeled to inflict that torture in Satan's name. Destiny has bound us forever. All hail the 'Seven of the Cross'," Lucienne toasted.

All seven men poured the entire glass of the anise flavored liqueur down their throats. They had grown accustomed to the burning and the pungent flavor. They also welcomed the energized drunken fog the absinthe always seemed to provide. An immediate and guaranteed escape from the reality of who they really were, the vile deeds they were doing, and the evil one who they served.

"Tonight, we celebrate Satan's victory," Toribio congratulated. Then he, Lucienne, and Minister Arciga left so the others could make the final preparations.

ço   ço   ço

"Oralia," Bishop Castillo barely croaked.
"God has answered my payers, you're still alive," Oralia cried in relief. "Try not to talk. I know God will send us help."
"Oralia, it's you who God has sent to save us," the bishop moaned.
"Please Monsignor, save your energy," Oralia pleaded.
"It's you, it's you, it's you," the bishop repeated almost incoherently.

"He must be delirious," Oralia thought. "He doesn't even remember that I'm imprisoned along with him."

"Our Father…," Oralia began but remembered Bruno's words.

"*Latin, you must pray in Latin.*"

"I hear you Lord," Oralia said and this time began the Lord's Prayer in Latin.

"Shouldn't we get back to see what Kevin has found out from Oralia?" Francois asked.

"I've got to see what's going on in the dining room. Zapatero may be in danger and those seven men are somehow behind it," Romero explained.

"Oralia and the Reverend Father may also be in danger," Francois replied.

"This will just take a few minutes," Romero assured him, as they arrived on the Hotel Atlantico rooftop.

Romero held the camera to his eye.

"This is bad, really bad," Romero said handing the camera to Francois.

"What is it," Francois asked as he lifted the camera to have a look. "That's Lucienne!"

"I told you it was really bad," Romero replied. "What's happening now?"

"Lucienne is walking around the table talking. I wish I could read lips. She's holding a glass in her hand as are all the men. It looks like they're getting ready for a toast."

"Let me see," Romero said, taking the camera back from Francois.

"It is a toast." Romero watched quietly for a moment. "It looks like Lucienne, the bishop, and Minister Arciga are leaving. I think it's time we visit the dining room," Romero said.

"But isn't your comisario still there?" Francois asked.

"He is, but now I know for sure whose side he's on," Romero replied.

"We can't go there without Kevin," Francois insisted.

"I know, but we've got to hurry. We've got to find out what they're up to."

"Maybe Kevin has discovered something that might help us," Francois said, as they headed back down the elevator.

"I pray to God he has," Romero replied.

"I never thought I'd say it, but so do I," Francois responded.

CHAPTER THIRTY-THREE

"Ignorance"

"**Oralia would've never gone** through here on her own accord without telling anyone," Kevin thought. "Somebody had to forcibly take her. That has to be why she set off the fire alarm."

"I should've brought a flashlight," Kevin said to himself looking into the crypt. He climbed in slowly feeling his way towards the rear of the crypt. When he touched the back, another door swung open, but at the same time the entrance closed behind him.

"Maybe I shouldn't do this without telling someone either," Kevin said knowing he had no other choice but to keep going.

"These must be the old catacombs that Bruno Mancini predicted were here," Kevin said to himself.

A dim light from somewhere down the catacombs pierced the darkness ever so slightly. Kevin could hear a soft buzzing.

"That's the sound of a ballast going out on a fluorescent light. I guess there have been a few upgrades," Kevin said, continuing his nervous habit of talking to himself.

Unfortunately for Kevin, he didn't know the extent of the upgrades.

The soft dinging of the bell and flashing of the light startled Diaz.

"Somebody just came through the mausoleum passage," Diaz exclaimed, looking at the two men who had been sent earlier to kill the prostitute and summon forth Lucienne.

"I guarantee it's not that church secretary. Neither of us touched her. When we left she was still in the stocks," one of them said.

"And Bishop Castillo was as close to dead as a man can be. He was far too weak to even talk, let alone free himself from the garrote," his partner replied.

"Well somebody who shouldn't be is in the catacombs and we better find out who and stop them damn quick before Lucienne or Toribio find out about it," Diaz warned.

"Maybe it's Lucienne or the bishop checking on the prisoners," the first man suggested.

"He would have told us if that was his plan. Besides, even if they did change their plans they wouldn't enter from the mausoleum. You two come with me. You two finish checking the gas valves in the tunnels and get the trucks ready to go. I'm sure none of us want to end up like the librarian."

Just the thought made each man shudder.

৯   ৯   ৯

"God be with you," Reverend Father said to the overflowing crowd.

"And also, with you," they responded in unison.

Francois and Romero stood impatiently at the back of the sanctuary as the Reverend Father made his way back to his office.

"Reverend Father, have you seen Kevin or Oralia?" Francois asked.

"Oralia has been missing since yesterday. I left Kevin here in the office before Mass. He was reading from Bruno Mancini's journal. See, it still lies on the desk. He discovered that the ring he took from the librarian is a key that may unlock a secret passage in the mausoleum. The ring is identical to the one acting-bishop Toribio wears."

"Comisario Diaz also wears one with the same symbol on it," Romero replied. "Did Kevin learn anything else?"

"No, but Oralia discovered the meaning of the green emblem and cross. It is the emblem of the Spanish Inquisition. Kevin was planning to tell you this."

"So where is Kevin?" Romero asked again frustrated.

"I would guess he went to find Oralia," Francois replied. "Probably through that secret passage."

"Do you plan on searching the mausoleum?" Reverend Father asked.

"We don't have the ring nor do we have the time," Romero replied. "I believe there are men who are plotting to kill él Presidente Zapatero at tonight's processional," Romero explained.

"And you believe Toribio and your comisario are part of this plot?" Reverend Father asked.

"I do," Romero replied. "And I believe these men are also responsible for Oralia's disappearance."

"Do you have proof of any of this?" Reverend Father asked.

"If we tried to prove it we'd be too late to stop it," Francois interjected.

"What do you intend to do about it?" Reverend Father asked.

"We intend to stop them," Romero replied bluntly.

"Just remember what Peter says," Reverend Father warned. *"Be self-controlled and alert. Your enemy the devil prowls around like a roaring lion looking for someone to devour."*

"Satan's already had enough to eat around here," Francois replied. "It's time for us to send him and his evil servants back where they belong."

"You are truly God's warriors," Reverend Father assured them. "I'll pray for God's wisdom to guide you in your spiritual battle."

Both Romero and Francois knew they could use all the help God could give them.

*   *   *

"It seems that Comisario Diaz' comments put you on the defensive today. I must say that chill you brought into the room left quite a fright in some of the 'Seven'," Bishop Toribio remarked.

"Yourself included?" Lucienne asked.

"Satan turned my heart to ice years ago, although, admittedly, when you changed from the chill to that glowing warmth, more than my heart was stirred," Toribio said, with a sly smile.

"Save it for your whores," Lucienne snapped back. "We have much to prepare for tonight's processional."

"You worry too much. Everything's in place and my men are making the final preparations as we speak," the bishop assured her.

"I fear Comisario Diaz has become lax in his supervision of his own men. Inspector Romero was working with Kevin Bridges in Ronda."

"What makes you so sure?" Toribio replied.

"I was there. I arranged for Kevin and Francois to come there. My plan was to kill the French prefect and place the blame on Kevin Bridges," Lucienne explained.

"Then you succeeded, for Diaz told us Bridges is in jail," Toribio replied.

"I'm not so sure," Lucienne said.

"You said you arranged for them to be there. How did you manage that?"

"The Interpol woman you've been so concerned about brought them to me."

"She what?"

"Elizabeth Purdue, I forget her true name. She's also an earthly Nephilim, or should I say was an earthly Nephilim. She's condemned to Tartarus until the day she submits to the reality that her only way out is to wander the earth as a demon, just as God ordained."

"She has been working with you?" Toribio said surprised.

"Not entirely, and that I'm sure she now regrets. Foolishly she sacrificed her own freedom pulling me back to Tartarus in an attempt to save Bridges and Romero. She had a deluded belief that if she tried to do what was right in God's eye then perhaps God would see fit to have mercy on her pitiful soul. A fool's dream, for Satan holds tightly her heart. She didn't realize that the 'Seven' were pledged to constantly summon me forth. A mistake she no doubt wishes she could undo."

"Even if Romero and Bridges are working together what danger do they pose to us in Ronda?" Toribio asked.

"None, if indeed they are in Ronda as Comisario Diaz claims. However, I doubt that Diaz is as well informed as he leads us all to believe."

"Are you suggesting Comisario Diaz has failed in his duties to the 'Seven of the Cross'?" Bishop Toribio asked.

"Perhaps he has or perhaps he will, I really don't know at this point, but I do intend to find out," Lucienne replied.

"Comisario Diaz is a valuable asset in his leadership role with the Cuerpo Nacional," the bishop reminded her.

"And I'm sure when Minister Arciga becomes él Presidente Arciga, Diaz will be assigned even greater power," Lucienne replied. "However, I sense a weakness in his heart that may require my attention."

"I hope it doesn't come to that," the bishop replied, "but who am I to question what Satan commands?"

"Or what I desire," Lucienne whispered, as once again a warmth began to radiate within the Bishop.

CHAPTER THIRTY-FOUR

"Doubt"

"Well, what have we here?" Kevin said picking up the cross that he had last seen in Oralia's desk drawer.

"I'm not sure if this is a good sign or a bad sign. At least I know she had to have come this way."

As his eyes adjusted to the dim light, Kevin scanned the small chamber behind the wall of crypts looking for any other clues that may lead him to Oralia. After a quick perusal, and seeing nothing of importance, he cautiously peered around the corner and down the catacomb to where the buzzing seemed to emanate. He saw darkened areas along the corridor walls indicating either bisecting catacombs or other chambers.

"I got a bad feeling about this," he whispered, then sighed and headed down the catacomb keeping his back to the side wall. When he reached the first opening he could see it was another chamber.

"Remember your training, count to three and just pop in and out a couple of times," Kevin told himself. He knew if somebody was waiting for him inside a moving target would be harder to hit.

"One, two, three," he said then quickly ducked in and out of the doorway. The room was empty, at least empty as far as any living people. There were several alcoves piled high with bones and mummified corpses. He stepped in the room to have a closer look when he heard what sounded like the shuffling of feet.

"That's not good," he whispered softly, holding the cross as a potential weapon.

He repeated his three count and reentered the catacomb in the same manner he had entered the chamber. This time with cross in hand poised to strike.

His movement startled several rats that were running down the catacomb, causing them to scatter in all directions.

The next doorway was several feet ahead on the opposite wall of the catacomb. He wasn't as cautious this time walking down the center of the catacomb until he was just shy of the opening. After his three-count, he popped in and out as he had before, discovering this to be another chamber. However, this one had been cleared of all but one skeleton which was laid on a table as if it were a shrine. A cross identical to the one he held in his hand was driven into the wooden table above the skeleton's head. Behind the table was large marble stone inlaid into the chamber wall inscribed with the same scripture from Matthew that was on the crypt leading to the secret passage. However, this marble plaque bore the name of the person whose skeleton now lay on the table.

"Jayro Toribio, freer of the 'Light' and first of the 'Seven of the Cross'," Kevin read. "Soul claimed by Satan 1725."

Kevin again heard some shuffling and turned just as something bit him on the neck. The last thing he remembered before everything went black was seeing Comisario Diaz holding a taser and smiling.

੭ଡ଼   ੭ଡ଼   ੭ଡ଼

"Are you sure you can't see anyone?" Romero asked.

"Not from this angle. The only way we're going to know for sure if they are there, is if we go back on the roof of the hotel," Francois explained.

"We can't take the time," Romero replied.

"Well I hope you have some sort of plan for getting us in there," Francois said.

"No, but I'm sure one will come to me," Romero replied pulling his car into the underground parking garage for El Corte Inglés.

"There's a space," Francois said, as Romero drove by yet another free spot. "Just what is it you're looking for?"

"I'm looking for official government vehicles," Romero replied.

"Like the one we're driving?"

"Yes, but a lot nicer. If Minister Arciga is still here we should be able to find his car. We also should be able to find the comisario's car as well."

"Turn down there," Francois quipped.

"What for? That says deliveries only."

"Do you really think Arciga or Diaz or, for that matter, any of the others, are going to park among the customers cars. I don't think so. If they're still here, we'll find them parked someplace with a little more privacy," Francois suggested.

"You're right," Romero asked turning down the ramp the wrong way.

"There's the comisario's car," Romero noted, "but I don't see Arciga's."

"That one belongs to the store's vice-president," Francois noted.

"How do you know that?"

"The placard on the wall in front of the car says so," Francois smiled.

"That leaves four more men but only three cars are here," Romero said.

"Don't forget about Lucienne," Francois said.

"I very much doubt she came in a car," Romero replied.

"Liz does, or did," Francois remarked. "Hey, if Lucienne has returned from this Tartarus place, maybe Liz will come back too."

"I don't understand how that works, but from what Kevin told us, I wouldn't count on it."

"You're probably right. My guess is Lucienne went with the bishop. He seems to be the man in charge," Francois said. "And right about now he should be getting ready for the Mass he holds before the processional."

"What do you think these trucks are doing here?" Romero asked. "*Petit Forestier.*" Romero read on the side of the truck. "Isn't that a French truck rental company?"

"I think they rent all over Europe, but I've never seen one in Spain before, but then again, I don't get here too often," Francois replied. "Maybe they're delivering some French wine to the store."

"Not on Sunday, and why four trucks?"

"Spaniards must drink a lot of French wine," Francois joked.

"Not this Spaniard," Romero replied snidely.

"Want me to take a look?" Francois offered.

"No, I think we need to park and head up stairs to the dining room," Romero replied. "We've got to find out what they're planning."

"Shouldn't you call for some backup?"

"You are my backup," Romero replied, opening the glove compartment and handing Francois a semi-automatic Glock 21.

"Will this stop a Nephilim?"

"I don't know about that, but those 45 caliber hollow points will pretty much remove a man's head."

"Let's hope that doesn't become necessary," Francois replied, as the two men exited the car.

"Now what was your plan again?" Francois joked.

"Let's go discuss it over lunch," Romero replied wryly, as they stepped into the public elevator.

Oralia heard a feint shuffling sound somewhere above her. "I think someone's coming," Oralia whispered to the bishop, but she heard no reply.

"Please Lord, don't let him be dead," she prayed.

The bolt snapped free from the torture chamber door echoing through the room.

"Pretend you're asleep," the bishop barely wheezed.

Oralia wished the stocks were turned so she could see who was entering but her only clue was the shadows reflecting on the far wall. Torches were lit at the top of the stairs.

"Use the strappado," Diaz ordered, "and put the fork on him to keep him quiet. I don't want him talking to that secretary woman."

"Yes Brother Diaz," one of the men replied.

The medieval fork was actually two little forks set against each other that were connected by a neck collar which allowed for the forks to be adjusted up and down. The collar was placed around Kevin's neck. One fork was rammed into the flesh under his chin while the other stuck in his chest just above the breast bone. No vital points were penetrated. Its only purpose was to keep the victim quiet and calm while prolonging the torture and suffering.

As the two men struggled to place the fork on the unconscious Kevin, Diaz checked on the two other prisoners.

"Did you miss me?" he said to Oralia running his hand across her hips.

"Don't you dare touch me," Oralia hissed, rattling the stocks as she tried to free her hands.

Diaz pressed his body hard against Oralia leaning over to whisper into her ear.

"Get away from me," Oralia began to scream, so frantically thrashing her wrists in an attempt to free them that they began to bleed.

"Leave her alone," the bishop attempted to cry out but started to cough uncontrollably.

"You better shut your mouth, old man, before you kill yourself," Diaz called to Bishop Castillo.

The two men still trying to adjust the forks on Kevin laughed at the scene.

"She's a feisty one," the first said.

"Maybe we'll find out just how feisty later," his partner grinned.

Diaz wandered back over to see the progress the men were making. He laid the cross he had taken from Kevin on the table and poured three glasses of absinthe.

"I never get used to the smell of putrefying flesh," Diaz commented

"The absinthe will help with the smell," one of the men said.

"This thing's all rusted, these adjustment screws barely turn," the other complained.

"I don't think Mr. Bridges will need to worry about contracting blood poisoning from a rusted fork," Diaz laughed. "You boys finish up here then place the explosives next to those gas release valves in the tunnels under the plaza. I need to find the Bishop and Lucienne to see what they want to do about this intrusion." Although he didn't say it to the two other members of the 'Seven', Diaz could feel things were beginning to spiral out of control. If Kevin was able to return to the templo and enter the catacombs, then it was a good bet that Romero is working with him just as Lucienne suggested. If Romero had figured it out, whom else could he have told? Diaz's stomach began to knot up at the thought of what Lucienne would do when she found out.

"Or does she already know?" Diaz said softly to himself.

Perspiration started to run down the comisario's face as he looked down at the chamber of horrors below him.

"Lord, what have I done?"

He exited the torture chamber closing the heavy stone door and locking the steel bars in place. Then he pulled a special key from his pocket. This was a regular key and fit into a special lock hidden several feet down the wall behind a loose stone. He inserted the key and turned it. Instantly several more steel bolts slid into the doorway sealing the chamber from anyone leaving or entering. Next to the key was a valve. Only he and Toribio knew about this secret lock and valve.

"You two get the easy way out," Diaz said and turned the valve.

CHAPTER THIRTY-FIVE

"Irreverence"

"**You any good at picking locks?**" Romero asked when the reached the door leading to the rooftop dining room.

"Yes, but not in front of an audience," Francois said, noting the security cameras covering the door. "Let's try the kitchen. There must be a service elevator or at least another staircase leading up there."

The two men walked through the public dining room and into the kitchen, just like they knew what they were doing.

"Pick out an important looking person, but not the most important looking," Romero said.

"That one there," Francois said, pointing to one of the chefs shouting orders.

Romero pulled out his badge. "Cuerpo Nacional, I need to access to the roof immediately."

The chef looked at Romero's badge then picked up a long butcher knife. Francois reached for his Glock but Romero lifted his hand signaling him to relax.

"Eet's loked," the chef replied with a heavy accent. "but I haf key." He held up the knife and grinned.

The three men walked to the back of the kitchen to a locked door next to a double dumbwaiter.

"Key," the chef said and stuck the butcher knife blade between the door and the jamb. With a quick upward lift the door popped open.

"Thank you," Francois offered, but the chef just nodded and began shouting out orders to his kitchen staff.

"I don't think he'll be telling anyone," Romero said, as the two men headed up the steps wondering what lay ahead.

❧   ❧   ❧

"What say you we have a little fun with the secretary?"

"The bishop said not to touch her," his partner reminded.

"Yes, but that was earlier and if Diaz can play why can't we?" his partner argued.

"Maybe we could have just a little fun without hurting her too badly," the other man agreed.

"Damn, the screw broke on this old rusted fork," the man said.

"Forget about it," his partner replied, as he wandered over to the stocks to tease Oralia while the other finished tying Kevin's hands to the strappado.

Oralia did her best to ignore the taunts pretending to be asleep as the man unlocked the stocks. "Let's chain her to the bed."

"Better give me a hand here first. I'll hold him while you pull the rope."

The strappado in the torture chamber had been upgraded since the days of the Inquisition. It now consisted of a chain attached on one end to a strong rope which tied to the victim. The other end connected to a rope that ran through a complex pulley system which could be tied off on the opposite wall. It made lifting the victim extremely easy. The rope binding Kevin's hands needed to be hooked to the chain so he would be lifted about ten feet above the floor.

"I need more slack," the man attaching the chain to Kevin said.

"The other man was still staring at Oralia, imagining what he planned to do to her, paying little attention to his partner and Kevin.

"Alright, give it a pull," his partner ordered.

Both men failed to notice that the drugs given to Kevin when he was tasered had worn off and Kevin was feigning unconsciousness. As the man began to pull the rope Kevin yanked the chain into the air and wrapped it around the man's neck just as the second man began to pull. Instead of lifting Kevin off the ground, the first man was yanked by his neck into the air.

"Argh, stop, stop," came the strangled cries. However, still focusing on Oralia the second man assumed the sounds came from Kevin.

When the other man finally looked and realized what he had done he rushed over to stop Kevin who was racing to free his hands from the rope.

"No, you don't," the man said grabbing a small wooden club and striking Kevin in the back of his legs knocking him to his knees. The next blow was to Kevin's side, bruising ribs and knocking Kevin to the ground.

"Time to die," the man said kicking Kevin in the side and raising the club for a final blow to the head.

Kevin was helpless unable to protect himself. "Please God," was all he could say as the man prepared for the final blow.

"No!" Oralia screamed.

As Kevin braced himself, the strike came, but instead of the club smashing into his head, the man himself fell heavily upon Kevin. The club dropped from the man's limp hand and rolled slowly across the floor.

Kevin squirmed from beneath the man who lay gurgling on the floor. Blood poured from his mouth and from the deep wound that had severed his spine and pierced his heart.

"Lord forgive me, Lord forgive me," Oralia cried over and over as she stood above the body. In her hand was the cross that the librarian had used to kill Adela.

Oralia dropped the cross and stood frozen in place as if in a trance. Then she began to cry.

"Oralia, Oralia!" Kevin screamed. "You need to untie my hands. The other man may yet be saved."

The other member of the "Seven" had been thrashing about as asphyxiation quickly overcame him. He now moved very little.

"Oralia!" Kevin screamed again, and this time she snapped from her transfixed state.

She untied the rope binding Kevin's hands as fast as her own shaking hands would allow. Kevin ran to the wall and released the rope that dangled the man dropping him roughly to the floor.

Kevin pulled the chain from his neck to feel for a pulse.

"He's still alive, but just barely." Kevin said, but Oralia remained transfixed on the man she had killed.

"The bishop," Oralia suddenly remembered breaking the spell.

Kevin hurried over to the garrote and loosened it from Bishop Castillo's neck. "Bring me some water."

"There is no water, only this," Oralia replied bringing over the bottle of absinthe.

Kevin smelled it and grimaced.

"It's okay, it's absenta," Oralia said. "I saw these men drinking it. It's what Bruno Mancini drank."

Kevin poured a little into his hand and wet the bishop's lips.

"We'll get you out of here soon," Kevin assured him as he carried him to one of the beds laying him carefully down. "Just lie here, we'll be right back."

The bishop nodded that he understood.

"I hate to leave the bishop here alone, but there's no way I'll leave you here while I go for help," Kevin said.

"What about him," Oralia said pointing to the man who was still wheezing heavily but seeming to slowly recover.

"Help me," Kevin said, dragging the man as gently as possible towards the stocks.

"With pleasure," Oralia replied, helping to place the man in the stocks then placing the lock on the latch but not fastening it.

Kevin picked up the cross as a weapon and ran up the steps towards the door. He easily sprang the original locks but the door wouldn't budge. For several minutes he struggled with no luck.

"It looks like there are several more bolts holding it closed but I can't seem to find any way to free them," he called down.

Oralia came up to help.

"Do you smell that? It's gas. I can even hear it coming from someplace over there." She said, pointing high on the wall next to the landing.

Kevin sniffed the air. "It is gas. Hurry, put out those candles."

"Diaz must've done this when he left," Oralia said, as she rushed back down the stairs and blew out the candles then wet her fingers and snuffed the wicks.

Kevin stood on a chair that was on the landing above the chamber. "I can really smell it up here. It's slowly filling the room."

"What are we going to do?" Oralia asked.

"Definitely not light a match," Kevin said as he climbed down slowly from the chair and felt his way back down the stairs in the total darkness.

॰   ॰   ॰

"It was indeed a fine way to spend a Sunday afternoon, but as they say, duty calls," Toribio laughed.

"You just did your duty?" Lucienne said coyly.

"It is to our master Satan where my duty lies," Toribio snapped back gravely.

Lucienne watched as he dressed. He first put on his chasuble which was embroidered with gold crosses on both sides. It was a common garment worn by bishops for Mass. Next, he pulled on his silken Episcopal stockings and shoes, but instead of the customary violet, Toribio's were emerald green.

"Nice touch," Lucienne commented.

Next Toribio put on a golden pectoral cross, smaller but identical to the framework of the crosses worn by the 'Seven of the Cross'. It was a symbol of dignity reserved for the bishop and was thought to provide prophylactic powers.

When Lucienne saw the next piece of vestment Toribio was preparing to add, she gasped as she sat up in bed.

"You don't dare wear a pallium," she said shocked.

Toribio held up the three-inch-wide woolen band for Lucienne to see. "Notice that there are seven, not the usual six silken crosses interwoven into this pallium. And you should also notice the crosses are green not black," he explained as he placed it over his shoulders.

"I hope it was not deposited in the grave of St. Peter for special consecration as authentic ones are," Lucienne replied.

"Of course not."

"I thought only archbishops and special privileged bishops were allowed to wear one."

"What, I'm not special or privileged?" Toribio laughed.

He next placed the highly jeweled miter upon his head. After staring at himself in the mirror for several minutes and making adjustments to his vestments he turned and faced Lucienne.

"Well, what do you think?"

"Absolutely stunning," she replied.

"Shouldn't you be getting dressed soon?" he asked.

"I think I'll pass on the Mass," Lucienne replied. "I'm going to drop by the Prado. Minister Arciga has invited me to join him and I think I'd like to meet King Juan Carlos."

"Never satisfied, are we?" Toribio joked.

Lucienne smiled, "Just remember, Zapatero must die. I want nothing to go wrong."

"Nothing will go wrong," Toribio assured her. "By this time tomorrow Satan will rule Madrid and soon we will rule all of Spain."

Something about the word 'we' didn't quite sound right to Lucienne.

CHAPTER THIRTY-SIX

"Desperation"

"**Do you have any ideas?**" Oralia asked.

"Maybe there's a drain or sewer line for that pit I saw," Kevin suggested.

"I think that pit is full of dead bodies. Besides, how are you going to find it in the dark? "Oralia asked.

Kevin didn't answer. He stood up and tried to walk to where he remembered it being and ran into the wall.

"Ouch," Kevin said, causing Oralia to giggle.

"You find that funny?" Kevin said.

"It's either laugh or cry, and as bad as things are, I still think I'd rather laugh," Oralia replied.

"Good point," Kevin responded. "There's a rope here. Maybe I can climb up and plug up the gas valve."

"Don't even think about it," Oralia warned.

Kevin pulled on the rope, but it didn't give. He just heard a click, then a swishing sound.

"What's that?" Oralia asked.

"Uh oh," Kevin said. "Now I've done it."

"Done what?" Oralia asked. "I think I just hit the release on the pendulum."

The swishing turned to a swoosh as something swung within inches of Kevin's head. He dropped like a rock to the floor.

"Kevin, are you okay?" Oralia called.

"Yes, but whatever you do don't stand up. Crawl over towards me. We should be safe against the wall."

Oralia did as instructed and the two of them laid up against the wall listening as the pendulum swung back and forth.

"You know," Kevin finally said, "when that pendulum hits the floor the blade is going to cause a spark and this whole place is liable to explode."

"Well that's reassuring," Oralia quipped.

"Sorry," Kevin replied.

"Maybe Francois and the inspector will find us," Oralia suggested.

"I wouldn't count on it. I don't think they even know about this place," Kevin replied.

"Swoosh," the pendulum cut through the darkness somewhere overhead.

"Yes, but neither did you till you found it," Oralia replied.

"If you recall, I didn't find it, I was brought here unconscious."

"Then maybe Liz will find us. You said she had special powers," Oralia said.

"Liz is gone. When we were in Ronda, she saved us by taking Lucienne back to Tartarus. Neither of them will return," Kevin explained.

"You're wrong," Oralia snapped back. "Lucienne returned from Tartarus and appeared here several hours ago. Those two men were sent here to summon her forth after killing the prostitute."

"How do you know that?" Kevin asked.

"How do I know what? That she appeared or that they were sent here to summons her?"

"Both," Kevin said incredulously.

"As the men were leaving one of them said that he almost forgot what they came here to do. Then he said some mumbo-jumbo about Satan commanding them to sacrifice someone so his servant Lucia can return. They left, then a little while later the bishop and I watched as Lucienne seemed to fade into existence."

"Lucienne. Are you sure?"

"Swoosh," the stillness was ripped apart as the pendulum drew nearer.

"If that was Lucienne who we saw on the video at the church, then I'm sure it was her," Oralia replied. "She even greeted both Bishop Castillo and me. She complained that the 'Seven of the Cross' had summoned her back to such a foul place."

"If she was able to return, perhaps I could summon Liz back," Kevin said excitedly.

"Not unless you plan on killing someone. From their conversation you cannot summon someone forth unless you sacrifice someone," Oralia explained.

"That's right, Liz explained it to me once." Kevin was quiet while he thought about it.

"You can do it," he finally said.

"I can do what?" Oralia replied.

"You could summon Liz from Tartarus."

"No way," Oralia snapped. "There's no way I'll do that." "Either we're going to suffocate from the gas or a spark from the pendulum will blow this whole place apart. Liz could save us. You could save us."

"It would be like making a pact with the devil himself," Oralia cried.

"The reality is that you did kill the man. He's the sacrifice we need to summon forth Liz. It's our only chance for survival."

"Swoosh," the pendulum drew nearer.

"I don't know if I could do it. I don't know what to say." Oralia said softly.

"Sure, you can. Just think about what you heard them say and repeat it," Kevin assured her. "I know you can do it."

"It's just so wrong," she said.

"Think of it as deceiving the deceiver," Kevin encouraged.

"Alright," Oralia whispered, "if I must."

Kevin felt in the darkness for Oralia's hand. He held it tightly.

"As Satan commands, I have sacrificed a body so his servant, Liz Purdue, can return and his will be done." Oralia burst into tears while Kevin held her.

"Swoosh," the pendulum rushed past in the darkness growing ever lower.

"Now what?" Kevin said.

"We wait. And while we wait, we pray."

֍ ֍ ֍

The two men walked quietly up the staircase. There was much yelling and ambient noise, but it all seemed to be coming from the kitchen they had just left.

"Have you got a plan yet?" Francois asked.

"This is my plan," Romero replied.

At the top of the stairs was a large service kitchen for warming, storing, and serving food, but no cooking facilities. An antique china cabinet held three sets of very expensive looking dishes.

"I don't think anybody is home," Francois said.

"At least not in the kitchen," Romero replied.

"Look at all the soundproofing in here," Francois noted.

They walked over to a swinging door that led into the dining room.

"You think they'd at least have a window in this door," Francois commented.

"I think privacy was more important than convenience," Romero replied.

Very slowly Romero pushed the swinging door open just slightly.

"Great, all I can see is a view of the Gran Via out the window." Impatiently he pushed the door wide open and stepped into the room.

"No one's home," Francois commented.

"Maybe not, but you can be sure someone will be back. There are three sets of car keys and a cell phone on the table," Romero observed.

Francois picked up the cell phone and pushed a button.

"What are you doing?" Romero said.

"Seeing if there is a number for the 'Seven of the Cross', I thought I'd give them a call," Francois joked. "This must be your comisario's phone."

"It does look like his. How do you know?"

"Your number is listed here along with Arciga and Toribio, but no number for Diaz," Francois replied.

Romero picked up the keys. "Yeah, these are his car keys."

At that very instant, one of the elevators silently opened behind them without the customary 'ding' of warning.

Diaz pulled a blackjack and taser from his pocket. He could tell it was Romero but he was unsure who the second man was. He moved quickly before either man could react firing the taser into Francois' neck and smashing the blackjack into the back of Romero's skull. Both men dropped unconscious onto the inlaid walnut dining table.

❧ ❧ ❧

"There's enough gas in those tanks to blow up half of Old Madrid," Guidino remarked to the other member of the 'Seven'.

"And burn the other half down," his partner laughed.

"Are you sure all the remote-control valves are working? We don't want the kind of problems we had torching the whores the other night." Guidino said. "The 'Light' was none too happy about that."

"My valves worked fine. It was Diaz who screwed up. If he'd gotten rid of that Vatican investigator like he was supposed to have everything would've been fine," the man replied.

"You try to tell that to Diaz," Guidino laughed.

"I think I'll pass on that offer," the man replied, "but if I was Diaz, I'd be watching my back. Lucienne doesn't like failure."

"Lucienne won't mess with Diaz, he's too important," Guidino replied.

"Nobody's too important. When Arciga is él Presidente, he can assign or promote anyone Lucienne tells him to into a lot more powerful position than comisario of the Cuerpo Nacional," the man explained. "No, Diaz needs to watch his back."

"All of us need to watch our backs," Guidino added.

"You having second thoughts about this?" the man asked.

"No, I sold my soul to Satan just like the rest of us did. Even if I did want out, Satan now owns me and I'm his servant until the end," Guidino said resolutely.

"As are we all."

"Are the detonators set?" Guidino asked.

"That was Diego and Juan's job. They were supposed to set the explosives in the tunnels under the Plaza Mayor after we checked the gas valves. The detonators are already built into the explosive bundles. Diego was showing one to me. As soon as Toribio calls the cell number, they'll explode. I'm sure glad the truck detonators are all on timers. I wouldn't want some wrong number blowing me apart while I'm driving," the other man laughed.

"I didn't see your car when we left the garage," Guidino said.

"No, I parked it over by the Plaza Provencia, that's near the entrance gate I'm supposed to block tonight. As soon as we're finished here, I'm taking the truck assigned to me and moving it closer to the Plaza. Once I put the truck in place, I'll be able use my car to get out quickly and back here so I can see the fireworks."

"Good idea. I'm assigned the entrance off of Calle Mayor so I should be able to walk back in time," Guidino replied. "Why don't you go ahead and set the timers on the truck detonators while I make sure Diego and Juan set up the explosives under the plaza."

"Are you sure?" the man asked.

"Certainly, besides I want to make sure they don't mess with our gas valves. We can't afford to have anything go wrong."

"Things are sure going to change after tonight," the man said.

"Yes indeed, and by this time next week the 'Seven of the Cross' will be in complete control of Spain," Guidino exclaimed.

CHAPTER THIRTY-SEVEN

"Expectations"

"**Gabriel it's so nice of you** to invite me as your guest to such a formal affair," Lucienne purred.

"I'd have it no other way," Arciga replied.

A waiter presented a tray of champagne to Lucienne, she reached, but then hesitated.

"Go ahead, it's an excellent vintage," Arciga encouraged. "Besides, we have so much to celebrate."

"I could get use to this," Lucienne said, taking a glass.

"You know, you'd make an excellent first lady," Arciga said.

"With your predilections, I don't think so. You forget, I've already had that pleasure and didn't live through it," Lucienne replied.

"But that's what would make you my perfect first lady. If things got a bit out-of-hand and you died, no matter, you'd be back the next day," Arciga explained.

"Actually, I thought I'd make a better queen than a first lady," Lucienne replied. "Why don't you introduce me to Juan Carlos."

"He's much too old for you," Arciga replied.

"On the contrary, perhaps I'm too old for him," Lucienne joked. "After all, I've been able to take human form for almost three hundred years now."

"And you don't look a day over twenty," Arciga assured her.

"You're such a bad liar," Lucienne replied. "You'll make a great él Presidente."

"Speaking of él Presidente, there goes Zapatero and his security team now. They must already be headed for the processional. The King will just have to wait till another day for the honor to meet me."

"Then I'm afraid I must be going too," Lucienne said. "I promised Bishop Toribio I would join him at the cathedral before the processional."

"Let me drive you. I think I'll get a jump on the crowd and go back early to El Corte Inglés, have a drink, relax, maybe do a little reading of the Libro de Reglas."

"Protect the book with your life," Lucienne warned. "And pay special attention to the part about what happens to those who fail me."

"I'll do a better job than Carlos, I can assure you of that," Arciga laughed. "It should be quite a show tonight."

"A truly unforgettable evening for all, I'm sure," Lucienne purred and grabbed Arciga's arm as they headed out of the Prado.

"*The light shines in the darkness, but the darkness has not understood it,*" Bishop Castillo rasped.

"Your Grace, do not talk. There is little air left in here," Kevin advised.

"Swoosh!" The pendulum continued its downward track just inches from the torture chamber floor.

"But the light, it begins to shine, just as John the Divine tells us," the bishop continued.

"Kevin, there is a light," Oralia exclaimed. "Liz, thank God you've returned. You've got to help us, we're trapped and there is so little air."

Liz rushed up the stairs to the bolted door. The room grew frigid as some of the gas turned to liquid droplets, then solid tears.

"Don't touch anything or the cold will burn you," Liz warned.

Kevin was too weak to open his eyes. Death seemed so easy. There was little oxygen left in the room and he knew they were all but seconds away from entering God's Kingdom. He had surrendered to the inevitable and the cold felt warm.

"Kevin!" Oralia screamed, "Wake up we're saved."

Kevin heard an echo in the distance. He too, saw the light and headed towards it.

"Kevin! Kevin!" Oralia began to slap Kevin's face.

"*No, too late, too late, too cold, what?*" Suddenly Kevin's eyes popped open. "I can't breathe."

"Kevin, she's back. Liz is back." Oralia cried.

Kevin was too dazed to understand. A dim glow emanated from somewhere above and Kevin could barely see Oralia's face.

"You've got to get up. We've got to get the bishop out of here, you must help me," Oralia ordered.

Kevin continued to lie next to the wall confused and shivering.

"Damn it, Kevin, wake up." Oralia yelled in frustration, and slapped him hard across the face.

"Cold, why is it so cold?" Kevin asked, beginning to come around.

"Liz is freezing some of the gas, but if she freezes it all it'll freeze us too. We need to get out of here," Oralia explained.

"But the door..." Kevin began to say.

"...is no longer a problem," Liz called down, as the brittle steel bars securing the door shattered from the intense cold.

"Swoosh." the pendulum glided by just inches from the floor.

"You two get the bishop, I'll get the other man," Liz ordered.

"You might consider stopping the pendulum," Kevin replied.

"No problem," Liz said, "but let's please hurry, I only can do so much."

With the pendulum frozen in place Kevin and Oralia carefully lifted the shivering bishop onto Kevin's back. With Oralia steadying Kevin, they slowly climbed the chamber stairs.

"Liz, it's too cold, I can barely breathe," Kevin gasped.

"Just keep going." Liz ordered. Kevin could feel the cold slightly subside.

"I'm smelling gas again," Oralia warned, as they reached the top of the stairs.

Kevin, Oralia, and the bishop turned to the left and headed down the catacomb towards the mausoleum when Liz screamed.

"Swoo…" the pendulum broke free when Liz eased the cold and hit the torture chamber floor creating a spark and igniting the gas that was no longer frozen.

A fireball engulfed the torture chamber and blew out into the catacomb just as the three freed captives ducked into the side chamber holding the bones of Jayro Toribio.

"Oh my God, Liz is still in there," Oralia shrieked.

When Romero came to, he and Francois were both handcuffed to chairs in the dining room.

"What's going on?" Romero asked.

"That's exactly what I was going to ask you," Comisario Diaz replied. "How long have you been working with Lucienne and Liz?"

"Me! It's you who are the traitor," Romero insisted.

"Don't lie to me." Diaz screamed. "I know you're working for the 'Seven of the Cross'. Why else would you have helped Lucienne and Liz escape? They believe they are angels sent by Satan and you and your friend are working with them."

That's ridiculous," Francois interjected, finally coming around.

"Just what is it you have planned for tonight's processional? Do you really intend to kill él Presidente Zapatero? Tell me." Diaz demanded.

"Us? It's you who tried to keep us out of Madrid and in Ronda so you and your sick perverted brethren could kill él Presidente and replace him with Minister Arciga," Romero replied.

"So that's your intentions. Arciga is the one behind this whole plot and it's him you are working for," Diaz exclaimed.

"Is this guy for real? How gullible does he think we are?" Francois asked. "If you're not part of the 'Seven' just why have we seen you here and why are you here now?"

"I'm trying to stop a tragedy from occurring. Do you forget that I'm the Superintendent Inspector of the GEO of the Cuerpo Nacional?" Diaz said in disbelief.

"GEO, what's that?" Francois asked.

"Grupo Especial de Operaciones, the special operations tactical unit. If anyone, they'd be the group assigned to investigate such a high-profile case." Romero explained.

"I still don't buy it," Francois said. "I don't believe you're not part of the 'Seven of the Cross'."

"Just how is the Vatican involved in all of this? Are they behind the overthrow of Zapatero? Is that who you work for?" Comisario Diaz questioned.

"Bishop Toribio is the one calling the shots. You know that as well as us. We've seen you in this very room eating with him and the other members of the 'Seven of the Cross'. We even saw Lucienne in here earlier today," Francois said accusingly.

"And you arrived in Madrid with this other woman Liz. From what I've been told she is responsible for several murders here in Madrid, New York, France, and Poland," Diaz replied.

"She's only a suspect in those murders," Romero replied.

"She had nothing to do with any of those murders and you know it," Francois said to Romero.

"Are you telling me you two have nothing to do with the 'Seven of the Cross'?" Diaz asked, incredulously.

Francois and Romero looked at each other. Francois knew Diaz was scamming them but Romero wasn't so sure. Either way, they both were handcuffed and the only way out of the situation was to go along with Diaz.

"I swear we have nothing to do with Lucienne or the 'Seven of the Cross'," Romero said. "We were convinced it was you who was involved."

Diaz glared at the two men for what he hoped was the appropriate length of time.

"Do you have any idea how long it has taken me to infiltrate this organization? We first heard rumors about the plot to assassinate Zapatero fourteen months ago and began working the case. And you two along with that Vatican investigator just about ruined everything."

"So how do you intend to stop this 'Seven of the Cross'?" Francois asked.

"I was hoping you might have an idea. We found out early that somebody in the Cuerpo is dirty so there will be no back-up until the very last minute," Diaz explained.

"You'd be a lot more believable if you took these cuffs off of us," Romero said.

"You I'm not worried about," Diaz said, unlocking Romero's cuffs and handing him back his gun. "I think 'Frenchie' and his partners tricked you from the beginning."

"'Frenchie'! Is that the best you can do? You better damn well keep me cuffed, cause once I'm loose, I'm going to knock you into tomorrow," Francois warned.

"I've already taken out two of 'Seven'," Diaz said to Romero. "And the one they call the librarian was killed by that Liz woman who arrived with our friend here,"

"Romero, you know as well as I it wasn't Liz who killed the librarian," Francois reminded him.

"You need to shut your mouth before I shut it for you," Diaz said threatening to backhand Francois.

"Nice ring," Francois said, "I saw one just like it on the dead librarian and the Reverend Father told us Bishop Toribio has an identical one. A strange coincidence, don't you think?" Francois continued facetiously.

"Does the Reverend Father know you are here?" Diaz asked.

"Is that a problem?" Romero replied, starting to again question where Diaz' loyalties lie.

"Kevin knows all about you and your little group too," Francois added. "It all's starting to fall apart isn't it?"

"Shut up," Diaz ordered, "and you sit back down," he said shoving Romero back into the chair.

Romero went for his gun but the bullets had been removed earlier by Diaz.

"Damn it, I was hoping I could trust you," Diaz said, pulling out his taser and firing it into Romero's neck. Romero instantly went limp.

"You got in too deep and now that things are starting to fall apart you're looking for a way out," Francois mocked. "We were going to be your ticket to freedom. You really screwed up. Had you been smarter you might even have been able to pull it off."

"Oh, I'll pull it off alright, and in the process, I'll make sure you and your friends take the blame," Diaz said.

"Kevin will stop you" Francois said.

Diaz laughed. "Your friend Kevin is already dead. I killed him along with the real bishop and the church secretary over an hour ago. Unfortunately, two of the 'Seven' had to die in the process."

"You're lying," Francois accused.

"Why should I lie? Especially, since you'll be joining him as soon as I decide how your deaths will best benefit me," Diaz replied.

"You belong to your father, the devil, and you want to carry out your father's desire. He was a murderer from the beginning, not holding to the truth, for there is no truth in him. When he lies, he speaks his native language, for he is a liar and the father of lies. You know you'll never…" Francois began.

"You really talk too much, 'Frenchie'," Diaz interrupted and zapped Francois with the taser.

Diaz walked to the sideboard and unlocked the cabinet. Inside were several bottles of Pernod Fils 'post-ban' vintage absinthe made in Tarragona, Spain. Each bottle had cost the 'Seven of the Cross' more than two thousand Euros. However, it was the bottle in the back that Diaz preferred. It was a bottle of Pernod Fils 'pre-ban' vintage absinthe distilled in Pontarlier France sometime before the ban went into affect in 1915. This bottle had cost several thousand Euros and there was little chance of finding another.

"I see no point in saving this any longer," Diaz replied, even though he knew Toribio would seriously object.

Diaz took one of the specially designed antique glasses and poured a hearty amount of the emerald green fluid in the bulbous base of the glass. He then placed on it a sterling silver absinthe spoon specifically designed to fit the lip of the glass. On the spoon he placed a sugar cube. He removed a pitcher of cold water from a small refrigerator built into the cabinet and slowly poured the cold water on top of the sugar. As the sugared cold water mixed with the absinthe, it began to form billow-like clouds, an effect the French called the "louche".

Comisario Diaz gently sipped the mixture and smiled.

"Well 'Frenchie', I must say your people knew what they were doing when they made the 'Green Fairy'."

Diaz walked to the window overlooking the Plaza Mayor. "They say this sharpens your mind. Bruno Mancini swore to it in his journal," Diaz said to the two unconscious men.

As Diaz stared at the old city below a plan started to form. "You know, it just might work. I guess Bruno knew what he was talking about."

What he failed to remember from the journal and from the Libro de Reglas was that it was the absinthe that clouded Bruno's mind when confronted by, and ultimately killed by Lucienne. A fate Diaz might share with the ancient investigator, if he wasn't careful.

CHAPTER THIRTY-EIGHT

"Endurance"

"**Stay here!**" Kevin ordered, as he ran back to the door of the torture chamber. Even though the gas burned cleanly there was much smoke from the burning wooden stocks and rack. Kevin backed away from the deadly smoke coughing.

"Liz, Liz, are you in there?" Kevin called through the black haze. The dim fluorescent fixture barely illuminated the smoke-filled catacomb let alone shine into the torture chamber.

"Maybe she went back to Tartarus before the explosion," Oralia suggested, as she joined Kevin in the catacomb.

"If she did, we have no way of getting her back," Kevin said.

"Do you hear that?" Oralia said, "Someone's coming up the stairs."

"Liz," Kevin shouted and hugged her tightly. "You look like nothing happened. How is that possible?"

"It took most of my strength and ability to create a frozen cocoon around my body. Unfortunately, I wasn't able to save the other man. I'm so sorry," Liz gasped, almost in tears.

"But you were able to save us," Oralia heartened.

"And there are many others that you can help save," Kevin assured her.

"That's right," Oralia chimed in, "I heard the comisario tell those two men to check the detonators by the gas release valves under the plaza. He must have meant the Plaza Mayor."

"But then why did he condemn two of his own men by sealing them in the torture chamber with us?" Kevin asked.

"The comisario must know Satan's Kingdom is beginning to crumble and he is desperately seeking a way out," Liz surmised.

"The catacomb must somehow connect to the tunnels Diaz was referring to," Kevin said.

"We've got to stop them from blowing up the Plaza Mayor. It's just about time for the processional to begin, thousands will be in the plaza and will die if the gas explodes," Oralia said.

"Do you think you can get the bishop back through the mausoleum by yourself?" Kevin asked Oralia, as the reentered the small chamber where the bishop rested.

"I'm sure of it," Oralia replied.

It was then that she noticed the shrine set up on the table with the cross and the plaque behind it.

"Oh my God!" Oralia exclaimed, as she read the inscription. "*Jayro Toribio, freer of the 'Light' and first of the 'Seven of the Cross'. Soul claimed by Satan 1725*. It was my ancestor who started this," she cried.

"Yes," Liz replied, "but together we can end it now and forever." Liz pulled the cross from the wooden table and handed it to Kevin.

"What's this for?" Kevin asked.

"It was this cross that first freed Lucienne from Tartarus." Liz paused as if in thought. "I don't know, perhaps you'll need a weapon."

"I pray it won't come to that," Kevin said.

"As shall we all," Oralia seconded.

"Liz and I will see if we can find the gas valves Diaz was talking about. You let Romero and Francois know what's happening. And tell the Reverend Father to stop the processional."

"I'll take care of it," Oralia replied, helping Bishop Castillo to his feet. "Remember, there are still five more members of the 'Seven of the Cross' out there."

"Our struggle is not against flesh and blood, but against the rulers, against the authorities, against the powers of this dark world and against the spiritual forces of evil in the heavenly realms," Liz corrected.

"Put on the full armor of God, for the day of evil has come," Bishop Castillo whispered in a raspy growl. "Stand firm and declare your faith in God fearlessly and His Kingdom shall prevail."

"Amen!" Kevin said as he and Liz headed down the catacomb.

∾ ∾ ∾

"Where's Guidino?" Diaz asked the other member of the 'Seven' when he reached the parking garage.

"He's in the tunnels checking the gas valves under the Plaza Mayor like you said to do," the man answered. "What was the trouble in the catacomb?"

"The Vatican investigator figured out how to access the catacombs. The secretary probably left him a note before she entered," Diaz explained.

"I thought you said Bridges was in Ronda until Monday. The bishop and Lucienne aren't going to be happy to hear this news," the man replied.

"I took care of it. Kevin Bridges, the secretary, and Bishop Castillo are all dead."

"Where's Juan and Diego?" the man asked suspiciously.

"Probably with Guidino. I sent them into the tunnels to set the detonators on the explosives. They should be back any minute," Diaz replied.

"I don't like it. How can we be sure no one else will discover the passage from the mausoleum into the catacomb? We need to let the bishop know what has happened," the man insisted.

"The auto de fe must go on as planned," Diaz warned. "Even if someone else discovers the catacombs they'll never find the bodies in the torture chamber."

"Yes, but they'll find our shrine and that could lead them to us," he continued.

"If all goes as planned tonight, the country will be too absorbed in anguish over the death of él Presidente and the thousands of other Spaniards killed in Plaza Mayor to worry about an ancient shrine," Diaz replied. "We must continue as planned."

"I don't know, I still think we should tell Toribio." The man recalled his recent conversation with Guidino about Diaz being the one who needs to watch his back.

"If we tell the bishop he will tell Lucienne and you know what Lucienne did to Carlos," Diaz warned.

"Yes, but Carlos was just a librarian. His usefulness to the 'Seven of the Cross' had ended. Besides, he failed in his assignment and in doing so put the 'Seven' at risk. The Libro de Reglas is very precise as to how failure must be dealt with," the man replied.

"And you believe our value is such that none of the rest of us is irreplaceable? I think not," Diaz exclaimed. "We must do everything in our power to insure all goes just as planned for the processional. If not, then we'll have to deal with Lucienne."

"If you say so," the man said still not convinced, but not wanting to be the cause of Diaz incurring the wrath of the 'Light'.

"Is the detonator set in the truck you're driving?" Diaz asked.

"I was just about to set it and move the truck to the staging area near the Plaza Mayor," the man replied.

"Isn't it too soon?" Diaz asked.

"Not at all. The Mass at Almudena started almost an hour ago and should be ending shortly. I was waiting for Guidino but perhaps I shouldn't wait."

"You're right; we should be moving the trucks. I wonder what is keeping everyone?" Diaz replied in a feigned concern, pondering what his next move would be.

"Maybe they're having trouble with the detonators," the man suggested.

"Move your truck into place then return here. I'll wait five more minutes. If they're not here by then I'll move one of the other trucks and if need be, we both can move the second trucks," Diaz suggested.

"If they're not here by the time we return, then something has gone seriously wrong and we must contact Toribio and Lucienne," the man warned.

"And we will." Diaz insisted. "But when we do, let's make sure we've done everything in our power to insure all goes as planned. Hail Satan."

"Hail Satan," the man replied and started his truck.

Kevin stopped at the entrance to the torture chamber to have a look at the door.

"What's the problem?" Liz asked.

"I want to see what the locking mechanism looks like. There will probably be a similar one somewhere down the catacomb that will get us out of here and into the tunnels under the plaza.," Kevin explained.

"We don't have a whole lot of time," Liz warned.

"See, right here, it's the same verse that was on the secret entrance in the mausoleum. We just need to look for the scripture from Matthew 7:7. Wait a minute," Kevin paused, "that lock is different from the lock that the ring opened at the crypt."

"So now what?" Liz asked.

"At least we know what the lock should look like. When we find it, you'll be the key," Kevin explained. "You can shatter the door just as you did this one."

"Not a problem," Liz replied, "but there's something you need to know."

"Do I really want to know?" Kevin replied.

"Yes, you do. It's just that, as powerful as I may appear, I do have my limits. We're all very lucky to have escaped from the torture chamber alive. That took much of my energy, energy that needs time to regenerate. There's no possible way I can stop all of the gas under the Plaza Mayor from exploding except by physically turning the gas valves off. If we run into trouble, I'll be able to take care of us, just as long as there aren't too many of them. If we run into Lucienne," Liz paused, "things could go really badly for us."

"Then we best avoid Lucienne and concentrate on turning off the gas valves," Kevin replied positively. "Let's start with this one."

Comisario Diaz had left the covering off the hidden gas valve that he had used in his attempt to kill Kevin, Oralia, and the two other members of the 'Seven'.

"Let's hope the rest will be as easy to find," Lucienne said.

As they hurried along the catacomb, the light seemed to grow brighter. They had gone several hundred yards when the catacomb turned sharply to the right and came to an abrupt stop.

"All of this looks much newer, like the rocks have been recently hewn and constructed," Kevin remarked.

"I bet this is your hidden door," Liz remarked, as Kevin came over to have a look. "Not hidden very well. Want me to freeze it?"

"No, let's see if we can find the lock first. Remember, we're saving you for later," Kevin said.

Liz smiled at Kevin's remark, but he failed to notice, concentrating on the task at hand.

"It looks like the ring will fit right here," Kevin said inserting the ring he was now wearing.

"No clank of releasing bolts was heard, but a definite electric hum began as the door rotated smoothly and opened into a sparsely furnished room.

"Looks like a holding room for those on the way to the torture chamber," Kevin commented, pointing to the shackles bolted to the stone wall and the restraints attached to the chairs.

Kevin quickly walked the perimeter of the room looking for possible hidden doors.

"Looks like this is the only way out," Kevin said, standing in front of an elevator door.

"Where do you think it leads?" Liz asked.

"Based on how far we traveled along the catacomb and what Romero showed me from the roof of the Hotel Atlantico, I'm certain this elevator will take us to the dining room at the top of El Corte Inglés."

"We don't have to go to the top, it's an elevator, we can get off on any floor we choose," Liz replied. "The tunnels under the Plaza Mayor must be accessible from another level."

"Regardless, we need to move fast. I just noticed the camera hidden in the air vent so Diaz probably already knows we're here," Kevin said as he lifted his ring to the elevator call button.

Liz disagreed. She doubted that Diaz or anyone else was monitoring the camera at this point. The processional was due to begin at any time, and being two men short, Diaz was probably hard at work handling their assignments or plotting a way out of the mess he had gotten himself into. She knew Lucienne wouldn't tolerate any screw-up and Diaz had certainly made several.

Suddenly, the whirring of the elevator motor kicked in.

"Stop," Liz warned, grabbing Kevin's hand. "Someone else has called the elevator."

"I hope it's not our reception party," Kevin remarked.

They listened as the elevator seemed to be coming closer. Kevin raised the cross to use as a weapon, but Liz signaled him to lower it. If there was to be a battle, she would handle it. The elevator came to an abrupt stop just above them.

"Now what?" Kevin asked.

"We wait," Liz replied.

Kevin wasn't very good at waiting.

"You awake yet," Romero asked as Francois' arm started to twitch.

Slowly Francois raised his head and groggily looked towards where the voice had come. "I got to get me one of those."

"Too high of voltage, you hit someone with a weak heart and you're going to kill them," Romero replied.

"Okay, so now what's the plan?" Francois asked. "And I hope it's better than your last plan."

"I didn't have a last plan, remember?"

"Is that blood on your shirt?" Francois asked.

"Probably. When Diaz first surprised us, I took a whack in the head from the blackjack he carries with him."

"Ouch, that had to hurt," Francois replied.

"At least we're still alive. Maybe I'll get the chance to pay him back," Romero remarked. "Let's just hope Kevin figures out where we are."

"Kevin's dead," Francois replied. "At least that's what Diaz told me after he tasered you."

"I don't believe it," Romero replied.

"He also said he killed Oralia and the real bishop along with two of his own men," Francois continued.

"You really think he did?"

"We know he's a liar, but if he was trying to distance himself from the 'Seven of the Cross' and Lucienne like he tried to do with us, it would make sense that he would take out the people who know he is really evil," Francois surmised.

"Then why are we still alive?" Romero asked.

"That's why I think Diaz is lying," Francois said. "He's keeping us alive until he figures out what to do. I don't think he would risk killing Kevin or the bishop for the same reason. He's too smart for that."

"You give him too much credit. If he was smart, he wouldn't have gotten mixed up with Satan in the first place," Romero replied.

"So where does that leave us?" Francois asked.

"My father once told me that God has a plan for all of us," Romero replied.

"Well at least somebody in this room has a plan," Francois remarked snidely.

CHAPTER THIRTY-NINE

"Sacrifice"

"**Guidino, where the hell** have you been and where's Diego and Juan?" Diaz asked.

"Doing my job!" he snapped back. "And the last time I saw Juan and Diego was when the three of you headed into the catacombs."

"We ran into some trouble. It was Kevin Bridges who set off the alarm. We had to kill him, the bishop, and the secretary," Diaz replied.

"The 'Light' isn't going to like that," Guidino warned.

"Toribio may not like it, but the 'Light' won't care, just as long as everything goes as planned tonight," Diaz replied.

"I'll handle my end," Guidino quipped.

"Well you're not doing a very good job of it. When I returned, I caught my own Inspector Romero and that French cop snooping around in your dining room," Diaz said.

"How's that possible?" Guidino gasped.

"It doesn't matter now. All that really matters is that we handle it and make sure it doesn't interfere with tonight's plans."

"What did you do with them?" Guidino asked.

'They're both still there, handcuffed to chairs," Diaz replied

"What do we do now?" Guidino asked.

"We're going to go get Inspector Romero and bring him down here. We'll stick him in the back of one of the trucks. He can be part of the fireworks," Diaz laughed.

"What about the Frenchman, do you want to put him in one of the trucks?" Guidino asked.

"No, let's leave him for the 'Light' to deal with. We'll need to find out who else knows about the 'Seven of the Cross' and Lucienne has a way of getting that information," Diaz explained.

"I hope you know what you are doing?" Guidino said.

"Of course I do," Diaz replied as he stuck his ring into the call button for the elevator.

"Somebody's getting on," Liz whispered.

Kevin stuck his ear against the elevator door trying to listen.

"The door is closing," Kevin said, backing away preparing for the intruders.

"The elevator is going up," Liz said.

They both continued to listen for several seconds as the elevator motor continued to whirr.

"They must've gone to the dining room," Kevin said, as the motor stopped and the doors opened and closed once again.

"Now what?" Kevin said.

"Call the elevator, we're running out of time," Liz replied.

Kevin placed the ring into the matching symbol on the call button and immediately the motor began to wind.

When the door opened both Liz and Kevin were prepared for battle, but the elevator was empty.

"Let's go up one level," Kevin suggested.

"Makes sense to me," Liz replied.

Again, Kevin and Liz were both prepared for conflict, but when the door opened, they found themselves alone in a loading dock.

"What do you think is in the trucks?" Kevin asked.

"It doesn't matter," Liz replied, looking around the garage, "we don't have time to look."

"Over there," Kevin said pointing to a door next to the loading dock, "the sign says service tunnels. Do you think that's what we're looking for?"

"I don't see any other possibilities and the next button on the elevator says parking. This has to be it," Liz agreed.

No sooner had the elevator door closed did the motor again start to wind.

"It's headed back up," Liz said.

"And I think I hear a car coming down the ramp. We better hurry into those tunnels," Kevin replied.

"Let's pray we still have enough time," Liz replied.

"We should still have plenty of time," Kevin guessed, as they ran to the tunnel doors.

"Why do you say that?" Liz said, as they hurried inside and peaked backed out of the doors to see if anyone was coming.

"Friday's processional didn't start until almost eight, and it's just now 7:30. It wouldn't make any sense to blow up the Plaza Mayor until after the processional and the place was packed with spectators and participants," Kevin explained. "That gives us a good two ..."

"Shhhh, there's a car coming," Liz interrupted.

૭ઃ   ૭ઃ   ૭ઃ

"Back so soon," Francois remarked, as Diaz and Guidino both stepped off the elevator into the dining room. "Who's your friend?"

"Shut up!" Diaz demanded.

"That's Señor Guidino. He's our host here at El Corte Inglés," Romero said.

"I said shut up!" Diaz screamed.

"Does Señor Guidino know you're having second thoughts about this 'Seven of the Cross' plot to kill él Presidente?" Romero asked.

"Or that you killed those two other members of your little club?" Francois added.

"What are they talking about?" Guidino asked, puzzled.

"Pay them no heed, they are trying to turn us against each other. It's a ploy all police are trained to use in such situations," Diaz explained.

"Go ahead, tell Señor Guidino how you killed your two friends when you killed Bridges, the bishop, and the secretary," Romero pushed.

"Or are you going to tell him how you've already sold out the rest of the 'Seven' to cover your own ass," Francois added.

"I told you two to shut up," Diaz yelled, pulling out his taser and shocking Romero once again in the neck.

"You know you're going to kill him if you keep doing that. His heart can only take so much," Francois said.

Diaz backhanded Francois hard across the mouth. "If you don't shut up it's you who'll end up dead."

Diaz unlocked Romero's handcuffs. "Let's get him down to the truck."

"What happened to Juan and Diego," Guidino asked.

"Nothing happened to them. I left them in the torture chamber with instructions to take care of the three bodies and then set the detonators on the explosives near the gas valves in the tunnel," Diaz snapped. "Maybe they decided to have a little fun with the secretary. How the hell should I know?"

"Yeah right," Francois remarked from his bleeding mouth.

"I don't like it," Guidino said. "Something's not right. None of the explosives were in place."

"If Diego and Juan screw up then they'll have to answer to the 'Light'," Diaz replied. "I've seen what she's capable of doing and don't want what happened to Carlos to happen to me. Let's get the inspector into the truck and the trucks to the Plaza Mayor."

"I'll get the elevator," Guidino said.

"Yeah, you do that," Diaz responded sarcastically.

"Hey, it's not me screwing up so lighten up," Guidino countered, beginning to get angry.

"Just open the damn elevator!" Diaz retorted. "What's the problem?"

"Somebody must have called it," Guidino replied.

"That's just great," Diaz snapped.

"Are we having fun yet boys?" Francois called from across the room.

If the elevator door hadn't opened at that exact moment, they both would have killed Francois.

෴ ෴ ෴

"What are the trucks still doing here?" Lucienne demanded.

"How the hell should I know? The trucks weren't my responsibility," Arciga replied. "One of them is gone. Maybe it's still too early to move them into place."

"I guess you're right it is a little early," she replied.

"Then perhaps you'd like to join me for a drink in the dining room before you meet Bishop Toribio?" he asked.

"That would be lovely," the 'Light' replied. "It'll give us a chance to look out over Old Madrid before it's changed forever."

"Kevin, it's Lucienne and she's with that man we saw at…" Liz started to whisper.

"That man is Minister Arciga," Kevin interrupted, now standing over Liz and peeking out the door. "Look the elevator is opening."

"It's Diaz and some other man. They're carrying somebody. It's Romero, they've got Romero, we've got to help him," Kevin said emphatically.

"No way!" Liz ordered, shoving Kevin away from the door. "I'm still too weak from the torture chamber. Lucienne could rip you and Romero to shreds and I would be unable to stop her. We've got to wait."

"She might kill him," Kevin replied.

"If that is God's will," Liz replied. "But if you go out there now, Lucienne will kill you. Of this I am certain."

"Comisario Diaz, I see my intuition has proven prophetic," Lucienne gloated, as Diaz and Guidino carried Romero from the elevator.

"You were wise in your warning to me," Diaz replied tritely.

"And you were wise to heed my warning," Lucienne replied. "Where is Kevin Bridges?"

"Bridges is dead, as is the secretary, and Bishop Castillo. Bridges found his way into the catacombs so I had Diego and Juan kill all three of them in the chamber," Diaz explained, while Guidino stayed silent.

"What about this one, your own Inspector Romero?" she asked. "Why is he still alive?"

"He won't be for long. I intend to place him in one of the explosive trucks." Diaz replied. "I found him and the French lieutenant snooping around in the dining room."

"Goodness, it seems the 'Seven of the Cross' has garnered considerable attention. What do they know of our plans and who else knows?" Lucienne demanded.

"That is something I thought you might want to ask the Frenchman yourself. I left him handcuffed in the dining room," Diaz explained.

"Please assure me that all will go as planned tonight," Arciga requested.

"If Zapatero marches in the processional and speaks to the crowd in the Plaza Mayor, as you have assured us he will do, then he and thousands more will perish as Old Madrid is reduced to a burning hell," Diaz replied. "In one hour the gas valves will open in the tunnels and the trucks will all be in place. At 10:00, evil will reign in Madrid."

ဢ ဢ ဢ

"Did you hear that? They plan on killing él Presidente Zapatero and destroying Old Madrid. Those trucks are full of explosives," Kevin said. "We've got to stop them."

"And we will, but we must be smart about it. The first thing we need to do is shut off those gas tanks in the tunnels," Liz started to explain. "Then we'll remove the detonators from the trucks."

"How will we even find the trucks? For that matter how will we find the gas canisters in the tunnels?" Kevin was already sounding defeated.

"Trust in God," Liz reminded him. "This is His battle now. Still, we must make some difficult choices."

"You're referring to Francois," Kevin whispered. "She plans to kill him, doesn't she?"

"I'm afraid she does," Liz replied.

"Is there nothing you can do?" Kevin begged.

"My powers are limited and Lucienne is strong," Liz replied. "Francois must pray for strength and have faith in God. If he does that the angels will protect him."

"Then I fear Francois is doomed. He doesn't believe in God," Kevin lamented.

"Then you must believe for him," Liz replied. "We must hurry. As Diaz said, the gas valves will open in an hour and who knows how long after that the explosives will detonate. We must make sure that doesn't happen."

Kevin watched as Romero was bound and gagged then thrown into the back of one of the trucks. Diaz jumped in behind the wheel and raced up the delivery ramp with Guidino in a second truck right behind him. Lucienne watched as the two men pulled away then entered the elevator with Arciga.

CHAPTER FORTY

"Salvation"

"So, we meet again," Lucienne said as she stepped off the elevator.

A sudden chill engulfed the dining room.

"Actually, I don't believe we've really ever met," Francois replied. "I only got a glimpse of you as you toppled off the Puente Nuevo in Ronda, though I must say, you look much nicer in person than you did on the hotel video when you killed the security guard."

"Some of my finer work," Lucienne replied, smiling.

Francois could feel his heart begin to slow and tighten as his body temperature plummeted.

"Minister Arciga, I think you're beginning to run with the wrong crowd," Francois said hoarsely.

"I rather enjoy the company of the 'Light', he replied setting the Libro de Reglas on the table. "Is it a little cold here? I think I'll go pour a drink." He smiled and moved to the bar at the far end of the room.

"Tell me, who else knows about our plans tonight?"

"What plans?" Francois replied.

Suddenly excruciating pains seemed to sear his organs. "Agh, you must mean the "Seven of the Cross' plans to kill Zapatero," Francois wheezed in pain.

"That's right, who else knows about them?" Lucienne replied.

"Everybody," Francois answered, "We told Interpol, Cuerpo Nacional, the FBI, the Paris Prefecture of Police, even Zapatero's own security team."

"He's lying," Arciga said. "If Zapatero's security knows they wouldn't have brought him to the processional."

"Of course he's lying," the 'Light' snapped.

"Am I?" Francois gasped. "Did you actually see Zapatero at the processional? We're on to you. It's a set up, Diaz turned and has told us everything."

"I knew that son-of-a-bitch Diaz couldn't be trusted," Arciga cursed

"Shut up, Gabriel," Lucienne ordered. "It's a trick. I thought you were smarter than this. It's a desperate attempt to save his own life and place doubt in our minds. Too bad it didn't work."

Lucienne turned and placed her hand on Francois' chest. He was too weak to resist.

"Time to meet your God," Lucienne said, "Oh that's right, you don't believe in God do you. I guess we'll be seeing you in hell."

"Rather ironic, don't you think," Arciga added and laughed.

Francois started to say a prayer but his head collapsed to the table as his heart stopped, frozen solid.

"How will we ever find the gas canisters, there are tunnels going every which way?" Kevin said. "Wait, what's that?"

"Looks like a gas canister to me, oh ye of little faith," Liz replied.

"Several gas canisters I'd say," Kevin said seeing the clutter of cylinders marked explosive stacked along the wall of the tunnel. "They all seem to be hooked to a central release valve with a timer. All we have to do is turn off the valve on each individual tank. Then when the timed valve releases there will be no gas to release."

"But how were they going to ignite the gas?" Liz asked.

"That's right. Those tanks in the Plaza Mayor had automatic igniters. These don't have that," Kevin replied.

"They didn't just want to ignite the gas, they wanted to explode it. There must also be explosives somewhere in the tunnels," Liz surmised.

"These had to be wheeled in here, they're much too heavy to carry," Kevin guessed. "Look, you can see tire marks in the dust on the floor. All we need to do is follow the trail."

"Let's just hope it leads us to the explosives as well as the gas canisters," Liz added.

§ § §

"What the hell," Romero tried to say, but only a muffled growl emerged from his taped mouth, as the sudden jarring of the truck running over the curb awoken him.

"This is bad," he thought to himself. He was obviously in the back of one of the trucks that had been parked in the loading dock and from the smell he could tell that the barrels that surrounded him were likely filled with a large amount of ammonium nitrate and nitromethane."

The truck suddenly came to a stop and he heard the driver's side door open and close. He waited for someone to open the rear door, but after a few moments, it became obvious that it was not going to happen.

"This is one big bomb," he thought and then realized that the three other trucks were probably filled with the same explosive material. "Looks like the 'Seven of the Cross' are planning quite a reception for él Presidente. I need to get out of here."

As he listened, he could hear crowd noise coming from someplace nearby so he began kicking the door hoping to draw attention to the truck.

ം   ം   ം

"It's a miracle," one of the monks at the Templo Eucarístico de San Martín shouted, as he and several others prostrated themselves before the large marble icon of the Virgin Mary next to the sanctuary.

"God has returned Bishop Castillo to us and the Madonna no longer cries the bloody tears," another monk cried hurrying to find the abbot.

"What, what is it you say?" the abbot asked.

"Oralia has returned with Bishop Castillo and the Virgin no longer cries," the monk explained.

"Thank you, Lord," the abbot said dropping to his knees, "It truly is a miracle. Has Reverend Father been notified?"

"Reverend Father is at the Mass being held at Almudena Cathedral and then he'll participate in the processional. We're not able to contact him."

The monk picked up the phone and called for an ambulance.

"The bishop's very weak and has been tortured, he needs immediate care," the monk explained to the abbot.

"What about Oralia, is she okay?" the abbot asked.

"Oralia too has been tortured, but she's in much better shape than the bishop," the monk replied.

"Where are they now?"

"They're in the sanctuary. As weak as he is, the bishop insisted he be first taken to the Monstrance to receive the Eucharist. I believe he is now lying on one of the pews. Oralia is by his side," the monk explained, as they rushed to the sanctuary.

"Oralia, thank God you and Bishop Castillo are safe," the abbot said.

"Where's Reverend Father, I must speak to Reverend Father. Has Francois and Inspector Romero been here?" Oralia gasped.

"I'm sorry, but I've not seen Francois or the inspector and, as you know, Reverend Father is at the processional for the final night of the Fiesta de San Martín," the abbot said.

"The processional! We must stop the processional," Oralia said in a panic.

"You need to relax and let a doctor have a look at you," the abbot said gently.

"No, no, you don't understand. Thousands will die if we don't stop the processional," Oralia was becoming frantic.

"You've been through a lot, you need..." the abbot began, but was interrupted.

"Bishop Toribio plans to destroy the Plaza Mayor with a massive gas explosion in the tunnels beneath Old Madrid, Kevin and Liz are in the tunnels trying to stop him right now," Oralia insisted.

"That' makes no sense," the abbot replied, "Bishop Toribio will be leading the processional into the Plaza Mayor."

"Actually, he won't be leading tonight's processional," the monk piped in. "I heard Reverend Father say that he will lead the processional along with él Presidente Zapatero. Él Presidente plans to speak to the faithful after the processional in the plaza."

"Toribio wants to kill Zapatero," Oralia realized. "It was Toribio and his men who kidnapped Bishop Castillo and me and locked us in the torture chamber in the catacombs. We've got to stop the processional."

"I'm sure it has already begun," the abbot said.

"Ring the bells," Oralia said. "That's how they stopped the processional the last time the Virgin cried the blood of Jesus in 1725. Start ringing the bells and send all the monks to find Reverend Father and stop the processional."

"Should we tell them about the gas explosion?" the abbot asked.

"No, it could cause a panic. Just have them say that Bishop Castillo has returned and a new miracle has occurred at the templo. The bishop has ordered the faithful to all come to the templo at once."

Bishop Castillo lifted his head from the pew. "In him we have redemption through his blood, the forgiveness of sins, in accordance with the riches of God's grace that he lavished on us with all wisdom and understanding Jesus came to show the world he was God in flesh-he came to undo the works of the enemy. This he has done through the Madonna's bloody tears. The battle isn't over, do as Oralia requests," the bishop ordered.

Immediately the bells of the cathedral began to toll and dozens of hooded monks were sent scurrying towards the streets of Old Madrid.

As the member of the 'Seven' who drove the first truck away returned to the garage, he was pleased to see that two other trucks were now gone and hopefully in position.

"It's about time Diego and Juan got their asses in gear and did their job," he swore.

He parked his small Citroën next to Diaz' car.

"Time to join the party," he said and placed his ring into the call button of the elevator.

The motor kicked in instantly as the car made its way down to the garage. He was about to step in when he heard someone walking down the parking ramp.

"Guidino, how's it going?" the man asked.

"Bad, really bad," Guidino replied.

"What's the problem, isn't everything still on schedule?" the man asked.

"Maybe, I really don't know, but I think Diaz killed Diego and Juan," Guidino replied.

"Why would he do that, it makes no sense?" the man replied.

"A lot of things are making no sense. When I double-checked the gas valves the explosives still had not been put in place."

"Diaz told me Diego and Juan were probably with you in the tunnels."

"Diaz has been saying a lot of things that make no sense or are outright lies. He screwed up bad and now is maneuvering to try to cover his own butt so the 'Light' won't waste him," Guidino explained.

"As long as all goes as planned there should be no problem," the man insisted.

"We're way passed the point of everything going as planned," Guidino replied. "Diaz caught Inspector Romero and that French cop in the dining room. They seemed to know all about the "Seven of the Cross' and what we're up to. Who knows who else they have told?"

"Does the 'Light' and the bishop know about this?"

"Lucienne is upstairs, or at least was upstairs when I left to move the truck. Diaz left the Frenchman for her to question. She'll find out who else knows," Guidino replied. "Arciga is with her, but I know Toribio hasn't returned yet because when I drove by the cathedral the procession still hadn't started."

"What happened to the inspector?"

"Diaz locked him in the back of the truck he moved into place. We won't need to worry about him," Guidino replied.

"Are you sure? Are you sure Diaz can be trusted?" the man asked.

Both men were suddenly distracted by the continual tolling of the bells at the Templo de San Martín that was just two blocks away.

"Why are the bells tolling? Are they announcing the start of the processional?" the man asked.

"I don't believe so. I've never heard them ring so incessantly," Guidino commented.

Suddenly, both men heard footsteps of someone running down the service delivery ramp. It was Comisario Diaz.

"Diaz, what's going on?" Guidino asked.

Diaz was pale and visibly distraught. "Is Lucienne still here?"

"We don't know, we both just returned. I was about to move the other truck into position when Guidino arrived," the man said.

"Have you seen Diego or Juan yet?" Guidino said, trying to gauge Diaz' reaction.

"Juan and Diego are dead," Diaz replied flatly. "Kevin Bridges somehow overpowered them and killed them both."

"How do you know that?" the other man challenged.

"Do you hear the bells of the Templo de Eucarístico? Those bells are tolling to announce a new miracle," Diaz began,

"What new miracle," Guidino asked,

"The miracle that Bishop Castillo and the secretary have safely returned to the templo and that because of that the Madonna has stopped shedding the bloody tears," Diaz finished.

"How do you know all this?" Guidino demanded.

"There are dozens of monks from the templo spreading the word through the streets at this very moment. They are also telling everyone to leave the Plaza Mayor and the processional and come directly to the templo."

"What are we going to do?" the man asked.

"The explosives for the tunnels were never moved into place. They are still just behind those doors. I want you to take them down into the catacombs and move them into the mausoleum of the templo," Diaz ordered.

"I can't blow up the templo," the man replied, shocked.

"It may be the only way to save us from arrest and the death penalty," Diaz replied. "Bishop Castillo or the secretary has seen every one of the 'Seven'. We must kill them."

"I think I'd rather be arrested," the man replied.

"If you don't do it, the 'Light' won't let you live long enough to be arrested," Diaz assured him.

"And you," he said turning towards Guidino, "You take this truck and park it behind the templo. If there's time, move as many of the other trucks there as well."

"What do you intend to do?" the man asked.

"I'm going to tell the 'Light' what has happened," Diaz replied, "unless one of you two would rather do that job?"

Both men shirked away from Diaz' challenge.

"I didn't think so," Diaz replied. "Now let's get going."

Guidino opened the door to the truck, but hesitated while he watched Diaz call and then enter the elevator. The other man headed to the doors to where the explosives were stored. They were on a dolly so he rolled them out onto the loading dock by the elevator. He too was moving at a slow pace.

"I don't like it," he called over to Guidino.

"Me either," Guidino replied. "I say we get the hell out of here."

"I'm with you," the man replied.

"Here, take this tarp and cover up the explosives, nobody will know what they are. I'll move the truck up into the public garage area in case Diaz comes back down."

"Let's take my car," the man said. "I'll follow and pick you up. Where are we going?"

"As far away from Spain as possible," Guidino replied.

"Do you think that's all of them?" Kevin asked.

"We can only pray it is," Liz replied. "Anyway, we're almost out of time and we still need to find those explosives."

"I think the two men from the torture chamber died before they could put them in place," Kevin guessed.

"Then they should probably still be somewhere back near the loading dock," Liz suggested.

They walked quietly back through the tunnels. Finally, Kevin asked. "So, how are you feeling?"

"Don't you mean have I recovered enough to take on Lucienne?" Liz replied.

"Well...yeah," Kevin replied sheepishly.

"She's a very powerful Nephilim. I've the strength to take her back to Tartarus, but would that really do any good? Chances are she would be summoned back to earth shortly."

"What are you saying, is there nothing you can do?" Kevin asked.

"No, there's much we all can do. I can battle her, but I cannot destroy her. God has known all along that we would fight this battle and has given us the weapons necessary to defeat Satan," Liz explained.

"Yet you say you aren't capable of defeating Lucienne. What weapons has he given us?" Kevin asked.

"You are his weapon," Liz replied.

"What can I do to destroy Lucienne that you cannot do?" Kevin said in doubt.

"For centuries Satan and his evil disciples have waged a battle for the souls of humankind. When a major battle looms, God in all his wisdom, has sent the weapons necessary for good to prevail," Liz explained.

"You're speaking about the miracle of the Madonna's bloody tears aren't you," Kevin realized. "That's why you took a jar of the blood with you when you went to face Lucienne in New York and that's why Bruno Mancini had it with him in 1725."

"Ephesians 2:13," Liz recited, *"But now in Christ Jesus you who once were far away have been brought near through the blood of Christ."*

"So, this blood will send Lucienne back where she belongs?" Kevin asked holding the blood he had collected in a plastic instant coffee jar.

"I don't know," Liz said.

"You don't know?" Kevin replied in shock. "Then why did you take it with you to fight her the first time?"

"I've never used it or know of it being used," she replied, "but God has sent it for a reason and I believe that reason is to defeat evil."

Kevin was starting to get a bad feeling about the battle to come. "What about the cross you gave me, is it a weapon from God? When you handed it to me you said now we can end this forever."

"It is a weapon, but not from God. It was wrought by the hands of one of Satan's disciples. It was what Jayro Toribio used to bring Lucienne out of Tartarus," Liz explained.

"So that's it? We are headed to battle with a cross from Satan and a coffee jar full of what we think is the blood of Jesus that may or may not have any special power over evil," Kevin huffed.

"No, we have one very strong weapon," Liz replied. "We have the power of prayer."

CHAPTER FORTY-ONE

"Affirmation"

"**Of course, I'm sure** this will get us to the Plaza Mayor. It's a short-cut," Gabe explained to his wife.

"Like your last short-cut," his wife Pauline laughed. "We would still be lost if you hadn't run into that other American couple. We passed the same butcher shop five times from four different directions."

"Let me look at the map," Gabe said, turning it ever which way hoping it would reveal where they were.

"Thump, thump, thump," a pounding came from a truck parked in the alley that was supposed to be the shortcut.

"It sounds like there's a horse in that truck," Pauline said.

"It's probably tonight's dinner at one of these restaurants," Gabe joked nervously.

"Thump, thump," Romero kicked again. He thought he heard voices right outside the truck. "Ummmh," he tried to call out but the tape covering his mouth stifled his cry. "Thump, thump, thump."

"I think someone's stuck inside," Pauline said nearing the back of the truck.

"Stay out of it," Gabe warned her, "It'd be our luck to interrupt some Mafia kidnapping."

"We're in Spain not Italy," Pauline reminded him.

"Okay, some Basque separatist kidnapping then," Gabe joked.

"Hello, is anyone there?" Pauline called out.

"Thump, thump, thump, thump, thump," Romero kicked wildly having heard the voice.

"I told you somebody was in there," Pauline said. "Maybe they need help."

"Stay out of it," Gabe repeated. "I think we need to go that direction."

"If anyone is in there, knock twice if you need help," Pauline called out ignoring her husband.

"Thump, thump," Romero replied.

"Someone needs help, we need to open this door," Pauline insisted.

Gabe knew there was no point arguing. Pauline wouldn't leave till he opened the truck and as much as he wanted to deny it, this was just like he had dreamed it would be.

"We'll probably be arrested for this," Gabe said looking around suspiciously to make sure no one was watching.

"Go stand over there in case you have to run for help," Gabe said.

Pauline moved back but not as far as Gabe wanted. The door wasn't locked so he turned the handle and lifted up on the door.

Romero came tumbling out the back of the truck.

"Are you hurt?" Pauline said running up to pull the tape off his mouth.

"I wasn't until you ripped the tape off," Romero replied.

"Sorry," Pauline replied.

"What's going on?" Gabe asked before assisting any further.

"I'm Inspector Romero with the Cuerpo Nacional. That's the federal police. You've just saved the lives of thousands of Spaniards. This is a bomb set to go off after the processional. There are three more somewhere around here."

"A bomb?" Pauline cried.

"There's a key for these handcuffs hidden in the cuff of my pants," Romero said.

Neither Gabe nor Pauline rushed to find the key.

"My badge is in my wallet if you don't believe me, but please we've got to hurry."

Within seconds Romero was free and had called the local police from Gabe's cell phone to warn them about the three other truck bombs and the plot to kill él Presidente.

Romero jumped back into the truck and began looking at the bomb. Within a minute he was back with a digital alarm clock in his hand.

"When the police arrive tell them the bombs have alarm clocks as detonators. This one was set to go off at 10:00."

Pauline and Gabe were both stunned but understood the message. "Where are you going?" Gabe asked.

Suddenly bells began to toll from several of the churches in the area causing all three of them to look up.

"I'm going to stop the people responsible for this," Romero replied and ran off.

൦ൟ   ൦ൟ   ൦ൟ

"God be with you," Bishop Toribio said.

"And also, with you," the congregation responded in unison.

"Now, I would like…" but before he could finish his sentence, a flurry of activity took place around where él Presidente Zapatero had been sitting in the cathedral.

A phalanx of suited security guards grabbed él Presidente and with guns drawn plowed their way through the crowd towards an armored limousine that had pulled up next to the cathedral.

Almost simultaneously bells began to toll at several of the other cathedrals and templos in Old Madrid.

"What's happening?" Bishop Toribio asked one of the other priests standing near him.

"I don't know my Lord, but I shall find out at once," the priest replied and hurried into the crowd.

The congregation sat momentarily stunned by the frantic removal of él Presidente. The tolling of the bells seemed to awaken them and they exploded into a chaotic frenzied exodus.

"It's a bit chilly in here now, would you mind if I opened the door to the terrace?" Arciga said, handing Lucienne a glass of absenta.

"It is a lovely evening, why not," Lucienne replied.

The dining room had been designed to be soundproof so as Arciga opened the door the auditory shock of the tolling bells felt like a blow to the face.

"What's happening?" Lucienne said, rushing out onto the terrace. "Why do the bells toll?"

"Perhaps it is part of Toribio's plan for this evening," Arciga speculated.

"He said nothing to me about this," she huffed.

"Maybe he believes it will draw more people to the processional and to the Plaza Mayor, you know, the more the merrier," Arciga laughed.

"Then why are the streets filled with people leaving the plaza and heading this way?" she demanded.

"You're right, they are headed this way. That is very strange," Arciga replied.

"You idiot," the 'Light' shrieked, "something has gone horribly wrong. Go find Toribio and bring him to me."

"Toribio will be here soon enough," Diaz said stepping off the elevator hearing Lucienne's last order to Arciga.

"What do you know about this?" Lucienne fumed.

"Diego and Juan failed me," Diaz began. "They allowed Kevin Bridges, Bishop Castillo, and the church secretary, to escape from the torture chamber."

"They shall die for that," the 'Light' hissed.

"They already have," Diaz replied. "Bishop Castillo has ordered the processional stopped and for everyone to come to the Templo Eucarístico de San Martín. That's where all these people are headed."

"What are we going to do? They'll discover who the "Seven of the Cross' are and we'll all be arrested," Arciga blubbered.

"You pathetic sniveling piece of trash," Lucienne said, turning to Arciga. "Satan's glorious plan is collapsing and you're worried about going to jail. You make me ill."

Lucienne raised her hand, and as if launched by a catapult, Arciga flew off the roof, plummeting towards the street below and was impaled on the decorative iron work of a kiosk along the Gran Via.

"All is not lost," Diaz continued. "I've ordered two others to move the explosives meant for the Plaza Mayor through the catacombs and into the mausoleum at the templo. They were also told to move the explosive laden trucks into place behind the templo. There should be enough explosive power to level the templo and several blocks around it. Thousands will still die, including the ones who could identify us," Diaz explained.

"I'm impressed," Lucienne replied coyly.

"Don't be too impressed yet. Kevin Bridges is still out there somewhere and I've got the feeling he's not alone."

"You think Elizabeth is helping him?" Lucienne asked.

"I don't know any other way he could have escaped. He had to have her help," Diaz replied.

"How interesting. For her to return from Tartarus, someone would have had to summon her forth after murdering another human," Lucienne explained.

"I see Francois wasn't very cooperative," Diaz said, noticing the frozen body still cuffed to the table.

Lucienne ignored his comment. "If Kevin and Liz are out there as you say, I expect we'll be seeing them before long. Liz has this misguided notion that God will forgive her if she fights evil and continues to do good deeds. She's a Nephilim just like me. She forgets Satan is our Father, not God. She'll come to challenge me, but she'll lose."

"I'm sure Toribio is scared to death at what has transpired. I would imagine that he'll be arriving at any moment," Diaz surmised.

"Then why don't we enjoy the drinks that the recently departed Minister Arciga had prepared," Lucienne said with a smile.

"An excellent idea," Diaz replied. "But allow me to prepare the 'green fairy' correctly."

"I think we should be using the Pontarlier France pre-ban vintage absinthe."

"I have to agree," the 'Light' replied. "But can we move inside, these damn bells are driving me crazy."

When Bishop Toribio heard the news of the miracle at the Templo Eucarístico and about Bishop Castillo returning, he knew that God was all powerful. What a weak fool he had been to be taken in by Satan's temptations, but he knew what was done could not be undone and that he had chosen Satan willingly and eternally.

It was obvious that él Presidente's security team had learned of the assassination plot. He knew it wouldn't be long before they came for him, but he swore, as a disciple of his lord Satan, that he would spread evil and take as many lives as possible before he died. Death was assured for he knew he would never surrender.

"Out of my way," he demanded, pushing people aside as he rushed towards El Corte Inglés.

"The 'Light' was correct when she said Diaz had failed us. How could I have been so foolish not to listen," Toribio moaned as he rushed to meet the 'Seven of the Cross'. His garments were not conducive for traveling at such a quick pace nor was he in the best physical condition causing him to sweat profusely.

The mitre was the first part of his Holy robes to be discarded. The jewels inlaid into the hat were worth more than most Spaniards made in a year. It had been knocked askew as he pushed his way out of the cathedral and was gone before he reached the Palacio Real. By the time he reached the garage entrance to El Corte Inglés, Toribio had shed or lost both his pectoral cross and pallium to the mêlée.

As he approached the elevator, Liz and Kevin walked up behind him.

"Looks like you're having a bad day," Kevin said, startling Toribio.

"You! I thought you were in Ronda," Toribio declared.

"I guess they've kept you out of the loop. Everyone else seemed to think that we were dead," Kevin replied.

"Mind if we join you in the dining room?" Liz asked.

"Of course, he doesn't mind," Kevin replied for him. "The entire plot of the 'Seven of the Cross' to assassinate él Presidente and kill thousands in Plaza Mayor has collapsed all around him. Why would he mind if we joined him for dinner?"

Kevin stuck the ring into the elevator call button surprising Toribio.

"Wow," Kevin exclaimed, "you've got a ring just like mine. Did you get yours off the finger of a dead librarian or out of a Cracker Jack's box?"

It was a joke neither the bishop nor Liz seemed to understand.

"You know the 'Light' will be waiting for you," Toribio said in an ominous tone.

"We certainly hope so," Kevin snapped back.

"You fool," Toribio said, "you're headed to your death."

"We all are headed towards our death," Kevin replied. "It's where we end up afterwards that really matters."

Just then the elevator door opened.

"After you," Toribio said politely.

"No, after you," Kevin insisted.

"Ladies first," Liz said, and pushed past the both of them.

Romero had lived in Madrid half of his life and still couldn't find his way around.

"I should've borrowed his map," Romero said, standing at a corner trying to decide which way to turn. He had asked someone on the street how to get to El Corte Inglés and they had directed him to where he now was, right in front of El Corte Inglés. The problem was it wasn't the right El Corte Inglés.

As he stood there, dozens of people streamed past him.

"Where's everyone going?" he asked.

"There's been a new miracle at the Templo Eucarístico de San Martín. Bishop Castillo has returned and he has called everyone there."

"Bishop Castillo has returned? Are you sure?" Romero asked excitedly.

"That's what the templo monks have been sent out to say. The processional has been canceled and the faithful have been ordered to the templo," the man explained.

"Yeah," Romero screamed. "If the bishop escaped, Kevin must still be alive. Are you headed towards the templo?"

"Yes, yes, I am," the man replied hesitantly.

"Well that's the direction I'm headed too, lead on."

Romero's faith in God had never been stronger.

CHAPTER FORTY-TWO

"Conviction"

"Oralia, are you okay?" Reverend Father asked as he rushed into the sanctuary. "I heard the news and couldn't believe it. May God forgive me for doubting His infinite powers."

"Liz saved us," Oralia started to explain.

"Bishop Castillo," Reverend Father said, kneeling down and kissing his ring. "God has answered my prayers and returned you safely to us."

The bishop nodded his head in acknowledgement.

"The Madonna has stopped crying the bloody tears," the abbot interrupted. "What does it mean?"

"The tears were God's warning that a great evil had come to Madrid," Oralia explained.

"And now that evil has passed?" Reverend Father asked.

"Not at all. The evil is greater and more powerful than it has ever been. The tears are no longer necessary because God knows we now understand what we are up against. Madrid is under siege by Satan's Kingdom. He calls upon us all to fight for the Kingdom of God and defeat this evil," Oralia explained.

"Where are Kevin and Liz?" Reverend Father asked.

"They went to stop Lucienne and her evil group the 'Seven of the Cross' from blowing up the Plaza Mayor. That's why Bishop Castillo ordered the processional halted and everyone to come to the templo," Oralia explained.

"How can we be sure we'll be safe here?" the abbot asked, growing very concerned.

"This is God's house," the Reverend Father replied, "and we are God's warriors. We too must fight this battle."

Two paramedics hurried into the sanctuary to prepare Bishop Castillo and Oralia for transport to the hospital.

"I cannot leave yet," the Bishop insisted as they tried to put him on a gurney.

"Nor can I," Oralia added. "Not until the battle is over."

"Leave them," the Reverend Father said to the paramedics. "We'll bring them to the hospital when this is over. God needs them here for now."

"I think that's a bad idea," one of the paramedics said, "but who am I to argue with God." The paramedics did what they could for the superficial wounds on both Oralia and the bishop, but insisted they both be taken to the hospital for a complete check-up as soon as possible.

"I'll bring them personally," Reverend Father assured the man.

The sanctuary was now full and thousands of people continued to gather on the streets outside the templo.

"What can we do to prepare for this battle?" the abbot asked.

"Tell your monks to go out among the people who have gathered and lead them in prayer," Bishop Castillo whispered.

"Yes, your Grace," the abbot replied.

"In Latin" Oralia added, "Satan hates it when we pray in Latin."

※ ※ ※

"Bishop Toribio, we've been expecting you. And I see you brought guests," Lucienne said as the elevator door opened to the dining room.

Toribio began to exit the elevator, "don't move," Kevin ordered, grabbing the back of Toribio's chasuble, wanting to keep Toribio between himself and Lucienne.

"It's okay," Liz assured him. "She cannot harm you as long as I'm here."

"Thank you," Toribio replied, haughtily, striding out of the elevator over to where Lucienne and Diaz were sitting.

Still on edge Kevin moved slowly out of the elevator keeping a tight grip on the cross.

"Francois," Kevin blurted out when he saw the blue frozen body of his friend lying at the far end of the dining table. "What've you done to Francois?"

"I'm afraid the Frenchman wasn't very cooperative," Lucienne replied. "But why should you care, he won't be joining your God."

"He was on the path towards his salvation," Liz replied, sharply.

"I guess he should've run a little quicker," Toribio joked.

Liz and Kevin both walked over to where Francois lay.

"You could at least uncuff him," Kevin urged.

Liz touched the cuffs and they fell away. Kevin sat the cross on the table to grab Francois' still icy body and laid him across two chairs.

"I'll take that," Lucienne said and the cross slid across the table coming to rest in front of her.

"I see you've found Jayro Toribio's original cross," Lucienne began. "That was the cross Satan used to first free me from Tartarus."

She picked it up and handed it to Bishop Toribio. "I believe this family heirloom belongs to you. I'd feel safer if you hold onto this."

Kevin didn't care about the cross, he was grieving for Francois.

"Is there nothing you can do?" he said to Liz.

"Oh, there's plenty Liz could do," Lucienne said. "It's just a matter of how far is she willing to go."

"What is she talking about?" Kevin asked.

"Go ahead, tell him," Lucienne prodded. "Tell him how you could bring the Frenchman back to life."

"Forget the Frenchman," Toribio roared, "We need to figure out what we're going to do. Kill these two so we can get out of here."

"What's your hurry," Diaz said.

"What's my hurry? Are you insane? Bishop Castillo has escaped, él Presidente has escaped, the processional has fallen apart, and where's the rest of the 'Seven'?" Toribio roared.

"I can confirm that two of them are dead," Kevin piped in.

"What?" Toribio said.

"Three," Lucienne added. "Don't forget about Minister Arciga."

"What happened to Arciga?" Toribio asked, but was ignored.

"Can you really bring Francois back to life," Kevin asked Liz.

"Of course she can," Lucienne interjected.

"It is possible," Liz admitted, "but as before, I would lose much of my power."

"Do it," Kevin insisted. "God is on our side and when God is with you who can be against you. We won't need your powers."

Liz wasn't so sure.

❦ ❦ ❦

"Finally," Romero said as he ran into the parking garage of the El Corte Inglés.

"Sorry sir, but we're closing early because of the miracle," a security guard informed him as he tried to enter the door.

"I'm Inspector Romero with the Cuerpo Nacional. See that truck parked over there?"

"The *Petit Forestier* truck? Yes, I see it," the guard replied.

"Well it is full of explosives. You need to get this building evacuated immediately and contact the local police and tell them one of the four truck bombs is here in the garage. Do you understand?" Romero said.

"Yyyyees sir," the man stuttered.

"Then do it now," Romero demanded.

Immediately the man smashed the fire alarm and got on his radio.

The loudspeaker system in the store blared the instructions for an orderly exit advising everyone to exit out the main doors and stay away from the parking garage. Fortunately, very few patrons remained in the store and it was mostly cashiers and staff that headed out of the building. Romero was the only one going against the flow as he ran up the escalator towards the top floor.

When he reached the restaurant the last of the kitchen help was headed out the door. He already knew where the stairway to the rooftop dining room was located.

"I better grab a key," he said to himself as he picked up a large butcher knife one of the chefs had left on the counter.

"*Eets loked*," He said mimicking the voice of the chef who first let them in. He slipped the knife into the door just as the chef had done and lifted it up quickly. The door gently swung open.

CHAPTER FORTY-THREE

"Atonement"

Liz placed her hand on Francois' frigid chest. "*I will give you a new heart and put a new spirit in you; I will remove your heart of stone and give you a heart of flesh.*"

Soothing warmth encompassed the dining room as Liz prayed over Francois.

"Why's that light flashing?" Toribio asked, pointing to a strobe light in the corner of the room.

"It's the fire alarm," Diaz replied.

"Then why don't we hear it?"

"The room is soundproof so we wouldn't hear it from below and Guidino turned off the alarm in the dining room," Diaz explained.

"Why's the alarm going off in the first place?" Lucienne asked.

"Perhaps the police have arrived to arrest you all," Kevin speculated.

"I'll put a stop to that," Toribio said pulling a cell phone from beneath what remained of his bishop robes.

"Before you call that number, I should warn you we've made a few last-minute changes," Diaz said.

"What kind of changes?" Toribio asked.

"Shhh," Lucienne whispered, "You're missing the show."

The two men stopped talking and turned to see what Lucienne was talking about.

Liz had continued to pray over Francois and now his arms and legs began to twitch. Suddenly he bolted to his feet, swayed back and forth for a minute in a daze, then collapsed to the ground as if his entire insides had liquefied.

"What's happening?" Kevin demanded. "What have you done to him?"

But as Kevin questioned her, Liz's eyes seem to roll back in her head and she collapsed onto the floor next to Francois.

"Well done, well done, indeed," Lucienne said, standing to applaud.

The three men stared at Lucienne completely baffled by her reaction to what was happening around them.

Then slowly, Liz stood back up.

"Took a little more out of you than you thought it would, don't you think?" Lucienne said to Liz.

Liz held the edge of the table to steady her balance.

"Enough of this nonsense," Toribio demanded. "What are these changes you are talking about?"

"The explosives meant for the tunnels under Plaza Mayor have been moved. They are now in the mausoleum and catacombs beneath the Templo Eucarístico de San Martín," Diaz explained.

"That's excellent," Toribio replied.

"And at least one and possibly two of the trucks are now parked behind the templo," Diaz continued.

Francois suddenly leaped to his feet. "What happened, what's going on? Kevin, you're alive."

Francois grabbed Kevin in a bear hug.

"And thanks to Liz, you are once again alive," Kevin said hugging him back.

"How is this possible? I remember now. Lucienne froze me and, and, I died," he realized the magnitude of what he had just said.

"You were healed by faith," Liz replied.

"But I had so little faith," Francois said.

"You are healed by your faith, someone else's faith, or

God's faith," Liz went on to explain. "Though I believe your faith is greater that you'll admit, I'm sure Kevin and God had something to do with your healing."

"You make it sound like I was just sick. I had died! You brought me back to life."

"And now you'll get the chance to die a second time," Lucienne laughed. "Although I must say, Liz, you put on a superb show."

Kevin had moved closer to Lucienne as her attention was on Liz. He'd pulled the jar of the Madonna's bloody tears from his pocket and unscrewed the jar. "I've had just about enough of you," Kevin said and threw the blood at Lucienne.

Lucienne lifted her hand and the blood stopped in midair then splattered onto the walnut inlaid dining table.

"You fool! Do you actually think the blood of your Jesus Christ would have any affect on me?" Lucienne sneered.

She reached over to the table and smeared the blood with her index finger. She then wiped the blood on her forearm.

"Enough of this," Toribio said, looking at his watch. "It's time to light up the night."

He began to dial his cell phone.

Liz was still weak from saving Francois, but she grabbed his hand and motioned for him to kneel down next to her. She began to pray.

> "*In you, O LORD, I have taken refuge;*
>   *let me never be put to shame.*
> *Rescue me and deliver me in your righteousness;*
>   *turn your ear to me and save me.*
> *Be my rock of refuge,*
>   *to which I can always go;*

> give the command to save me,
> for you are my rock and my fortress.
> Deliver me, O my God, from the hand of the wicked,
> from the grasp of evil and cruel men."

"It's show time." Toribio said and pushed the send button on his phone.

༄ ༄ ༄

Inspector Romero was trying to decide when to burst through the doors and into the dining room. He was also trying to decide just exactly what he was going to do when he did. He had very slowly and carefully eased the swinging doors slightly askew so he could at least hear what was going on. What he heard gave him hope. Kevin was alive and so was Liz. He recognized Lucienne's voice from their meeting on the bridge in Ronda and he heard Comisario Diaz. He knew there was at least one other member of the 'Seven' inside as well. He knew two had died. At least Diaz said he had killed two of them, so that left the possibility of three others that could be there as well but hadn't spoken while he was listening. He quietly allowed the doors to close so he could consider his next move. Diaz had taken his gun earlier in the day but he did have the butcher knife he had used to unlock the stairway door. "Lord, give me a sign," Romero prayed.

And the Lord did!

༄ ༄ ༄

Seconds after Toribio pushed send on his cell phone to detonate the tunnel bombs, the building began to shake violently.

"What's happening?" Lucienne screamed.

"Those fools never moved the explosives into place. They must have still been in the parking garage," Diaz replied.

Several glass panels shattered as the timer on the explosives in the truck parked in the garage below detonated, causing even a greater rumbling and shaking.

"It's going to collapse, we've got to get out of here," Toribio yelled.

"Thank you, Lord, for the sign," Romero said and burst into the chaotic scene.

Kevin took advantage of the mayhem and leaped over the table to grab Diaz.

Diaz saw him coming and backed away tripping over a chair but managed to pull his gun.

Romero went for Toribio, who saw Romero coming at him with the butcher knife.

"Stay back, stay back," he screamed, flailing the cross wildly trying to keep Kevin and Romero at bay.

Lucienne had ducked under the table when the building first began to shake. When she heard Toribio scream she climbed out from under and stood up just as he swung the cross, smashing it into her forehead.

"Look what you've done," she screamed, and grabbed his robe. His entire body instantly turned to a solid block of frozen organs and bone. With a flick of her wrist the block flew out one of the shattered windows and exploded into millions of sand size frozen granules.

"Nobody moves," Diaz ordered, holding his gun on Kevin and Romero, but they like Liz and Francois were staring at Lucienne who had sat down with the cross still embedded in her forehead.

"This is just great," Lucienne said facetiously.

"Are you all right?" Diaz asked her.

"Do I look alright?" Lucienne snapped back, and then began to laugh. "You all will pay dearly for this."

But as she spoke, the blood she had smeared on her forearm began to flow up her arm towards the wound in her head.

"What's happening here?" Lucienne said nervously.

The Madonna's bloody tears that had been splattered across the table began to boil, then suddenly congeal into a single puddle and leap off the table and onto Lucienne's body.

"No, no," she screamed as the blood ran up her limbs and into the wound from which the cross still protruded.

She began to writhe, twisting and contorting, screaming in excruciating pain. Each individual cell in her body began to implode, collapsing on itself, causing immeasurable pain. All watched as Lucienne's body eventually disappeared.

Through the shattered windows came the sound of thousands praying in the streets below.

"Now what are you going to do?" Romero said to Diaz, who still held the gun.

"Once I kill all of you, I'll be the hero," he laughed. "And with Lucienne gone, I have nothing to fear."

"I think you have once again underestimated the power of God," Liz advised him. "Look around, what do you see?"

The sound of the prayers grew louder, as Diaz looked out across Old Madrid, every rooftop, including El Corte Inglés, were covered with legions of angels in white shining armor, each holding a glistening white sword before him.

"The time has come," Liz said. "The kingdom of God is near. Repent and believe the good news! Christ just doesn't want to change your actions; he wants to change your heart."

"It's too late for that," Diaz replied. He stuck the barrel of his gun in his mouth and pulled the trigger.

EPILOGUE

"Redemption"

"**Where's Liz?**" Oralia asked. "I was hoping she'd be here."

"Liz returned to Tartarus," Kevin said.

"Why in the world would she do that?" Francois asked.

"She said it was where she belonged, where God meant for her to be," Kevin explained.

"What if Lucienne returns?" Oralia said.

"Lucienne can never return. Satan arranged for her to be brought onto earth by your ancestor Jayro Toribio and God sent her back using the blood of Christ and your cousin, Bishop Toribio."

"Acting-bishop Toribio, may he rest in pieces" Oralia reminded Kevin.

"Do you honestly believe that Liz and Lucienne were these Nephilim creatures they claimed to be?" Francois asked.

"You don't?" Oralia piped in.

"I never said that," Francois replied. "I was asking the Vatican expert for his opinion."

"I'm no expert, I'm simply a miracle investigator," Kevin reminded Francois.

"Speaking of which, did all this really have to do with hiding the miracles supporting the beatification of Pope John Paul II?" Reverend Father asked.

"I'm not really sure. Liz once told me it had more to do with Satan trying to cast doubt about me, for whatever reason I don't know. I submitted my report to the Vatican and it met with quite a bit of skepticism. Fortunately, your report,

Reverend Father's, and the report from Bishop Castillo, did give mine some validity, but like usual, I'm sure by now it has been buried in some obscure archive deep in the bowels of the Vatican."

"Sorry I'm late," Comisario Romero said rushing into the mausoleum.

"You're not late," Oralia replied. "Actually, you are late, but it really doesn't matter. I asked you all here to thank you. If it wasn't for you, Raul Toribio would never have been given the sacraments and burial he truly deserved. The Libro de Reglas of the 'Seven of the Cross' included a detailed history of what really occurred back in 1725. It wasn't Raul who killed Bruno Mancini, it was Lucienne or Lucia as she was then called. Jayro Toribio also killed his brother Raul and the other monk in the courtyard, so Raul never committed suicide like everyone believed."

Oralia began to cry as Reverend Father removed the cloth covering the crypts head plate.

BROTHER RAUL JESUS TORIBIO
1692-1725
One of God's true warriors

"They placed him right next to Bruno Mancini's crypt," Oralia sobbed.

"I'm sure he's finally at peace," Francois said, comforting Oralia.

Reverend Father said a prayer and after everyone paid their due respect, the group of friends left the mausoleum.

"What's going to happen to the catacombs and torture chamber," Francois asked.

"Much of the catacombs collapsed when the bombs exploded in the garage of the El Corte Inglés," Reverend

Father replied, "but the torture chamber and cells housing the remains of those long-forgotten monks still remain. The Vatican is considering a plan to open it up as a tourist attraction. They think people would be interested in a historical exhibit about the Inquisition and the auto de fe."

"I think that's a ridiculous idea," Oralia huffed.

"Did they ever find Señor Guidino and that other member of the 'Seven'?" Kevin asked Romero.

"We found Guidino," Romero replied, obviously not wanting to share anything further.

"And," Francois said, pushing for more information.

Everybody looked at Romero.

"He had made it to Romania."

"Are they going to send him back," Kevin asked.

"They already sent the body back," Romero replied, sheepishly.

"How did he die?" Oralia asked

Romero hesitated. "They found him impaled on a stake."

"Impaled on a stake! What did he do, trip and fall off of something?" Francois asked.

"Not quite. The stake went through his anus and came out of his mouth. I was told he lived for almost two days stuck like that on a hill overlooking Budapest."

"My God, who would do such a thing?" Oralia gasped.

"Only a disciple of Satan would be capable of such an atrocity," Reverend Father insisted.

"Isn't that how Vlad Dracula crucified his victims?" Oralia asked

"Sounds like a case for you, Kevin," Francois suggested.

"What about the other man?" Kevin said, ignoring Francois' comment.

"We've no idea who the other man was. The name and information about him in the 'Seven's' Libro de Reglas was completely made up. We've been unable to find any fingerprints on the trucks or in the dining room that might help," Romero said. "The man is a complete enigma."

"So evil lives on," Oralia whispered.

"God knows who he is," Reverend Father replied. "And someday he'll have to answer to God for what he has done."

"What about you Francois," Romero said, changing the subject. "How's your walk going with God?"

Francois blushed. "It's going," he replied, "but I have to admit my Christian walk isn't down the Catholic path."

"Neither was mine," Kevin reminded him.

"When Liz brought me back from the dead it was like I was born again," Francois explained. "I've accepted Jesus as my Lord and Savior."

"Congratulations," the Reverend Father said and Oralia gave him a hug.

"Will wonders ever cease?" Kevin joked. "Now if you'll excuse me, I hate to run off like this but I've got to get back to work."

"What, is there another miracle somewhere that can't wait a couple of hours until we have lunch?" Oralia asked.

"No miracles, just duty. I've been asked to fill in temporarily as security chief at the Vatican and I've got to be back by four this afternoon. I guess somebody doesn't like me running around fighting Nephilim and Satan," Kevin explained.

"A desk job?" Francois and Romero said at the same time and laughed.

"Better you than me," Comisario Romero added.

"I know, pretty pathetic," Kevin replied.

"I'll pray for you," Francois said.

Everyone turned and looked at Francois.

"What? You've never prayed for somebody before?" Francois said, and everyone laughed.

࿔ ࿔ ࿔

"First class, no way," their daughter said.

"I swear to God," Pauline said. "Ask your dad."

"It's true. We were heroes," Gabe joked. "Well, kind of heroes. All we really did was let the man out of the truck and take the handcuffs off of him."

"We did get to spend several extra days that we hadn't planned for in Madrid," Pauline said.

"That must've been tough," the daughter replied. "Did Spain pay for the extra hotel bill too?"

"They even paid for our meals," Pauline said.

"The police were able to find two more of the trucks and diffuse the detonators before they exploded," Gabe said, "but one truck did blow up in the parking garage of some department store."

"Did they ever find out who did it?" she asked.

"When we got home I saw on CNN that Spain was blaming some terrorist group called the ETA for the whole mess," Pauline said. "It was supposedly an assassination attempt meant for their president, Zapatero. He got away, but one of his cabinet members or ministers, I guess they call them, was killed, as was a priest."

"Well, I read on the internet that it was some group of religious fanatics or devil worshipers called the 'Seven of the Cross'," Gabe countered.

"Which was it, devil worshipers or religious fanatics? There's a big difference you know," his wife scolded.

"Does it really matter?" Gabe replied.

"Well, yeah, it does," she replied.

"I just can't believe you opened that truck and freed that policeman before the bomb exploded. It's a miracle!" Gabe's daughter exclaimed.

"Your mom made me do it," he replied, but he knew it was more than that. He had dreamed such a thing would happen. And the dreams were only getting more troubling.

"I just thank God you're home safe," their daughter said.

"Amen to that!"

www.ingramcontent.com/pod-product-compliance
Lightning Source LLC
Chambersburg PA
CBHW030105100526
44591CB00009B/285